INTRODUCTION TO
PSYCHOLOGICAL RESEARCH
*Logic, design,
analysis*

Under the Editorship of

WAYNE HOLTZMAN

INTRODUCTION TO

PSYCHOLOGICAL RESEARCH

Logic, design, analysis

RICHARD G. LATHROP
Chico State College
California

HARPER & ROW, PUBLISHERS
New York, Evanston, and London

Acknowledgment

Appendixes C, E, and F: I am indebted to the Literary Executor of the late Sir Ronald A. Fisher, F.R.S., to Dr. Frank Yates, F.R.S. and to Oliver & Boyd Ltd., Edinburgh, for permission to reprint as Appendix C: Table III, "Distribution of t"; as Appendix E: Table VII, "Values of the Correlation Coefficient for Different Levels of Significance"; and as Appendix F: Table IV, "Distribution of χ^2" from their book *Statistical Tables for Biological, Agricultural and Medical Research* 6th ed. (Edinburgh: Oliver & Boyd Ltd.), 1963.

Appendix D: An adaption of Table 10-7, "5% (roman type) and 1% (bold-face type) Points for the Distribution of F" from G. W. Snedecor, *Statistical Methods*, 6th ed. (Ames, Iowa: The Iowa State University Press), 1967.

Contents

Contents

Preface

I cannot, in good conscience, claim that this text would have been possible without the willing cooperation of a great number of people. Although much of this assistance came from my own campus, both Nelson Hanawalt (Douglass College) and Daniel Weintraub (University of Michigan) reviewed the manuscript in draft form and made suggestions for change. Robert B. Freeman (Pennsylvania State University) reviewed two forms of the manuscript and his detailed comments led to major revisions in Chapters 1, 2, and 8. At Chico State College, Jay Caldwell and Persis Sturges used a draft copy in their classes and, with the teaching assistants for that course, made suggestions for improving student understanding of the material in addition to helping with the task of reading galley proofs. William Kalberer used draft copies for two successive classes and assisted with the rewriting of Chapter 6. Emmett Anderson was largly responsible for the production of the initial draft copies and assisted with reading of the galley proofs. Credit for collection of the actual data for the sample experiment given in Chapters 2 through 7 belongs to three assistants: Barbara Peters, James Piper, and Phillip Slattery.

Three people were especially helpful in the actual production of the various versions of the manuscript. Jean Harvery typed all of the "finished" material, corrected spelling, and kept style as nearly consistent as possible given the material available. Patricia Donaldson (a coauthor of the *Study Guide* which accompanies the text) produced the first draft of this text from my dictation and wrote most of the test question material in the *Instructor's Manual*. Finally, a true coauthor of this book is Ann Lathrop. Each of the draft copies and the final manuscript were critically reviewed by her and willing help was given in rewriting nearly every page.

My deepest gratitude to them is meager repayment for their assistance.

RICHARD G. LATHROP

To the Student

So you are about to embark upon a study of the scientific method as applied to behavior. Just what will be expected of you? For one thing, you will be expected to do some *independent* thinking. Some people seem to complete an entire college career without doing a great deal of independent thinking. They go to the classroom, take notes, read their texts, memorize endless facts, and take exams. One recalls, in this connection, the old saying about course material going from the professor's lecture notes to the student's notebook without going through the heads of either.

By the time you have finished this course, you should be able to apply some method of critical analysis to your course material. Perhaps it will seem to you that a particular point is being made from an "I think that . . ." or "Generalizing from these facts . . ." basis. Or perhaps you just don't agree with the point being made. You should be able to define the problem, search the relevant literature, formulate a research study, collect and analyze the data, and arrive at some meaningful conclusion. Acquisition of the ability to investigate a problem scientifically is the specific aim of this text.

Tangential to this specific aim, it is hoped that your experiences in the laboratory may also communicate to you the sheer joy of discovery. One can only assume that the great explorers enjoyed a sense of discovery as they opened the new frontiers of our world. Yet such physical frontiers are diminishing daily and very few of us will be qualified to search, say, the new frontiers of space. To the scientist of behavior, however, the limitations on physical explorations are of but small personal concern. For him, the whole new frontier of mental, emotional, and behavioral characteristics is open. Indeed, rather than shrinking, this boundary seems to expand with each exploration. And when a particular exploration has been completed, the behavioral scientist also has the thrill of being the first to view and to know the new frontier.

There are several prerequisites for beginning the exploration of behavior. The necessity for independent thinking has already been touched upon. One must also be able to integrate information, derive new approaches, or formulate new problem areas in order to contribute significantly to psychological science. Much of scientific endeavor is conceptual and should be recognized as such.

Coupled with conceptualizing ability is training. Undoubtedly some of the notable physical explorations were made by individuals who, one day, just decided to see what was on the other side of the mountain. But, from Columbus to the astronauts, most of our knowledge of the world has come through systematically planned explorations by trained explorers. Similarly, one may expect that the notable discoveries in behavioral science will be made by well-trained individuals. The material in this book will begin this training by introducing you to three areas. First, you will investigate some of the basic tenets and assumptions that underlie the scientific method—*philosophy of science*. As these concepts are being developed, you will also learn some of the basic "how to" of science—*experimental design*. Finally, you will be shown some of the simpler methods for deriving conclusions from data—*statistics*. Perhaps this study will be your introduction to a lifelong career in psychological science.

To the Teacher

This text evolved from an introductory research course which presents some of the basic concepts of philosophy of science, experimental
design, and statistics as an integrated subject area. Students meet this
course for two hours lecture and three hours laboratory during both
semesters of the sophomore year. Typically, the first seven chapters of
the text are covered during the first semester and the remaining six
chapters during the second semester.

The first chapters serve to introduce the student to some of the
logical and design considerations which underlie all of psychological
research, graphic and descriptive methods, inferential techniques for
single and multiple samples, and report writing. A sample experiment
is developed in Chapter 2 and serves as a generally cohesive agent for

these first chapters. If a correlated laboratory experience is provided, the student may gain sufficient experience in various aspects of psychological research to permit some student-designed research to be conducted during the second semester.

The second portion of the book is directed toward giving the student a broad background of useful statistical techniques with relevant research design considerations. Some of the previously discussed design and methodology concepts are reviewed from a statistical point of view in Chapter 8. This material is followed by three chapters on parametric analysis techniques: confidence intervals, correlation and regression, and correlated-scores analysis of variance. The book concludes with two chapters devoted to scales of measurement and nonparametric techniques.

It is not feasible to list here all of the factors that influenced the decisions of what material to include in the text and what material to omit. Many of these decisions (e.g., the decision to omit the *t* techniques and cover, instead, analysis of variance techniques) are discussed in the *Instructor's Manual*, which is available from the publisher. The manual includes (1) a guide to the text, (2) a file of test questions from the text—multiple-choice, true-false, completion, short answer, and essay, and (3) answers to the student *Study Guide* which accompanies the text.

INTRODUCTION TO
PSYCHOLOGICAL RESEARCH
Logic, design, analysis

1. Philosophical and Logical Background

SCIENCE AS AN APPROACH TO KNOWLEDGE

Science and Common Sense

Man has been experimenting in one form or another since he appeared on the earth. The earliest, or common-sense sort of "experimentation," led to the use of fire, the development of the wheel, and many other advances which we today take for granted. Why, then, do we emphasize the use of the scientific method in experimentation? It may appear that man has made rather astounding progress using nothing more than his common sense.

A partial answer to this question is that common sense often leads to contradictory predictions about the proper course of behavior in any given situation. For example, consider the following guides to behavior:

Look before you leap.

He who hesitates is lost.

A person who systematically tried to follow all such common-sense rules might find himself in a state of continual ambivalence. The short-comings of deductions arising from such uncontrolled sensory observations were noted very early in recorded history and various systems were devised to compensate for them.

Rationalism and Empiricism

One of these systems was rationalism, a philosophy which insisted that some aspects of knowledge could not be gained through observation but could be known only through the mental process of reasoning. Rationalism traces its roots to the Greek philosophies of Aristotle and Plato, and has since been vigorously advocated by Hegel, Kant, Spinoza, and other philosophers. These rationalists believed that man, as a rational being, should be able to logically deduce the true state of the universe.

As has been true of many systems devised by man, rationalism was occasionally carried to extremes. The story is told that a group of monks sat for several days debating the number of teeth to be found in a horse's mouth. When one of the young novitiates could stand it no longer, he respectfully suggested to his elders that they settle the argument by counting the teeth of a nearby horse. Sad to relate, the elders took such offense at this breach of rationalistic ethics that they immediately banished the young novitiate.

Possibly in reaction to such irrational rationalism, a second philosophical viewpoint, empiricism, attempted to formulate rules for establishing order in man's perceptions of his universe. The early Greek empiricists believed that only the study and analysis of observations could lead to knowledge, i.e., they denied the uniqueness of reason as a special approach to knowledge. During the seventeenth and eighteenth centuries, this argument was rephrased by the philosophers Bacon, Locke, and Hume. This new group recognized perceptions as the source of truth but saw reason as indispensable for organizing this truth into knowledge. Their integration of the concepts of rationalism and early empiricism laid the philosophical foundation for the development of science as we know it today.

Science, Metaphysics, Religion, and Art

Our modern scientific concepts, then, are based upon the orderly organization of observable phenomena. This very insistence upon observable events may seem to be a denial of religion (the conception of ultimate causes and reality based on faith) and of metaphysics (a rational approach to ultimate causation and reality). However, as Whitehead (37)* points out, the insistence of Western religion upon a rational divine being actually laid the groundwork for the acceptance of science. Since God was perceived as being systematic in His creation, an understanding of the rules of that creation was regarded as possible. Eastern concepts of theology, which emphasized an impersonal or arbitrary deity, tended to discourage the development of such ordered patterns of thought.

The rise of science may also appear to the casual observer to have caused a partial rejection of the arts. One who writes, paints, or sculpts may be regarded by some people as making less than an essential contribution to the nation's progress. This tendency to undervalue art's relative contribution may arise from the many pragmatic advantages that have accrued to our culture from the pure and applied sciences. The pure sciences produce new knowledge, technology utilizes and applies this knowledge, and the general standard of living is raised. Such technological advances may help explain the near deification of the sciences which has only recently been modified by a resurge of interest in the arts.

By now you may be wondering why we are discussing the relationships of science to other approaches to knowledge instead of going directly to the "how" of experimental design. One of the major points which you should accept before beginning your study of psychological research is that the scientific method is simply one more system developed as an attempt to order the universe. Science has a limited domain with both methodological and logical boundaries. As a consequence, even all of our advances do not permit us to look to science for final answers or ultimate truths. At your point of training it is important to recognize not only the tremendous strengths, but also some of the limitations which are inherent in the techniques that you will use.

---

* References (listed on pp. 269–271) will be indicated in this manner throughout this text.

FOUNDATIONS OF SCIENCE

The Development of Science

Let us investigate, then, the development of a science as a first step in clarifying these strengths and limitations. A systematic pattern of growth has been exhibited by most of our current scientific disciplines. At first the embryonic science may exist only as a collection of half-truths and popular beliefs centered about a particular area. For psychology, these would be the host of common-sense statements which focus on human behavior. Philosophical and pseudoscientific systems are slowly developed in the attempt to integrate some of these general beliefs into logical systems from which systematic predictions can be made. This second development in the history of psychology is illustrated by Freudian philosophy and by the pseudoscience of phrenology.

From these early forerunners the new science slowly emerges. Much of the effort of the new laboratories is spent in relatively simple classification of the phenomena to be included in the science. Subsequently, the development of laws interrelating those phenomena can be initiated. Many of these early laws, however, are related to gross observations and may be of value only insofar as they lay the groundwork for further developments. These early laws also serve the purpose of summarizing in an easily comprehensible form the major interrelationships between observations. General theories constructed during this period are usually accurate enough to sustain scientific growth yet sufficiently inaccurate to cause some feeling of discontent.

As a science matures its theories become increasingly complex and its orientation changes from gross observation to minute and detailed experimentation. A growing concern for adequate explanation of the basic concepts is also expressed. Einstein's formulation of the general theory of relativity is illustrative of this search for basic laws which are generally comprehensive. The growth process of a science should not be viewed as a slow, on-going, cumulative development but rather as a progression from discontent with the old method of viewing data to a period of new experiments and theories, followed by further discontent, etc. As Kuhn (22, pp. 117–118) has demonstrated, the growth of a science seems more an evolution from its past than a growth toward the future.

This adaptability to changing times and reliance on changing evidence is one of the greatest strengths of science, in that it allows a continuous revision of man's understanding of his universe. Consider the changing beliefs about the shape of the world. The earliest observations from transits, surveyors, and bubble levels led very naturally to the accepted "scientific" understanding that the world was flat. As science developed and additional facts became available, this belief changed to a new "scientifically based" belief that the world was nearly round. Thus the adaptability of science permits a changing conceptualization of our universe.

From this example, you can understand that a scientifically based "belief" is quite different from a belief in religion or metaphysics. Since these latter two systems involve the study of ultimate reality, belief implies final truth. A scientific belief is tentative, stemming from a statement such as "Within the limitations of the data presently available, it appears that. . . ." Thus, scientific belief is often more in the nature of a best guess than a statement of absolute truth. These beliefs become more and more accurate as a science progresses. Older theories tend to be discredited by new facts derived from ever-increasing scientific investigations. New theories are then devised to accommodate all of the available evidence.

Causation and Indeterminacy

The tentative nature of scientific belief may leave some question in your mind as to whether or not we will ever understand the ultimate *causes* of behavior. The concept of causation has given scientists endless concern. We must accept the premise that there are certain systematic modes of behavior or else there would be little point in attempting to develop a science of behavior. Consider what chaos would exist if all people in the world behaved completely erratically! That behavior normally proceeds in a more-or-less predictable manner can be accepted without a great deal of experimental sophistication. The primary problem arises when we begin to isolate bits of this behavioral sequence and argue that X causes Y. To do so suggests that we live in a deterministic universe. By a deterministic universe we mean that *if* all of the factors influencing a particular event were known, then the event itself could be predicted with absolute certainty.

All of the subtleties of this argument do not need to be discussed now. However, some brief sketches of the point of view may be helpful. For example, the German philosopher Gödel (28) has demonstrated that one of our complex logical systems (arithmetic) will never be sufficiently complete to eliminate all contradictory predictions. This, if extended to all logical systems, leads to the possibility that no theory of behavior which we may construct in psychology will ever be totally correct. If a system can neither be complete nor totally correct, then all possibility of absolute determinism is eliminated.

The fallacy of complete determinism is further illustrated in Heisenberg's (15) discussion of subatomic particles. He has shown that, due to the interference of the observer, one may have certain knowledge of either the position of a particle or its velocity, but not both. If the position of the particle is known, its velocity may only be predicted. If the velocity is known, the position may only be predicted. These predictions, furthermore, are probabilistic rather than deterministic because they are subject to error.

Let us extend these findings to psychology. Since we suspect that the behavior of an organism, like that of an atomic particle, may change as a function of observation, only a limited portion of behavior may be known. As a consequence, we see that total behavior can only be probabilistically rather than absolutely predicted.

What, then, can be our position? We have seen that one must necessarily assume order to build a science, but it is possible that such order cannot be complete and that absolute truth can never be known. A resolution of this seeming paradox is found in the construction of a probabilistic view of truth. Using a probabilistic frame of reference, we do not state that a particular stimulus will absolutely make an organism behave in a specific manner. We only state that there is a certain degree of probability that the organism will behave in the predicted manner. That probability, however, may be extremely high. A typical goal of psychological science is the determination of such probabilistic rules or laws.

STRATEGIES OF RESEARCH

Approaches to Science

There are, of course, many different approaches to scientific investigation and the determination of probabilistic laws. It may seem to you that the taxonomist in biology may be less of a true scientist than is the experimental chemist. The taxonomist who studies the characteristics of a plant in order to correctly classify it may not appear to be experimenting in the same sense as is the chemist carefully controlling the quantities of chemicals in a reaction. These are both examples, however, of orderly approaches to the organization of observable phenomena. The particular approach, or research strategy, to be used depends both upon the problem to be solved and upon the resources available for attaining its solution.

In psychology, as in the other sciences, several different research strategies may be used by investigators in trying to resolve specific problems. Each of these approaches has some strengths and also some limitations. As we investigate four basic strategies of psychological research, try to relate each of them to specific problems that you personally might be interested in investigating.

Naturalistic Observation

Naturalistic observation is the collection of behavioral data in real-life situations with as little interference from the investigator as possible. One example of this research is Lott's (25) investigation of fighting signals in American bison. His observation of the behaviors which terminated fights between adult male bison led him to conclude that the submission signal of a defeated bison was the turned head and exposed flank. This signal usually terminated the attack by the dominant male and prevented serious injury or death to the defeated male.

Such studies have a minimum degree of artificiality in that the behaviors being recorded are those which one might expect to occur whether or not an observer is present. The less the observer intrudes, the greater is the assurance that the recorded behaviors are naturalistic. In Lott's study, since the bison appeared to be sensitively aware of men either on foot or on horseback but relatively undisturbed by motor vehicles, all notes were taken from the vantage point of an automobile.

This research strategy permits the scientist to accurately describe in some detail those naturally occurring behaviors that he has observed. However, explanations of the causes of this behavior are relatively weak. Since the observer must interfere as little as possible, the use of this research strategy permits only a minimum of control over either the environment or the behavior. For example, in Lott's study, it would be almost impossible to reproduce the observed behavior under laboratory conditions where prior experience with "losses" and "wins" could be systematically manipulated.

As a consequence, although Lott favors the "prior experience" ex-

7

planation of the dominance–submission signaling in bison, he recognizes as an alternative explanation that the signaling may be an innate, species-specific behavior. It would be difficult to test the accuracy of either explanation.

In general, then, naturalistic observation provides accurate descriptions but seldom yields explanations of the causes of the observed behavior, although possible alternative explanations may be derived for further study by other research strategies.

Correlational Studies

A second strategy often used in psychological research is the correlational study. The object of such a study is the determination of the degree of relationship which exists between two variables. Many correlational studies were presented in your introductory psychology course. One commonly cited study explores the relationship between IQ scores of parents and their children (7). Although the necessity for measuring the two variables involved in such a study usually implies a greater degree of artificiality than is found in naturalistic observations, the quantitative results of such a study permit descriptions which are more accurate than is verbal description alone. Then, too, when a reliable relationship is found to exist between two variables it becomes possible to predict the strength of one trait through a knowledge of its correlate.

Let us consider the concept of prediction as it relates to correlational studies in psychology. For example, if we know that a person has an IQ of 80 as measured by some standardized intelligence test, we may predict that he probably will not succeed in college. The general statement underlying this specific prediction is that there tends to be, over the population as a whole, a positive relationship between IQ scores and college achievement (8). This, and related problems, are essentially correlational in nature. The practical advantages of predictive relationships should be immediately apparent.

One serious limitation to the use of this research technique lies not with the stated relationship, but with the user of the relationship. Causation is too often inferred from prediction. In the example above, this distinction may not be perfectly clear. It may seem reasonable to state that the *reason* the person with an IQ of 80 will not succeed in college is *because* he lacks the requisite intelligence.

Perhaps if the example is changed, the fallacy of arguing causation from prediction will become more apparent. We might find that the amount of diaper rash in babies in the United States is significantly related to the number of miles of highway built in Ireland. From this general statement, we could make the specific prediction that if diaper rash in the United States is increasing, the number of miles of highway being built in Ireland is also increasing.

The fallacy of arguing that the *reason* highways are built in Ireland is *because* babies are having diaper rash in the United States should be obvious. In this particular case, a more nearly reasonable "explanation" might be that both diaper rash and highway building tend to increase in summer months and to decrease in winter. You should note, however, that even this explanation might be incorrect. Such predictive relationships are always open to alternative explanation.

A survey of correlational studies may reveal other questionable explanations that seem to have been similarly derived. Possibly you recall one study usually discussed in introductory psychology which shows a significant relationship between the severity of weaning and later psychological adjustment (32). The relationship usually inferred is that severe weaning *causes* psychological maladjustment. Are there alternative explanations that you could advance?

Correlational studies are similar to naturalistic observations in that it is risky to infer causation from either. Use of the correlational study usually implies a greater degree of artificiality than exists with naturalistic observation, due both to the preselection of the variables to investigate and to the necessity for accurate measurement. This disadvantage, however, may be offset by a gain in the quality of description and by the advantage of quantitative prediction. The correlational technique, like other research strategies, should be used only when it appears to be the one most appropriate to the solution of the problem under investigation.

True Experiments

The true experiment in psychology is at an opposite pole from naturalistic observation in two respects: It has both maximum artificiality and maximum control. The necessity for maximum control is found in the logic underlying the simple two-group experiment. If maximum control has been exercised, the performance of the two groups to be tested should initially be exactly equal. If the two groups are then treated identically in all respects except one, any subsequent differences in performance should be attributable to the one way in which they were treated differently. For example, assume that we have been so fortunate as to have available for an experiment two groups exactly equal in all respects. The results of any test that we might administer would show no difference between the two groups. Suppose that we now treat these groups in two different ways, administering a stimulant to one group but not the other. If the results of a test then indicate some difference between the two groups, it is logical to assume that the administration of the stimulant caused this difference. This true experimental approach is the primary method for formulating the probabilistic laws of psychology, as it overcomes that inability to determine causal relations which is one of the severest limitations of both the naturalistic observation and the correlational study.

Let us investigate the structure of the simple psychological experiment in more detail. An experiment is usually designed in terms of its dependent and independent variables. The distinction between these two variables may be clarified if you consider them from the point of view of the person who participates as a subject in the experiment. The dependent variable is that variable which is dependent upon what the subject does in the experiment; the administration of the independent variable is independent of what the subject does. It is important to recognize that the manipulation of the independent variable must represent purposive intervention on the part of the experimenter in the true experiment. That is, two initially equal groups are treated differently *by the experimenter*.

As an example, if we are trying to determine the effects of a stimulant on test taking, the administration of the stimulant is the independent variable. We say that the administration of the stimulant is independent of what the subject does because, once he has agreed to participate in the experiment, the subject will either receive the stimulant or not receive it as directed by the experimenter. The dependent variable in this case is test-taking performance. This is called the dependent variable because the subject himself determines what score he gets on the test, i.e., his score is dependent upon his performance. Note that this experiment, if properly controlled, should lead to the development of some lawful relationship or causal statement that can be made within a probabilistic framework.

A third type of variable may inadvertently enter into the true experiment if control has not been complete. These are termed extraneous variables because they are unwanted or "extra" variables which may lead to erroneous conclusions concerning the results of the study. Good experimentation should, insofar as possible, control those extraneous variables that might affect the outcome of the study. In the study of the effects of a stimulant upon test-taking ability, as outlined above, assume that all subjects in the control (or normal-condition) group were tested in a quiet room with sufficient lighting. Assume also that all stimulant-treated subjects were tested in a darkened and noisy room. At the end of this experiment, it would be extremely difficult to tell whether any recorded differences between the two groups were due to the stimulant administration, to room lighting, to room noise, to some other variable, or to some combination of these factors.

When extraneous variables have been controlled, the true experiment yields the strongest conclusions of any of the various research strategies. When this method is coupled with what Platt (29) termed strong inference, maximum progress in the development of psychological theory may be expected. Essentially, strong inference means the theoretical formulation of mutually exclusive predictions for a given set of conditions, the design of an experiment which will eliminate all but one of these predictions (and placing limitations on the theories from which these incorrect predictions were made), then reformulation and the testing of more advanced possible explanations which include the new data. To use an analogy, the process of strong inference is the most direct route to experimental truth—at each fork in the road the correct alternative is chosen on the basis of experimental evidence, while theory serves to guide the exploration, suggest alternatives, and interpret findings.

The true experiment, then, is quite dissimilar to either naturalistic observation or the correlational study in that the inference of causation is possible. Note that this great advantage of the true experiment is coupled with the disadvantage that maximum control is requisite if the conclusions are to be valid. Maximum control also implies maximum artificiality in that we cannot be certain that the behaviors observed in the laboratory are identical to those which would occur outside that situation. It is obvious, however, that subjects do exhibit behavior in the laboratory. If this laboratory behavior can be adequately explained, we may predict that a majority of nonlaboratory behavior will follow similar patterns.

Ex Post Facto *Studies*

The fourth research strategy, the *ex post facto* study, closely resembles a true experiment, except that probabilistic causation cannot be inferred from the results. As the name implies, an *ex post facto* study is one in which the independent variable is chosen "after the fact" or without direct experimental manipulation. That is, with the true experiment, an experimenter begins with initially equated groups and then treats these groups differently. In the *ex post facto* study, the experimenter begins with groups which are initially different in some respect and then treats these groups identically.

An example may help to illustrate this difference. Suppose that an investigator were interested in determining whether blondes would exhibit higher anxiety than would brunettes. He might administer a standardized anxiety scale to one sample of natural blondes from the population and administer the same test to an equal number of natural brunettes. The investigation would be an *ex post facto* study because the groups were selected on the basis of an *initial difference* (natural hair color) rather than beginning with *initially equal* groups which were subsequently treated differently. For purposes of this illustration, let us assume that the results are in the direction predicted by the investigator, i.e., the blondes score higher on the anxiety scale. May this investigator conclude that high anxiety scores are *caused* by having blond hair? No, for he cannot know that hair color is the *only* difference between the two groups. If, in fact, hair color *is* the causative agent, it would be possible for a brunette to raise her anxiety level, or for a blond to lower hers, simply by changing the color of her hair. Possibly some unidentified factor, such as a biochemical compound, causes both blond hair and anxiety. The *ex post facto* study is similar to a correlation study in that alternative explanations may always be advanced as the cause of the existing relationship.

The fact that causation cannot be inferred from a single *ex post facto* study should not lead you to reject this research strategy. Many of the phenomena that we might like to investigate are not amenable to direct experimental manipulation in the laboratory. Suppose that we wished to study the differences in patterns of responses to a personality test for groups differing in socioeconomic background. To design a true experiment to investigate this problem would be extremely difficult, for we would have to begin with initially equal groups and then administer some experimental treatment which changed their socioeconomic background. A more appropriate method for investigation of this problem is an *ex post facto* study; the groups to be studied will be initially different (selected because of the varying socioeconomic backgrounds) and then treated identically (measured on a standardized test).

12

It is relatively easy to see that we could not infer causation from such a study even if the groups were found to exhibit different personality patterns. We know that the selected groups are systematically different in many ways other than socioeconomic background. For example, intelligence-test scores tend to be higher for the higher socioeconomic groups. Perhaps the differences that we observe in personality patterns are caused by this difference in IQ scores rather than by the difference in socioeconomic status.

A similar situation is presented to the psychological scientist in his search for facts concerning differences between the sexes, between races, or between other naturally occurring groups. Obviously it would be impossible to experimentally treat a randomly sampled group of individuals in some manner to make them females or Caucasians or shorter than average. Perhaps it is not so obvious, however, that we may also use *ex post facto* studies to determine the characteristics of groups which have differed with respect to some kind of behavior. For example, in what ways do those people who are involved in a riot differ from those who refuse to participate? What are the differences between people who develop psychoses and those who do not? In each of these cases, it is appropriate to select groups that differ initially on the variable we wish to study. Such studies would then be classified as *ex post facto*.

With respect to the other research strategies, the *ex post facto* study seems to occupy a middle ground. Like naturalistic observations and correlational studies, *ex post facto* studies permit accurate description. And, as with the true experiment, testing should be carried out under conditions of maximum control of extraneous variables.

CONTROLLING EXTRANEOUS VARIABLES

Systematic Extraneous Variables

In our discussion of research strategies, the need for careful control of extraneous variables has been either directly stated or implied. These extraneous variables, or unwanted variations in the experimental procedure, can be conveniently divided into two classes: systematic and nonsystematic. Systematic extraneous variables are those which uniformly affect a group of subjects participating in an experiment, causing a systematic distortion in the data collected for the group. This was illustrated by the experiment in which all of the "stimulant administered" subjects took the experimental test under one set of conditions (dark, noisy room) not related to the independent variable, and all of the subjects in the control group took the test under a different set of conditions (well-lit, quiet room) which were unrelated to the independent variable. The independent variable (drug administration), of course, should have been the only true difference between conditions for the two groups. If a difference was found to exist between these two groups it would be difficult to determine whether the difference was due to the independent variable or to the extraneous variable or variables. Reaching any valid conclusion becomes impossible in such an instance.

Systematic extraneous variables operating between two experimental groups may also cancel out the effect of the experimental manipulation of the independent variable, causing us to conclude that there is no difference between the two experimental treatments when, in fact, a true difference does exist. To determine the effect of vocabulary training upon subsequent vocabulary-test scores, for example, we might design an experiment in which one group of subjects receives vocabulary training while the other group does not. Both groups are then given the same vocabulary test. Assume that, in addition to the independent variable of vocabulary training, our two groups also differ with respect to the extraneous variable of sex—all subjects in the vocabulary training group are males and all subjects in the control group are females. In this case, the finding of no marked group differences between the test scores following the experimental treatment would not permit us to conclude that the training was ineffective. Possibly the males were initially inferior to the females and the treatment was successful in raising their vocabulary scores to a comparable level. Note that the extraneous variable in this example, sex differences, did not permit us to make the assumption that the two groups were initially equal and thus the study may not be accepted as a true experiment.

You may wonder why such a strong point is being made about situations that appear to be perfectly obvious. The particular examples that we have chosen as illustrations of the effect of systematic extraneous variables have been exaggerated. In actual experimentation, these effects may be very subtle. One group of student experimenters, for example, wished to study the effects of verbal suggestion on performance. They gave the experimental group a placebo (a dummy pill containing only starch) but made the suggestion that the placebo was actually a stimulant. The control group received only the general test instructions. Although the two groups did differ in their test performance, this difference could not be attributed to the effects of verbal suggestion, for the two groups also differed in another respect: one group had been given a placebo and the other group had not. It would be impossible to determine whether the observed difference was due to verbal suggestion, to administration of the placebo, or to a combination of both factors. A better way to study the effect of suggestion would be to give each group the same placebo but with different types of suggestion.

Another systematic extraneous variable which has a very subtle effect is that of experimenter bias. Even naturalistic observations, in which a minimum of control is desired, are not immune to the effects of this systematic extraneous variable. The investigator who begins his observation with some preconceived notions about the type of data he is likely to collect must guard against possible unintentional biasing of the results. All of his errors in recording or analysis of the data may unconsciously tend to favor the experimental group, and differences between the groups then become more a function of this bias than of true differences actually observed.

The effects of experimenter bias as a possible extraneous variable have been dramatically demonstrated by Rosenthal (30) in a study involving two groups of rats. Unknown to the student experimenters, the two sets of cages contained nearly identical animals, chosen so that litter mates (brother and sister pairs) were evenly divided. The students were told prior to beginning the study that Cage A contained "maze-bright rats" and that Cage B contained "maze-dull rats." At the end of the first group of test trials, when the results were analyzed, the effect of experimenter bias was very evident. The recorded data indicated that the rats in Cage A ran more accurately in the maze than did the rats in Cage B, when in fact the performances should have been nearly equal for rats which were almost identical. As a check on this unexpected result, another group of student experimenters was instructed that Cage B contained the maze-bright rats and that Cage A contained the maze-dull rats. The same experiment was performed; and, when these data were analyzed, the Cage B rats were shown to have performed more accurately than had those in Cage A.

Control of experimenter bias is extremely difficult because it usually operates to confirm the experimenter's predictions. When an experimenter is thoroughly immersed in a particular theoretical position, he is seldom skeptical of experimental results that confirm his predictions.

Consequently, the investigator may not bother to check for the influence of experimenter bias. Those investigators who are concerned about this influence have gone to great lengths to collect unbiased experimental data by using mechanized data collection or employing research assistants who are uninformed regarding the predicted behavior.

Methods for Controlling Systematic Extraneous Variables

Since systematic extraneous variables uniformly effect the performance of whole groups in the experiment, psychologists have developed several methods for their control. When it is relatively apparent that certain factors could cause an experiment to yield an incorrect conclusion, the methods of control tend to be fairly direct. A given experiment may, depending upon the possible occurrence of extraneous variables, use one or a combination of several of these methods for control.

One of the most desirable methods of control is to completely *eliminate* an extraneous variable from the study. This method is restricted to variables which may have a value of O (e.g., the amount of stray light present in a study of dark adaptation). Many of the extraneous variables encountered in research are difficult to control by this method.

A second method of controlling these extraneous variables is that of *balancing* the occurrence of the variable. Again with respect to possible sex differences, we might have an equal number of males and females in each group. Similarly, we might equate intelligence, educational background, hair color, eye color, weight, height, or any of a number of other possible variables. When balancing is carried to extremes, we find that we are limited in the type of subject we may select. For example, we might find that a brown-eyed, five-foot-four, IQ 100, weight 125, female with three years of college is required to complete a balanced group. Thus, balancing can be only partially effective; and, in general, the goal is to balance out the known effective variables. It would seem apparent, for example, that intelligence would be a more important variable in verbal test taking than would be eye color. As a consequence, the intelligence variable should be balanced prior to the balancing of eye color. In a study of color vision, of course, eye color may be more important than intelligence, and would therefore receive preference in balancing procedures.

A third method for the control of extraneous variables is to insure that *equivalent* conditions obtain for all subjects. It is probable that we cannot achieve completely soundproof rooms, and therefore we cannot totally eliminate noise as a background variable in an experiment. However, it might be possible to have approximately the same noise level for each group. One method of control is to test each group of subjects in the same room. In this way the color of the walls, the lighting of the room, the noise in the room, the size of the desk, the size of the room are all held constant for the subjects. Any variation in the behavior of the two groups would not then be attributable to changes in room conditions.

If we cannot control extraneous variables by any of these methods, we can perhaps use a *counterbalancing* technique in which each subject experiences the test procedure under both normal (control) conditions and manipulated (experimental) conditions. For example, one half of the group of subjects would first receive the stimulant before being tested, and would later repeat the test without having received the stimulant beforehand. The other subjects would first take the test under normal conditions and then repeat the test under the stimulant condition. Extraneous variables such as fatigue, practice, learning, and transfer may all be controlled to some degree by the use of the counterbalance technique.

When we have attempted some systematic control for all of the extraneous variables which prior research has shown to affect our proposed study, will our study then be error free? No, even when all of the known systematic controls have been applied one may never be certain that all extraneous variables are equal or balanced out for all subjects. In particular, consideration of differences in genetic inheritance and environmental background of subjects should make it readily apparent that our techniques for controlling systematic sources of error may be inadequate. In such circumstances, the technique of *randomization* may be used in addition to other techniques to insure that the groups are initially equated.

Randomization

Randomization is one of the control techniques used most often in psychological research. If subjects are assigned randomly into groups and the groups randomly assigned to experimental conditions, by chance alone we should have approximately equated groups. Then most extraneous variables should be approximately balanced for the two groups. This eliminates to some extent the necessity for more direct balance. However, the experimenter must insure that his own particular biases or influences do not enter into the selection of the subjects to be used. For example, if we have a male experimenter and a female experimenter their personal biases might dictate that all of the female subjects be assigned to the group being run by the male and vice versa. Such biasing of the randomization procedure might well ruin the scientific value of the experiment.

In careful studies (19, pp. 57–59) of the randomization process it has been found that relatively small samples will tend to balance out a large number of characteristics. For example, in random selections from the census list as few as thirty people will, in most instances, tend to have approximately the mean height of all people in the United States, the mean weight, even such minutia as the mean number of hairs on the left leg, mean number of atypical white blood cells, etc.

We have seen that it would be extremely difficult to balance by selection alone all of the possible variables that might affect the outcome of an experiment. With randomization, however, we may assume that large numbers of these extraneous variables are approximately equivalent for all the experimental groups. This procedure should be kept as nearly random a process as is possible. Special tables have been generated for the purpose of random selection and the student is referred to more advanced texts (10, 35) for such lists.

Nonsystematic Extraneous Variables

In addition to the systematic extraneous variables which uniformly affect a set of data, the psychological researcher must also contend with the action of extraneous variables which may vary from one subject to another. For example, the strength of the relationship between two variables in a correlational study might fluctuate depending upon the degree to which extraneous variables are present. Such fluctuating errors are primarily a result of sloppiness in research and can be eliminated by a proper attention to written procedures.

In one case an investigator might "wake up on the wrong side of the bed" and as a consequence be rude and gruff to his subject, ignore the printed set of instructions, and be generally uncooperative. It is very likely that this subject will have a low score on this test variable regardless of his true ability. Should this investigator follow instructions precisely with his next subject, any difference between the scores of the two subjects may be more a function of "experimenter condition" than of differences between the subjects' true ability levels.

Control of such unwanted variations in psychological research is partly a function of experience in following an explicit procedure. Your laboratory training in the actual collection of data will help you to gain this valuable experience. In addition, systematic planning of the experimental procedure, rigid adherence to instruction sheets, and some pretesting of subjects to insure familiarity with actual testing procedures are useful in eliminating these experimenter-oriented sources of experimental error.

A second major source of nonsystematic errors in an experiment arises from the selection of an unreliable test as the dependent variable. If subjects do not tend to retain their relative placement with respect to each other when the test is readministered under similar conditions, the test is not a reliable indicator of the subjects' ability. If this ability is not accurately measured by the test, it is unlikely that the test will accurately indicate differences in ability. Thus, where we are afforded a choice of tests to be used in measuring the dependent variable, the most reliable test should be chosen.

A third source of nonsystematic extraneous variables is careless processing of the data which have been accumulated. One group of student experimenters concluded, in their report of an experiment, that no systematic differences could be found between the performances of the experimental and the control groups. Several pages of their discussion were devoted to possible reasons why, although the graph of the results seemed to indicate differences, the actual computation did not support this conclusion. The instructor later found that one student had misplaced a decimal in his data, and that true differences between the groups probably did exist. Avoidance of such non-systematic errors implies care in following explicit procedure in recording all data exactly.

Some influence of nonsystematic extraneous variables is to be expected in any experiment. Even the control of all systematic variables can not insure that all subjects will be exactly equal in the way in which they react to the experimental treatments; although randomization helps to insure that, for the groups as a whole, such variables are balanced. Thus, an appropriate goal of precise experimentation is the minimizing of nonsystematic extraneous errors rather than their complete elimination.

EXPERIMENTAL RELIABILITY AND VALIDITY

Nonsystematic Error and Reliability

Accepting the fact that our control of nonsystematic extraneous variables cannot be complete, what will be the effect of these variables on the experiment? The primary effect of some of the nonsystematic extraneous variables is to reduce the reliability of the experiment. If the experiment were to be replicated using another sample of subjects, with different quantities of these extraneous variables operating, conflicting results might be obtained. Such an experiment is not reliable.

We can compare reliability in an experiment to an example of reliability in testing. A test instrument, as we know, should be reliable. Suppose that we have decided to use a rubber tape measure as a test instrument for measuring height. When we measure an individual at one time we may stretch this rubber tape measure more than at another time and, as a consequence, we would tend to obtain varying estimates of a person's height. Although this person may be, in fact, taller than another person the variability in our measurements will tend to obscure this difference.

A similar situation exists in the experiment. If our hypothetical study of the effect of the stimulant is not conducted in a precise manner, many possible extraneous variables may be operating to make our measures of verbal test-taking ability inaccurate. This corresponds to the varying measurements obtained with the rubber tape measure. Similarly, as differences between heights may be obscured by the variability in the tape measure, so may any true differences between the stimulant group and the normal group be obscured by these unwanted variations. A first requirement, then, for the psychological experiment is that it be reliable—that it be a *consistent,* or dependable, experiment.

Systematic Errors and Validity

The second general requirement for an experiment is that it be valid. Validity, in a psychometric sense, is how well the test actually measures what its name indicates that it measures. Thus, a valid intelligence test actually measures intelligence. This has been humorously redefined as the degree to which the test reports what it purports to report. The psychological experiment should also be valid. Obviously, an experiment in which systematic extraneous variables have caused a reversal of the true direction of results is not a valid experiment. That is, the experiment does not truly indicate that which it was intended to indicate. The same statement can also be made of those experiments or studies in which the anticipated effect is enhanced by the presence of systematic errors of control. In such an instance, the investigator may report larger differences between his groups than may actually exist if testing were unbiased.

Other Sources of Poor Experimental Validity

From our knowledge of probabilistic determinism, our inability to control all possible variations in the genetic background and environment of our subjects, and the possibility that all systematic extraneous variables may not have been controlled, it is apparent that we can never have complete assurance that any study is truly valid. The outcome of an experiment, then, should not be stated as "If *A*, then *B*" but rather as "If usually *A*, then probably *B*." It is from this lack of assurance of total validity that exists in every experiment that the scientist learns his degree of skepticism with respect to conclusions derived from even the most carefully controlled study. However, when one surveys the progress of science one must conclude that most experiments must be relatively valid, or else such astounding scientific progress could not have been made.

The lack of absolute validity, however, is usually less important than some of the ways that validity can be reduced. For example, if our experiment is concerned with verbal test-taking ability, then the dependent variable should be a valid measure of that ability. Perhaps the particular test that we have used involved comprehension, speed, mathematical ability, logical symbolism, or any of a host of other characteristics beyond the specific one of verbal test taking. Any conclusion that we might make from such an experiment might be in error with respect to our stated purpose. The validity of an experiment determines the generalizations we may make from that experiment.

If our test yields significant results, we may state with certainty that for the actual students tested in that specific room with that particular test, the results were as actually found. An experimenter, however, is rarely willing to limit his conclusions to one small group, one limited sample of conditions, or one particular measure. Frequently he wishes to generalize beyond the specific results, perhaps extending his findings to all college students. In view of some of the reports in the literature, it seems probable that some experimenters might even like to make some assertion that will be applicable to all people and for all times. If such sweeping generalization is the ultimate goal of an experiment, then we must assess the validity of the experiment. Are the results in fact comparable to those which would be obtained for all people? Is the particular test of verbal material a good measure of the dependent variable? These are questions which must be carefully considered by the experimenter.

Relationships Between Reliability and Validity

In some ways the relationship between the reliability and the validity of a research study is similar to that of a testing situation. If the study is not reliable, it cannot be valid. That is, if the study is likely to yield contradictory results when replicated, then the conclusions based on that study are valueless. Thus, control of nonsystematic sources of error is a requirement for any psychological research.

It is perhaps not so obvious that we may design a very reliable study which is not valid. Suppose that we wished to determine whether or not males have superior intelligence with respect to females. Since the two groups would be selected on the basis of a preexisting difference, this investigation is an *ex post facto* study. Let us assume that strength of grip in the right hand as measured by a hand dynamometer is used as the dependent variable. If proper care is used in the testing procedure (control for nonsystematic extraneous variables), a reliable difference between males and females could likely be found. Thus, the study is reliable. The investigators would, however, be in serious error if they concluded that males have superior intelligence since they demonstrate superior strength of grip. Thus, this very reliable study lacks validity in that generalizations about intelligence made on the basis of the study will be in serious error.

OPERATIONAL DEFINITIONS AND CONSTRUCT VALIDITY

Generalizations from Different Studies

Let us consider some of the other factors involved in generalization from experimental data. Suppose that two investigators wished to study the effect of anxiety on performance. Anxiety is a broad topic and it is unlikely that many of the related problems will be resolved by a single experiment. Consequently two quite different approaches to the problem may be undertaken. One investigator may decide to use two extremely different groups as his subjects in an *ex post facto* study. He may have several clinical psychologists select patients who show extremely high levels of anxiety. By selecting only these subjects as his experimental group, he hopes to maximize the effects of anxiety on performance. The performance of this group would have to be compared with that of a normal control group. As a dependent variable, he decides to measure simple reaction time to light. For purposes of illustration, let us say that this experimenter, using subjects clinically identified as "anxious," finds that highly anxious subjects achieve significantly poorer performance scores (i.e., react more slowly) than do normal subjects.

A second investigator, approaching the same problem, might choose college students as the subjects for a true experiment. Anxiety would be induced in the experimental group by warning each subject that he would receive a mild electric shock if his reaction time was slow. The control group would receive neither the warning nor the shock. Let us assume that this experimenter, using threat of shock, finds that highly anxious subjects have a significantly faster reaction time than do control subjects. If we accept simple generalizations from these two groups, we find an apparent contradiction. One experimenter, upon completion of his experiment, concludes that anxiety impairs performance, while the other concludes that anxiety improves performance. To build a systematic science, it is necessary that we have some means for the reconciliation of such results.

Operational Definitions

One technique used in psychology is that of the operational definition. By "operational definition" we mean that each word is defined in terms of the operations necessary to produce it. In our two studies, the first experimenter has defined high anxiety as that judged by clinical psychologists; the second experimenter has defined high anxiety as that produced by the threat of shock. The contradictory conclusions may result from the differences in the two definitions.

The use of operational definitions began with philosophy but very soon was expanded into the scientific realm. For example, Bridgman (5) has shown that the revolution from Newtonian to Einsteinian physics was due to inadequate operational definitions of time. According to Bridgman, "Explanation consists in reducing a situation to elements with which we are so familiar that we accept them as a matter of course, so that our curiosity rests."

In the two experiments discussed above, explanation of the effect of anxiety requires operational definitions for both "highly anxious" and "performance." Perhaps most of us will accept as a matter of course the statement that the use of threat of shock as an anxiety provoker will lead to quicker reaction time as measured by a standard instrument.

You have seen operational definitions used in psychology many times. For example, the preferred definition of intelligence stated in most introductory psychology texts is: Intelligence *is* that which a properly standardized intelligence test measures. This may seem to be leaving most of the "meat" out of what you consider to be the *real* meaning of intelligence. Intuitively, intelligence means some abstract form of reasoning caused by an unknown genetic process. Unfortunately an intuitive definition does not permit us to specify the operations needed to measure it. The very use of the word "intuitive" immediately rules out the possibility of an operational definition. Intelligence defined as "that which a properly standardized intelligence test measures" is a term upon which psychologists can agree. The conclusions that one makes using this operational definition are readily understood by others and easily integrated into the body of scientific knowledge. A psychologist who wished to define intelligence in some other terms might come to different conclusions. These different conclusions, however, would not necessarily stand in contradiction to those results previously found by other investigators who used a different definition of intelligence. As a consequence, most psychological reports in the literature specify in detail the operations necessary to produce the results.

The proper use of operational definitions saves much useless argument. One class in introductory experimental psychology had decided to test the effect of distraction on performance, using sound as the distraction. In their discussions of the basic design one student asked, "But how do we know whether a sound is distracting or not? I know some people can just completely ignore things like that." After some heated discussion about "tuning out" noise and distraction, this student then asked, "Aren't we supposed to keep the experimental conditions constant for all subjects? If the sound is distracting to some people and not distracting to others, how can we say that we are testing the effects of distraction?" This particular argument arose from the confusion between distraction as an individual experience and distraction as a physical quantity. The first meaning relates to the private world of the subject which can never be precisely known by another and therefore cannot be isolated as the object of an experiment.

Distraction in the latter sense, that of a physically manipulable quantity, is capable of operational definition. Had these students developed such an operational definition for distraction, they might have defined it as "the presence of a 90 db white-noise signal." With this definition, the problem of establishing uniform experimental conditions for all subjects is solved. The experimenter needs only to insure that each experimental subject receives exactly the same amount of 90 db white noise.

Construct Validity

Even the use of operational definitions in the experiment described above will not reveal the true inner state of the subject. One still never really knows whether or not the subject was distracted. Does this, then, imply that none of the concepts of psychological science can ever make intuitive sense or have rich meaning? No, quite to the contrary, operational definitions are but one step in psychological science. Higher-order definitions and meaning come with what is known as "construct validity" (9). By a construct we mean the definition of a rich psychological term, such as "anxiety," in sufficient detail to formulate a miniature theory of that term. With this construct, a method of measurement is usually also implied. For the anxiety experiment, a measure such as the Taylor Manifest Anxiety Scale could be employed. Predictions can be made from the theory surrounding the construct and subsequent verification of these predictions will lend weight to the validity of the construct. Unfortunately, none of the constructs will ever be completely proven in that new predictions will always be possible. Thus the process of establishing construct validity becomes one of converging evidence. The first one or two predictions verified may still leave some doubt regarding the validity, but as more and more predictions are verified, we become more certain of the inherent meaning behind a construct. Thus, construct validation is an infinitely long process, never absolutely complete. However, from one point of view, the validation of constructs *is* the total problem of psychology. If every possible psychological construct (intelligence, drive, emotion, love, hate, etc.) were ever to be completely validated, most of the current problems of psychology would have been resolved.

The relationship of this text and your studies to construct validity should be apparent. Validation of constructs requires the verification of predictions made from a given theory. As this text progresses, you will become increasingly familiar with the techniques of defining problems, designing studies, analyzing the results, and deriving sound conclusions. Each successfully completed study becomes one more step in the process of validating a given construct.

SUMMARY

The purpose of this section has been to introduce you to some of the philosophical, logical, and methodological issues underlying psychological research. We first looked for reasons why we use the scientific method and science in an attempt to order our universe. It was seen that many approaches to order have been used, some to excess. This reminded us that the scientific method is but one more attempt to organize our universe, and blind faith should not necessarily be placed in the experimental method.

Other approaches to the establishment of order included religion or metaphysics, and the arts and humanities. All have the same goal as science—understanding—but use different techniques. The scientific approach relies upon the rational organization of observable events, metaphysics and religion rely upon unobservable phenomena, and the arts and humanities emphasize the interpretive or intuitive understanding of events. These three current methods are not necessarily in opposition to each other.

Next, some of the various research strategies used in psychological research were explored: naturalistic observation, correlational studies, the true experiment, and the *ex post facto* study. The decision of which strategy to use was seen to be a function of the problem to be solved and the resources available for solving it.

In all of these approaches to understanding psychology, the presence of both systematic and nonsystematic extraneous variables was seen as undesirable. One of the most difficult systematic extraneous variables to control was experimenter bias, which could affect even a naturalistic observation study. The effect of other systematic sources of error could be reduced by using the five methods of: (1) elimination, (2) balance,

(3) equivalence, (4) counterbalance, and (5) randomization. One of the primary methods used to control nonsystematic error was the development of, and adherence to, a systematic plan for conducting the experiment.

The effect of the operation of these unwanted nonsystematic variables was demonstrated to be equivalent to the reduction of reliability in a test situation. The psychological experiment was also found to require validity. Validity in the experimental sense was directly related to the generalizations that are made from that experiment. These generalizations required operational definition of terms to reduce incompatibility of results.

As a final step, construct validation was seen as one of the important tasks of psychological science, involving all of the preceding steps—philosophy, logic, control, prediction, verification, experimentation, reliability, and generalization.

2. Designing an Experiment

PROBLEM SELECTION: SYSTEMATIC APPROACHES

Systematic vs. Nonsystematic Approaches

The basic procedures of psychological experimentation are the same as those found in other sciences. One designs an experiment, collects and analyzes the data, and reports any significant findings. In this chapter we shall examine the first step, that of experimental design.

To design an experiment, one must first have an idea which he wishes to test. To the experienced investigator in a field, this is often the least part of the problem. So many areas continually present questions that it is more often a matter of choosing among problems than of attempting to derive one. For the beginner, however, choosing a problem is often one of the most difficult steps in designing an experiment. It may appear to the inexperienced eye that almost every subject has already been the basis of some experimentation, and that truly "there is nothing new under the sun."

To help you overcome this initial feeling, let us look at some of the ways in which experienced investigators may select problems for experimentation. These methods tend to divide themselves into either systematic or nonsystematic approaches. In following a systematic approach to problem selection, the initial idea for the study is selected by a rational or logical process, usually after a relatively thorough study of some particular field of psychology. In contrast, when a nonsystematic or intuitional approach is used, the integration of the problem into a specific area of psychology often follows rather than precedes the initial idea.

We shall begin with four systematic approaches to the generation of research ideas: theory testing, extending the range of applicability of current studies, resolution of conflicting reports, and replication of previous experiments.

Theory Testing

The first approach, *theory testing*, is quite possibly the foundation for more reports in the psychological literature than any of the other approaches that we shall discuss. Marx (26) pointed to the reason for the preponderance of theory testing when he defined theory's dual role as both a tool and a goal. Theories are, in general, summary statements that interrelate the results of several experiments. Theories, however, also predict events not yet tested. An experimenter who is familiar with the current theories in a particular area may devise an experiment to test the validity of a specific theory. For science to move forward there must be a constant interchange between observation and theorizing.

We have previously seen that theory testing, coupled with strong inference (29), is possibly the most rapid method for a science to advance. When an established theory can be revised on the basis of experimental evidence, then a study has served a dual function by contributing the additional empirical knowledge connected with the actual results of the experiment and also by making possible the integration of many other studies. One of the most fruitful methods for gaining new ideas for an experiment, then, is to become thoroughly familiar with the existing theories relating to a specific area of psychology.

One excellent example of the combination of theory testing and strong inference is given in a study on expectancies by Carlsmith and Aronson (6). The actual procedure, as in many well-designed experiments, was relatively simple. The subjects (hereafter abbreviated as *S*s) were informed by the experimenter (hereafter abbreviated as *E*) that they were to serve in two unrelated experiments at the same time. The first problem was a study of how accurately the *S*s could interpret minor cues given by the *E*. In front of each *S* were 24 paper cups, each containing either a sweet solution or a bitter solution. The *S* was to try to guess, on the basis of some mannerism of the *E*, whether a particular cup contained a bitter solution or a sweet solution. The second problem that the *S*s were to complete was a rating of the relative sweetness or bitterness of each of the solutions after they had made their guess as to the contents. Unknown to the *S*s, the sweetness concentrations were identical in all cups as were all bitterness concentrations.

The signals used by the *E* were easily learned by each *S* in an average of three to five trials. After this initial learning period, the *E* would give an incorrect signal on some trials—signaling a bitter solution when a sweet solution was to be tasted or signaling a sweet solution when a bitter solution was to be tasted. As a consequence of this procedure, *S*s' expectations were confirmed about 80 percent of the time and disconfirmed about 20 percent of the time. The dependent variables for this study were the ratings of the relative sweetness or bitterness of each of the solutions tasted.

Prior to the analysis of the data, four mutually exclusive outcomes could have been predicted by different theories. The first of these stems from a simple associationistic theory which would predict that the anticipated taste will be additively combined with the actual taste. If one is expecting to taste a bitter solution but actually tastes a sweet solution, the expected bitter detracts from the sweet and thereby reduces the effect. A similar prediction would be made for the expectation of sweet coupled with the tasting of bitter. This theory would, then, predict that the ratings of both sweet and bitter will be more nearly neutral when an expectancy is disconfirmed than when it is confirmed.

A second theory would predict exactly opposite results based on a contrast model. This theory would predict that when a person is prepared to taste a sweet solution but actually receives a bitter solution, a contrast effect will heighten the bitter taste. A similar prediction would be made for the bitter-expectancy–sweet-taste situation. This theory, then, predicts more extreme ratings in the disconfirmation situation than in the confirmation situation.

A third theory (27) is based on experiments that have studied the effect of change in a monotonous situation. Typically, small amounts of change in the environment are more pleasant than a constant level of stimulation. If one equates these changes to the disconfirmation of an expectancy (the *S* expects his environment to remain constant), then possibly the disconfirmation of expectancy in this study will also be positive. If this pleasant effect were added to an already pleasant experience of the tasting of a sweet solution, the effect should be magnified. This theory would predict that when a *S* is prepared for a bitter solution but tastes sweet, the result would be an accentuated rating for the sweet solution. On the other hand, if the pleasant effect of expectancy disconfirmation were added to the unpleasant effect of the actual tasting of a bitter solution, the result should be a canceling out and consequently more neutral ratings of the bitter taste presented when a sweet taste was anticipated.

The fourth theory which yields a prediction of the results of this experiment is Festinger's cognitive-dissonance theory (11). As applied to this experiment, cognitive-dissonance theory states that the disconfirmation of an expectancy will lead to the negative feeling of dissonance (i.e., "I was wrong in what I believed. This is an unpleasant state of affairs."). The combination of this unpleasant feeling with the already unpleasant taste of a bitter solution should lead to enhanced ratings of the bitter solution when a sweet solution was expected. Similarly, the unpleasant feeling of being incorrect should reduce the pleasant sensation of a sweet taste, resulting in reduced ratings of the sweet solution when a bitter solution was expected. Thus the cognitive-dissonance theory predicts exactly opposite results to those predicted by the environmental-change theory.

The actual data from the experiment supported this fourth theoretical position. *S*s did tend to rate solutions more unpleasant when their expectancies were disconfirmed; the bitter solutions were judged more bitter and the sweet solutions less sweet. Standing by themselves, the results are interesting. Coupled with strong inference and theory testing, they have made a significant contribution to psychological science by adding credence to the theory of cognitive dissonance and requiring some revisions in the general applicability of the other three theories.

Theory testing, then, is an essential element in the growth and development of any science. Studies which evaluate current theories of a science have a potential contribution far beyond any particular results which may be derived. They may point toward many other investigations which should be made. And, from your point of view, theory testing requires a study of the various specialized theories of psychology which may lead to ideas for investigation.

Extension of the Range of Applicability

The second source of research problems—*experimental extension*—is related to the concept of experimental validity. Since a single study can not cover all possible variations in experimental subjects under wide ranges of stimulation, generalizations from the study may be very limited or even be in error. Multiple studies permit generalizations to be made with a greater degree of confidence.

Extension of research areas into broader and broader fields is illustrated by the progressive development of the concept of transposition. In one early transposition study (2), a chicken was presented with two shades of gray, one light and one medium. When the chicken chose the medium gray, it was reinforced. After a period of training trials the chicken consistently selected the medium-gray stimulus. Then, as a test trial, the chicken was presented with the original medium gray and a dark gray. If the chicken was responding simply to absolute stimulus characteristics, it should select the medium gray. If, however, the chicken responded in some relational sense, it should choose the darker gray. This was the reasoning of the earlier Gestalt psychologists. In initial studies of this phenomenon, experimental subjects did, in fact, transpose, i.e., select the darker gray stimulus.

In one of the first extensions of the range of applicability of this finding, Spence (33) used not only a different species (apes) but a different and wider range of stimuli as well. Initial training trials were with a small block (nonreinforced) and a medium-sized block (reinforced). The choice stimuli for some Ss were the medium-size block and a large block. On other test trials for different Ss, the test stimuli were blocks so large as to be huge by comparison with the initial training stimuli. In these investigations, Spence found that transposition breaks down when the stimuli are far apart. That is, the S would respond in a relational sense only when the size did not depart too far from the original stimuli. When the discrepancy was great, the S sometimes chose the smaller of the two blocks.

Later studies were designed to further extend these findings. Kuenne (21), used children of varying ages and found the behavior of very young children to be similar to that of the apes. With older children it was found that when the response could be verbalized transposition did not break down. For example, a subject who would verbalize the training responses as "choosing the darker one" would also choose the very, very dark gray in his test trial.

Similarly, many of the developmental studies reported in the literature were designed to extend the range of applicability of other studies. Possibly you can locate several studies of this type, perhaps a specific animal experiment that could be repeated with human Ss to determine whether the results are applicable to human behavior, or a study that used college sophomores as subjects and which might be repeated with children.

If we conceive of psychology as a broad map, largely unexplored, then an initial investigation defines only one point on the map. Studies which extend the range of applicability of this one finding may be thought of as detailed mapping within a particular area. And, to continue the analogy, as we extend the borders of the map, it is to be hoped that we will begin to see interconnections with other areas previously mapped. Thus studies which extend the range of applicability of existing reports in the literature are of extreme importance to psychological science.

Resolution of Conflicting Results

A third source of research ideas is presented by *two studies which report conflicting results*. Consider, for example, some of the early work of Hull (18) and his associates on the appropriate time interval for the reinforcement of a response. These reports seemed to indicate that learning was maximized if the reinforcement immediately followed the response that was being made. Relatively recent work (e.g., Brackbill, 4; Sturges, 35) indicates a quite different conclusion, that retention seems to be improved with delay of reinforcement. How may we resolve the conflict between these two reports? Upon initial reading we find that Hull and his associates used rats; Brackbill and Sturges have been using human subjects. Perhaps this is the crucial variable. If so, it should be possible to design nearly identical situations for both rats and humans to test this supposition.

We also note that Hull used a straight run in an alley as his measure of performance. Sturges and Brackbill, on the other hand, used a cognitive multiple-choice learning situation. Perhaps this is the significant variable. We could design studies requiring a simple motor response from children and test the results. We might also devise a multiple-choice situation for the rat. So many variables seem to be involved that possibly dozens of studies could be devised.

As you review the literature in a given area, similar discrepancies may become apparent to you. One should, however, proceed with caution when considering conflicting results reported by experimenters using almost identical techniques. Resolution of such conflicting reports may await identification of formerly unsuspected extraneous variables.

Replication

Let us close our preliminary investigation of the systematic approach to the generation of ideas for research with the fourth area, that of *replication*. Replication means the more or less exact repetition of a particular experiment. We noted in the previous chapter that reliability was a requirement for the psychological experiment. If the experiment is, in fact, a reliable one, it should yield similar results when tested again. Many of our research studies consist of just this kind of "doing again" or replication. Perhaps the phenomenon originally observed in a particular study was, in fact, unique to the two groups used by the original investigator. As we begin the study of statistics, we will find that any investigator takes a risk of error when he concludes that his results are meaningful. Perhaps this study was one in which such an error was present.

Too often studies are replicated only when the results are questioned by an experimenter and one may feel that he is wasting time if he replicates a noncontroversial experiment. Science, though, is designed as a self-correcting system. For self-correction to work adequately, repetition or replication of an experiment is necessary. This procedure is so important that some of our most respected scientists refuse to publish any study until it has been replicated.

NONSYSTEMATIC APPROACHES TO PROBLEM SELECTION

Influence of the Zeitgeist

To these systematic approaches we must add the nonsystematic approaches to problem development. Before beginning this discussion, however, we should look at what has been termed the *Zeitgeist,* or spirit of the times. One finds that discoveries often are accepted only if they occur "at the right time." For example, one can note the existence of the atomic theory of matter in the literature of the ancient Greeks, but these ideas were not accepted at the time. It seems that a culture is ready for a certain type of advance only at a certain time in its development. As a consequence, many ideas or investigations which are fruitful and worthy of note may be overlooked if they are ahead of the times—perhaps too new or too original.

The disadvantages of working within this framework are obvious. It is possible that we may overlook some valid areas of experimentation. Problems of extreme practical import may be ignored just because "the times aren't right." The advantages of working within the *Zeitgeist* may, however, outweigh the disadvantages. A scientist working in a particular area will usually receive stimulation, support, and knowledgeable criticism from others also working in the area. Indeed, the four systematic sources of ideas spring directly from the *Zeitgeist* as reflected in the current literature of a field. The nonsystematic approaches, on the other hand, are less directly related to this literature and may thus be rejected or overlooked as being "out of step" with the main body of psychological research.

Inspiration

Keeping this factor of the *Zeitgeist* in mind, let us turn to the first of the nonsystematic approaches to problem generation: *inspiration.* This is the method of deriving ideas that occurs to many people when asked about scientific discovery. Although most of us are intuitively familiar with the phenomenon of inspiration, its description is difficult. Inspiration exists only in the "private world" of the investigator and, in the initial stage, may not even occur as verbal symbols.

One example (16, p. 361) of nonverbal symbols which led to subsequent investigation is shown in the field of organic chemistry. An investigator was puzzling over the possible connections between carbon atoms in what is now known as the benzene ring. Sitting in front of his fireplace one night, he dreamed of six snakes joining themselves together, each snake biting the tail of the snake in front of him until a perfect ring was formed. The scientist awoke with a start and realized that this was a possible solution to the benzene ring, with the carbon atoms forming a circular chain rather than a linear chain. We should note that this visual imagery resulted from an attempt to solve a specific problem. If the investigator had not been aware of the current problems in his field, even inspiration would have been of little value.

Serendipity

Another nonsystematic source of experimental ideas is that of *serendipity*. Although we call ideas serendipitous because they seem to have occurred by fortunate chance alone, later investigation usually shows that the experimenter had a good background of training. Flemming's discovery of penicillin falls within this area. Undoubtedly many investigators prior to his time had noticed mold growing in their bacteria cultures and had observed that this mold was killing the bacteria. These other investigators, however, threw the culture out as being "contaminated." Flemming seized upon this particular phenomenon and from it developed penicillin. It might seem to the uninitiated that this discovery happened by chance. When we consider that Flemming was a trained bacteriologist and that the person without his training would not have been presented this opportunity, it is apparent that a wide background assists the serendipitous finding.

Curiosity

Curiosity is the third nonsystematic approach to the formulation of a research idea. This curiosity may stem from some unexplained observed fact, from an unknown relationship between two facts, or from the simple "What if?" The "What if?" approach to idea formulation has been the primary method of common sense. We think of such an outstanding inventor as Edison as exemplifying this approach. Consider, however, the tremendous amounts of energy that went into the trial-and-error process of determining an appropriate filament for the electric light bulb. Each new material was selected and tested primarily as a result of curiosity rather than through a systematic knowledge of its electrical and thermochemical properties.

Many of the most original contributions to psychological science had their origin in the method of trial and error. Also, we find that many of the ideas of beginning experimenters stem from this basic curiosity. We should realize, however, that such ideas may be neither original nor of practical significance. The question of originality may be answered by a thorough review of the literature to determine whether or not the experiment has been previously conducted. The practical significance of an idea, on the other hand, may be extremely difficult to assess. One might suspect, for example, that an investigation of the color preferences of muskrats would be of little ultimate value to society. The results, though, may be of great importance to ex- terminators of muskrats. Possibly any study of any subject enhances the total body of scientific knowledge and understanding. From this viewpoint, practical significance may be an irrelevant criterion for judging the merits of a research proposal.

DESIGNING A SAMPLE STUDY

Selecting a Problem

We have discussed several ways in which an initial idea for an experi- ment may be generated. Let us choose one of these approaches—the resolution of conflicting results—to illustrate the development of an experimental design from the initial idea. The analysis, interpretation, and reporting of this experiment shall be developed in the next five chapters of this text.

Our problem arises from a possible contradiction concerning the interrelationship of two areas of psychological investigation: visual acuity and adaptation. Visual acuity refers either to the ability to detect a small separation between two points or to the ability to detect a single small point. An optometrist is testing your visual acuity when he asks you to name a letter on his wall chart: as the distance between the open ends of the "C" becomes too small to be discriminated, that letter be- comes confused with the "O." Adaptation, on the other hand, refers to the adjustment of the eye to various conditions of background illumination. You are familiar with the process of adaptation through your experiences in a theater. As you enter everything is dark and you are likely to stumble about, but after a period of adaptation your vision seems to return to nearly normal.

Some of the material presented in your introductory psychology course regarding visual acuity and adaptation may seem incompatible. In particular, you may recall having learned that the retina becomes more sensitive to light following a period of adaptation in a completely dark room, i.e., a smaller amount of light is required to elicit a visual response as adaptation increases. This may be compared to the gradual return of nearly normal vision in the theater. On the other hand, you also learned that visual acuity becomes better as the illumination is increased. You can imagine how much more difficult it would be to read the optometrist's chart if the lighting was poor.

Now, let us suppose that we are required to determine which of two lights is the brightest. Let us further suppose that we make this test of relative brightness under two conditions: in a well-lit room and in a relatively dark room. Perhaps it seems that two quite different predictions might be made on the basis of your knowledge of visual acuity and adaptation. If sensitivity of the retina determines performance, then we should be able to discriminate small differences in the brightness of the two lights much better when we are dark adapted than when we are light adapted. If the ability to detect small differences in brightness is actually a test of visual acuity, then this ability should increase with an increase in room illumination. Let us design an experiment to determine which of these predictions is correct.

LITERATURE REVIEW

We should begin the study with a review of the literature on brightness discrimination. By literature, we refer to the collection of scientific writings in some specific field of science. The sources of the literature review for this study would include not only psychological journals but also texts, definitive works on the specific area of psychology, and handbooks of experimental psychology. Your reference librarian is trained to help you to locate these sources and will be an invaluable aid in assisting you with the literature review. Perhaps the relevant study has been completed and we have but to read the results to satisfy our curiosity. In this instance, either a replication of that original study or an extension of the range of those results may be desirable. If the experiment has not yet been performed, the problem area may be a fruitful one for a new study.

We will begin our survey with some of the texts in sensory processes and perception. As these texts are read in an attempt to discover some of the systematic relationships that have been studied in the area of light discrimination, this apparently simple problem quickly becomes a complex one. The question involves the whole field of psychophysics, i.e., the study of the relationship of changes in physical stimulation to the psychological world. Some of the more recent literature in the area involves the experimenter in higher mathematics and signal-detection theory. One book leads to another book until you are thoroughly immersed in the study of light discrimination.

This initial survey of books will also furnish citations to published reports in the psychological journals. Since these journals present research studies as originally reported, they are the true foundation of the literature review. One should rely upon a secondary source only when the original is not available, or when the original journal is published in a foreign language which is not read fluently by the investigator.

The Use of Psychological Abstracts

The most efficient approach to journal studies is through the use of the *Psychological Abstracts*, which reports short abstracts of articles published in over five hundred psychological journals throughout the world, with over 17,000 entries in the 1967 edition. In each monthly issue the abstracts are arranged under topical headings such as general psychology, methodology and research technology, experimental psychology, physiological psychology, animal psychology, developmental psychology, etc. These major headings are further subdivided into smaller groups in the brief subject index included in each issue.

In searching for reports of the study we have begun, the first subject checked might be vision. In the brief subject index there would be headings for: vision; vision, binocular; vision, brightness; etc. Under "vision, brightness" is a note which refers the investigator to "brightness." Checking under "brightness" we find headings for both "brightness" and "brightness discrimination." The numbers following the subheading "brightness discrimination" refer to specific abstracts published in that issue. In using the brief subject index it is important to check the related headings as well as the specific heading first selected. In our study, for example, some of the related subject entries would be "threshold," "differential threshold," "brightness threshold," and "psychophysics."

A cumulative author-subject index to *Psychological Abstracts* is published each December and is usually bound with the monthly issues to complete the annual volume. Use of this cumulative subject index enables one to rapidly survey the appropriate research for the entire year. For example, there are 14 different articles referenced under the heading of "brightness discrimination" in the 1965 subject index to *Psychological Abstracts*. We find that two of these might be of value in our study: "Simultaneous contrast and contour in brightness discrimination," identified by the number 9,116; and, "Brightness discrimination and visual data contrast," number 13,567. We now refer to the body of the annual volume for these two numbers and read the brief abstracts.

A comprehensive guide to the relatively early issues of *Psychological Abstracts* is the *Cumulated Subject Index to Psychological Abstracts, 1927–1960*. It is used in a manner similar to the annual index available for each year since 1960. An author index for the years 1927–1958 with a supplement covering the period 1959–1963 is also available. This may be useful in tracing several studies in one area by the same investigator.

If the subject matter of the abstract seems to be pertinent to our study, it is necessary to refer to the journal for the complete report. Each abstract provides reference to the original article by listing identification number, author or authors, the institution at which the study was performed, and the journal in which the article appeared, giving year, volume, and page numbers.

Other Reference Sources

A careful review of several volumes of *Psychological Abstracts* and the cumulated index provides a good background of reference on a particular subject. It is absolutely necessary to expand this general background by referring to the original journal articles which seem to be related to our study since the abstracts are necessarily short and may omit much essential information. The investigator will be concerned with method, procedure, subjects, specific conclusions, and generalizations, which are not normally given in the abstract. The original articles will also provide a list of related references, usually included at the end of an article. Tracing such references to earlier investigations will increase the thoroughness of the literature survey.

As abstracts may not appear for as much as a full year following the actual publication of an article, one must go directly to the appropriate current journals to survey the most recent literature. It should be possible by now for you to identify those journals most likely to contain reports of experimentation in your area of investigation. In each of these journals, issues of the current year should be scanned for relevant information.

Some gaps in the survey may exist despite the most careful use of books, journals, and abstracts. One doctoral student working in the area of olfactometry, the study of the sense of smell, found that many important references were not included in either standard texts or *Psychological Abstracts*. The references he needed were largely from publications of perfume manufacturers. Such "trade journals" or "house journals" often contain valuable information not referenced in the body of psychological literature comprised of texts and journals. As a consequence, one may never be completely certain that a study has not been done before. But if the intention is to publish in the recognized psychological journals, the omission of the studies from the standard literature may be a legitimate reason for conducting the study.

A review of the literature can be very time consuming. One large industrial concern reports that it is often more economical to complete a relatively inexpensive study rather than to research the literature. Advances are being made in the area of information retrieval, and the situation will eventually improve. Still, one should recognize that a completely comprehensive literature survey may not be required. As one example, it is usually unnecessary to search the literature prior to that listed in the *Cumulated Index* (1927). Many early studies tended to be reported without sophisticated statistical analyses and the conclusions were often based on the visual appearance of the data.

Results of the Literature Review

Our literature survey has been made in the area of our selected study, brightness discrimination. For purposes of this example, let us assume that this thorough review has failed to locate any particular study which exactly answers our question.* Of what value, then, has been our literature review? First, we have found that no comparable study has been reported. As a consequence our study may make a contribution to the field if satisfactorily completed. Moreover, this literature review has provided us with the background material necessary to the

* Actually a rather comprehensive study of adaptation level, test-object area, and the differential-brightness threshold was made at the Tiffany Foundation and is reported by Blackwell (3). Relevant information is also presented by Steinhardt (34).

design of our study, including an understanding of basic concepts and terms.

The first term that seemed relevant to the study was threshold, the psychological point at which discrimination between stimulus inputs is possible. We found that there are two general types of visual thresholds, the absolute threshold and differential thresholds. The absolute threshold for light is marked by the amount of visual input that is just discriminably different from no light at all, typically measured as that amount of light that can reliably be detected by an observer 50 percent of the time it is presented. Although this is a type of brightness discrimination in that the observer must discriminate between no brightness and some brightness, it does not seem to be an appropriate dependent variable for the study being designed.

The differential-brightness threshold, on the other hand, seems to suit the requirements of the study. The differential-brightness threshold is measured by determining that amount of difference in brightness which is necessary if an observer is to reliably detect a difference in brightness between two points of light. If the two points of light were exactly the same brightness, it would be impossible to tell the difference between them and the naming of either one as brighter should occur about 50 percent of the time just by chance alone. Suppose, however, that one of the two lights was made much brighter than the other. In such an instance, the S in an experiment should be able to detect which light was brighter with nearly 100 percent accuracy. One of the methods of measuring the differential-brightness threshold is to use that added amount of light that is required to just divide these two points; i.e., that the brighter light will be correctly identified 75 percent of the time. This is a measure of discrimination since a very sensitive S will be able to detect a lower amount of added light to reach this 75 percent accuracy level than will an S who has poorer powers of discrimination.

The literature review also revealed several methods for determining this brightness threshold. For example, one method (38, pp. 200–219) required showing the S two lights—a constant-brightness light and a variable-brightness light—and asking the S to pick the brighter light of the two. The variable light would be presented at settings ranging from just barely brighter than the constant light to considerably brighter than the constant light. An S's differential-brightness threshold could be determined from the particular setting of the variable light which is reliably detected by the S. This method removes the S from any active participation in the selection of the lights to be presented and, as a purely pragmatic issue, requires several trials to obtain a single estimate of the differential threshold.

An alternative method for determining this threshold was found to be the method of adjustment (38, pp. 199–200). With this technique, the constant light is again set at some specific value during all trials. The variable light, however, is continually manipulated by the S instead of being discretely presented by the E. The S is required to adjust the variable light until it appears to be exactly the same brightness as the constant light. As he approaches the point where he cannot discriminate the differences between the two lights, the S will stop making adjustments. Thus a measure of the brightness threshold for this S is given on each trial. By weighing the relative advantages (increased interest in the task by the S, conservation of trials information, etc.) against the relative disadvantages of this method (susceptibility to motivational factors, constant errors in task performance, etc.), as a matter of preference we may decide to use this particular method for measuring the dependent variable for our proposed research.

Our original question has specified that the independent variable of the study will be different background illumination conditions. The literature has supplied us with a reliable dependent variable (the differential threshold) and an accepted method for obtaining this measure. Many of the possible extraneous variables that we should attempt to control for have been pointed out in a review of signal-detection theory's criticism of the whole approach to thresholds. By a careful integration of this background research, we should be able to devise a rigorous, scientific investigation into the problem of brightness discrimination as a function of background illumination.

The Working Hypothesis

The literature survey has also provided us with a "hunch" about what the results of our proposed study might be. All studies of visual acuity seem to require a discrimination of two levels of brightness—between the dark portions of a line or point and its lighter background. Additionally, we now have located a specific study (14) which has indicated that visual acuity improves as illumination is increased. We might, therefore, predict that brightness discrimination will also improve as the background illumination is increased. Let us reword this initial hunch, or working hypothesis, by stating operational definitions for each term: The differential-brightness threshold as measured by the method of adjustment (brightness discrimination) is a function of the ambient illumination to which the subject is adapted (background illumination).

Of what value is this working hypothesis? Since it has been stated in operational terms, we should be able to proceed step by step in producing these operations. For example, the major pieces of experimental equipment to be used should either be directly stated or implied. Let us see what equipment needs are implied by this particular working hypothesis.

Since we are going to measure the differential-brightness threshold, we need some apparatus which will produce two spots of light. We have indicated that the differential-brightness threshold will be taken by the method of adjustment. Consequently, our apparatus must include some provision to allow the subject to adjust one spot of light until he perceives it to be identical in brightness to the other spot. Such test instruments are commercially available.

We should also note the relationship of the working hypothesis to the data which we will collect. Since the working hypothesis has stated that we will record differential-brightness thresholds as the measure of visual discrimination we must record those settings of brightness equivalence made by our Ss on the test apparatus. Finally, this working hypothesis specifies that room illumination will be the independent variable to be manipulated by the experimenter. We must be able to vary this room illumination, possibly by means of a light-dimmer switch. Thus, the basic structure of our study is defined by the working hypothesis.

MAXIMIZING THE EXPERIMENTAL EFFECT

In exploratory studies we often try to maximize the experimental effect. Since an exploratory study is often concerned with the question of "is the effect there or is it not there," we may choose extreme values of our experimental treatments to emphasize whatever experimental effects might be present. For example, the experimenter might have subjects discriminate between distilled water and salty water. If there were only three grains of salt per quart in the "salty" water, most subjects would probably find no differences. By making the water very salty, almost every individual is able to make the discrimination. For an exploratory study this is sufficient. Later, studies to extend the range of the applicability of these results may vary the concentrations in an effort to establish the curve of salt discrimination.

A similar situation exists with respect to the study we have just out-lined. The important decision we wish to reach is whether or not background illumination does, in fact, influence visual brightness discrimination. If we are able to find this effect, later studies may be developed to determine the range of applicability of this conclusion. Our experimental treatments, then, might be a high-brightness background and a low-brightness background to maximize the experimental effect. It seems apparent that if we choose background brightness levels that are barely discriminably different from our test spots, then visual brightness-discrimination thresholds for the two conditions may not be very different. By making our "dark" room condition very dark and our "light" room condition very light we emphasize those differences in discrimination which may be attributable to background illumination.

REFINING THE STUDY TO INCREASE RELIABILITY

The basic outline of our study is now complete. Subjects will adjust one spot of light until it appears to be equal in brightness to another spot of light. Since we assume that a subject who is capable of very fine discriminations of brightness will adjust the variable light until it is very nearly equal to the test light, our scores should reflect differences in brightness discrimination. By using two very different conditions of background illumination in the test room, we hope to determine whether or not discrimination is a function of the subject's adaptation condition. The only remaining task is to refine this basic design in terms of the reliability and validity of the experiment.

As you recall from the previous chapter, one factor influencing the reliability of the experiment is that of the reliability of the dependent variable—in this case, the differential-brightness threshold determined for each S. After some review of the literature in psychophysics, it seems apparent that 50 to 100 test trials may be required for each subject in order to establish a definite curve of discrimination. This use of multiple trials in a situation is one more example of the randomization process. We assume that on any one trial an error may creep in attributable to fluctuating motivational states of the individual, lack of attention, or a host of other extraneous variables. By giving many trials, rather than a single trial, we assume that those temporary states of the individual will tend to cancel out. What remains as an overall effect should be the measure that we originally intended to take, uncontaminated by temporary dispositions of the subject.

A second nonsystematic extraneous variable that we might wish to control is that of instructions to the subject. Clearly, if there are significant variations in the instructions given our subjects, the experiment will be unreliable. Similarly, if there is to be more than one experimenter, we should also develop systematic instructions to the experimenters. This is one of the methods for control of extraneous variables (holding testing conditions constant) and increases reliability by increasing the precision of the study. Below is a portion of a printed set of instructions for experimenters and subjects used in a task similar to the study that we are designing (24).

1. As soon as the subjects arrive, take them to the experimental room. Record the time that they begin the dark adaptation.

2. Record the subject's name, sex, and introductory psychology section number on the data sheet.

3. Read the following instruction to the subject: "The experiment which you are about to participate in is concerned with how well you can match the brightness of one patch of light to the brightness of another patch of light. Since we want you to be able to do your very best on this task, we will have a short waiting period for you to get used to the darkness of the room. While we are waiting I'll show you just what I want you to do. After this we'll have a few practice trials to let you get used to the apparatus. If at anytime during this period you have any questions about what you are supposed to do, please ask them."

4. Demonstrate the apparatus by pointing first to the control source of light. Say to the subject, "This is the light source that you are going to try to match. This will stay the same for every trial that you take. You can see that there is a small black knob below this light, but please do not move that knob. Remember that this light is the one that you will try to match."

5. Now point to the variable source of light. Start here with a relatively low setting. Say to the subject, "This is the light that you will try to make match the other light. Notice that the two lights do not appear to be equally bright. Now see the large knob below this light? Try turning it and you will see that it makes this light get brighter or darker. See if you can make that light just exactly as bright as the other light."

6. After they have made a match on that light return the variable source to a relatively low setting. Say to the subject, "That was very good. See this is not going to be a very difficult task after all. I have just a few more

things to say and then we will get on with your practice trials. First, there is one restriction on your turning of that knob. This is that you may only turn the knob in one direction on a particular trial. If you happen to overshoot the target, you may not turn the knob back the other way. Do you understand this?"

7. If they have questions, answer them as completely as possible. If they just give you an automatic "yes," ask them to tell you what they are supposed to do. Make certain that they fully understand that there is to be no retracing.

This particular set of instructions included five additional items. It may seem that the amount of detail regarding the procedure to be used in testing each subject is unnecessary. However, recalling that differences in the treatment of subjects creates unreliability, we should restrict insofar as possible the operation of such extraneous variables.

Perhaps as you become accustomed to testing subjects in an experimental situation such detail will become unnecessary. For example, instruction No. 2 (record name, sex, and introductory psychology section) might not be needed. However, most tasks that we undertake are more difficult when we first attempt them. If we are just beginning to learn to drive a car, we may need detailed instructions on each step of the driving task. If we have been driving for some time and wish to learn to drive a different type of car, many of the original instructions may be eliminated. Similarly, the procedures followed by an experienced investigator may not be appropriate for someone just learning the techniques of experimentation.

Refining the Study to Increase Validity

Let us investigate some aspects of the study which might affect its validity. Since we wish to define all terms operationally, we need some measure of the darkness or brightness of the room. The study might not be easily replicated if the only definition of our room conditions was simply "bright" or "dark." One might use a light meter to record the relative brightness or darkness of the room and specify these in the final report. Then an investigator who wished to extend the range of applicability of the study would have these known points upon which to base the new study.

Other conditions of testing should also be specified. For example, if we give all subjects exactly 15 minutes to adapt to the existing room conditions, other studies can either replicate or extend this range. A detailed procedure on conditions of testing should be developed for each experiment in advance of the actual testing of subjects.

Another method of increasing the validity of our study by control of possible systematic extraneous variables is that of random assignment of subjects to experimental conditions. Complete random assignment is usually unattainable. One might, for example (if he wished to generalize to all people in the United States), randomly select names from the census list for participation in an experiment, but this would undoubtedly be a very expensive and time-consuming process. Consequently, most psychological experiments use locally available subjects.

Often these subjects come from introductory psychology courses in college. (As an aside, one might wonder about the generality of the science of psychology based upon the introductory psychology student. Perhaps these are atypical individuals in more than one way.) Even so, it is probable that not all introductory psychology students can be utilized for a particular experiment. One normally takes only those students who volunteer for an experiment. Several studies have shown that people who volunteer differ systematically from people who do not volunteer. Again, we are placing limitations upon the degree of generality or validity of our study. As our population narrows down, perhaps we are left with "those introductory psychology students at Flunkout U. who will volunteer to participate in a psychology experiment to be held on Wednesday afternoons." Given these restrictions, it is still possible to randomly assign people from that population into our experimental conditions.

If a table of random numbers is not available, perhaps some other nonsystematic way of assigning subjects to conditions will be used. One method is simply to use a well-shuffled deck of cards. If the first card is a black card, the subject will participate in the "darker than" condition. If the card is red, the subject will participate in the "brighter than" condition. This approaches random assignment and should eliminate most of the experimenter bias in assigning subjects to conditions.

In our review of the literature on brightness discrimination and psychophysical methods, we found several other important extraneous variables which should be controlled. For example, the direction in which the subject turns the knob is important. Consequently, we may decide that all subjects will have both ascending trials (those in which the variable light is initially dimmer than the constant light) and descending trials (those in which the variable light is initially brighter than the comparison light). Use of both ascending and descending series increases the validity of our experiment. If we used only ascending series we would place one more restriction upon generalizations drawn from our results. By using both series we balance out the occurrence of this extraneous variable. Recalling that we wish each subject to participate in 50 to 100 trials to increase the reliability of the test measure, it seems logical that half of these trials should be ascending and half should be descending trials.

A further control is achieved by use of the counterbalancing technique. Since each subject has both ascending and descending trials, it should be possible to counteract the effects of practice and fatigue by properly counterbalancing the sequence of presentation. One effective method of counterbalancing is that known as the *ABBA technique*, which consists of an *initial ascending* trial, then *two descending* trials, and finally *another ascending* trial. Suppose that fatigue is present over one of these *ABBA* sequences so that although initial performance for the *A* treatment is 10, it declines on the second or *B* presentation to 8, on the third presentation (again a *B* trial) to 6, and on the final trial (an *A* trial) to 4. Note that the sum of the two *A* trials (10 and 4) equals the sum of the two *B* trials (8 and 6). Thus we have effectively counterbalanced or counteracted the linear effect of fatigue.

Note the effect of counterbalancing if the fatigue is nonlinear; for example, a 10, 9, 7, 4 decline. If we had the two *A* trials first, the sum would be 10 plus 9 or 19. If we had both *B* trials last, the sum would be 7 plus 4 or 11. By using the *ABBA* technique, our *A*'s occupy the first and last positions and sum to 14 while *B*'s occupy the second and third positions and sum to 16. Although the effect is not completely cancelled out, if both *A*'s had been first and both *B*'s last, the difference would have been 8 units. By use of the *ABBA* technique the difference is reduced to only 2 units. Consequently, counterbalancing is partially effective even though the effect that we wish to eliminate is not exactly linear.

Previously we have stated that it would be desirable if the subject had 50 to 100 trials. We might include 16 of these *ABBA* or *BAAB* blocks for a total of 64 trials for each subject. Note that it would also be possible to counterbalance these blocks of trials. Calling *A* trials the ascending series and *B* trials the descending series, we find that we have systematically organized the number and direction of the trials in our experiment.

We may consider one last variable to control, that of sex. Perhaps there are systematic differences in the way males and females react to background lighting. If such is the case, we might wish to use either all males (the method of elimination) or to use an equal number of males and females in each condition (the method of balance). Although the method of elimination may increase to some extent the reliability of our study, we should note that including both males and females increases the validity of the study. By including both males and females we have not limited the conclusions of our study to a single sex and are able to generalize our findings to a much greater population. Consequently we may decide to use an equal number of males and females in our experiment.

This additional control permits us to determine the number of subjects required for our study. We will have male subjects being tested under light-background conditions and dark-background conditions. We will also have females tested under these two conditions. If we decide that we must have at least 10 subjects in each of these conditions, we find that we need 40 subjects for our experiment. This is not an unreasonable number to test in a psychological experiment.

Let us briefly review the decisions that we have made. First, it will be necessary to use 40 subjects who volunteer from an introductory psychology course. These 40 subjects will be equally divided: 20 males and 20 females. Half of each of these groups will be tested while adapted to a dark background; the remaining half will be tested while adapted to a light background. All subjects will be tested in the same room using a commercially available differential-brightness apparatus as the test instrument. Standardized instructions will be given to each subject. Each subject will perform 64 trials which are counterbalanced between ascending and descending trials. Our final measure will be the differential-brightness thresholds computed for these Ss under these conditions.

THE PILOT STUDY

It may seem that we are now ready to begin testing our subjects. One note of caution must be urged here. In many instances it is worthwhile to run what we term a "pilot" study, or an initial tryout of the experiment. Often a pilot study will reveal serious defects in the experimental procedure which might not otherwise be noted. As you have seen in this short discussion, one must organize a tremendous amount of details in order to successfully complete a psychological experiment. Details neglected in the original planning may be detected in a pilot study.

In our pilot study we would note, first of all, that we have not specified the brightness of the constant light source. Next we note that when we begin to run a subject under the "dark" condition our attempt to maximize the experimental effect has failed. Turning the lights completely out may affect the differential-brightness thresholds that we collect, but it also serves the purpose of preventing the experimenter from reading the final setting. A third defect in our design noted in the pilot study is the lack of a systematic data sheet. In the pilot study, we find ourselves taking the records down on our shirt cuff, on the table top, and on any available scraps of paper.

The deficiencies that we have pointed out are easily remedied. We decide that an appropriate setting for the constant light is one-half of the total range of the variable light, permitting us to have wide ranges of adjustment in both our ascending and descending series. In order to completely specify these particular conditions, it is necessary to once again measure this light output. Several checks of this light intensity as the experiment progresses will prove of value in holding this particular value constant. With respect to room brightness in the dark condition, we adjust the lighting by a potentiometer (light-dimmer switch) so that the experimenter can easily read the settings made by each subject. This reduces to some extent the range of our experimental variable but is unavoidable. The new room brightness should also be measured to complete the operational definitions of the terms "dark" and "bright." Finally, data sheets are constructed to record the settings of each *S*. A good data sheet makes it easy for an experimenter to progress through his experiment in a systematic fashion. It should also simplify subsequent data analysis and minimize the risk of errors in analysis.

After correcting our experimental procedure, we are finally ready to begin the experiment. This experiment will be further developed in the following chapters.

SUMMARY

In this chapter, we investigated some of the criteria for designing a psychological experiment. Both systematic and nonsystematic approaches to the generation of research ideas were discussed. The systematic approaches were: (a) validating predictions of a theory; (b) extending the range of applicability of existing studies; (c) resolving conflicting reports; and (d) repeating or replicating current studies. The nonsystematic approaches were: (a) inspiration; (b) serendipity; and (c) curiosity. All of these methods for generating research ideas were seen to be influenced by the *Zeitgeist*, or spirit of the times.

A thorough review of the literature was found to be necessary for the further development of a research idea. This literature review was accomplished by a review of books in the field, *Psychological Abstracts*, relevant psychological journals, and other sources such as trade journals or house journals. The integration of this background was of considerable value not only in the actual development of the problem area, but in delineating extraneous variables which might influence the outcome of our study.

The basic structure of the research design was derived through the use of operational definitions in the working hypothesis. The working hypothesis was used to specify the dependent and independent variables, the expected relationship between them, and the general method of data collection. This, in turn, determined to some extent the equipment required, the data to be collected, and the values of the experimental variables.

Once the values of the experimental variables were set, design became a problem of increasing reliability and validity factors in the experiment. Some aspects of the experiment which would affect the reliability or the validity of the study included: (a) instructions to the subject; (b) conditions of testing; (c) random assignment of subjects to conditions; (d) balancing of possible extraneous variables; (e) counterbalancing when subjects participate under more than one condition; and (f) the integration of these factors into a well-controlled experimental design. Finally, a pilot study was shown to be of extreme importance when investigating a new area, especially in the detection of extraneous variables previously unrecognized.

3. The Graphic Methods

BASIC CONCEPTS

An initial survey of the data from the brightness-discrimination study developed in the previous chapter may tend to leave the beginning investigator feeling somewhat bewildered. We have taken 64 readings on each of 40 subjects—a total of 2560 scores and an impossible number to scan visually and arrive at any meaningful conclusion. One group of techniques for handling such large masses of data are the graphic methods presented in this chapter.

Since most college preparatory courses in mathematics include graph construction, the area we will study is not entirely new. We will find that graphs can be employed as a device for analyzing the data collected in an experiment as well as for displaying this information following analysis. The latter is probably the function most familiar to you at this point, but this should not overshadow your acceptance of graphs as a method of analysis.

Before proceeding directly to the data from our study, we will discuss some of the basic concepts associated with graphs. As you recall, there are only two general types of graphs—those showing relationships between two or more variables and those which indicate relative frequencies (or the number of occurrences) for values of a single variable. Examples of the first type include graphs of school achievement as a function of IQ, visual acuity as a function of adaptation level, etc. These are usually simple line graphs and are frequently used to display the results of experiments.

Graphs which indicate relative frequencies or amounts of a single variable are commonly used in psychology. Typical examples include graphs of the distribution of IQ scores in the population, frequencies of various answers to a questionnaire item, etc. These frequency graphs are usually either histograms (bar graphs) or frequency polygons (line graphs). Other methods, such as cumulative-proportion graphs, are occasionally used. Although these graphs are most generally used to display the results of an experiment, they may also be used to analyze data. Most of the early experiments in psychophysics (including brightness discrimination) used the graphic method as an instrument of analysis.

Regardless of which type is used, there are some general guidelines to follow in the construction of a good graph. The graphs that we will be constructing represent the relationship between two concepts. Thus the two axes of the graph should present the two concepts that are to be related. For example, if we are studying income over a period of years the graph will have the years studied displayed on one axis and income on the other. These axes are called the X axis (horizontal) and the Y axis (vertical). In psychology, the independent variable of a study is normally placed on the X axis of the graph and the dependent variable is placed on the Y axis.

Another general guide to the construction of graphs is that the height of the Y axis is usually designed to be approximately 60 to 80 percent of the X axis. The reason for this is illustrated in Figure 3.1. In the first

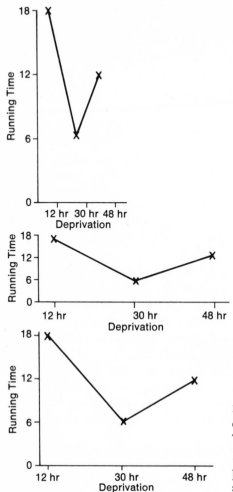

FIGURE 3.1. Graphs which use different *Y*-axis: *X*-axis ratios. The lowest graph (with the *Y*-axis: *X*-axis ratio between 60 percent–80 percent) is generally preferred.

graph, the vertical axis (running time in the maze) is three times the length of the horizontal axis (hours of deprivation). In the second portion of Figure 3.1, the inverse of this relationship is plotted. Here, the horizontal axis is three times the length of the vertical axis. Note the different conclusions that one might make following a brief scanning of these two illustrations. Systematic interpretations may best be made from the third graph shown in Figure 3.1, which uses the 60 to 80 percent ratio. That is, if one consistently plots *Y* axis : *X* axis ratios between 60 and 80 percent for all graphs, subsequent interpretation and comparison with similar graphs is facilitated.

False interpretations may also be designed into graphs by using a nonzero point on the vertical scale. Consider, for example, the data given in Table 3.1. This indicates the number of dollars spent for foot-

TABLE 3.1. Thousands of dollars spent on football recruiting for 1968 (fictitious data)

COLLEGE	AMOUNT
Flunkout U.	988
Lunkhead U.	1006

ball recruiting by the two colleges (in thousands of dollars). In this particular example, Flunkout U. spends only slightly less than a million dollars for the year on football recruiting. Lunkhead U., on the other hand, spends slightly more than a million dollars on football recruiting. Thus the two colleges spend approximately the same amount of money in this area.

In the left-hand side of Figure 3.2 we see a graph that might be drawn by someone in Flunkout U. who wanted more money for this activity. Note that the bar graph for Lunkhead U. is approximately seven times as tall as that for Flunkout U. At first glance, the implica-

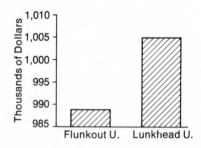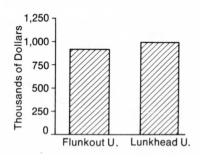

FIGURE 3.2. An illustration of the varying impressions that different baselines may have on the interpretation of a graph. The data plotted are those presented in Table 3.1.

tion is that Lunkhead U. spends seven times as much for football recruiting as Flunkout U. does. When we examine the axes, however, the inaccuracy of this interpretation immediately becomes apparent. We find that 985 thousand dollars has been chosen as the origin of this graph. Thus Flunkout U. spends 21 thousand dollars more. Although the total difference of 18 thousand dollars is relatively small with respect to the total amount, the graph gives a very different and misleading impression.

A more nearly correct version of this graph is presented in the right-hand side of Figure 3.2. Using a true origin of zero, we find that the two are almost identical. This interpretation is in keeping with the actual figures reported in Table 3.1. Thus, it is necessary that the origin indicate a truly meaningful relationship where frequencies or amounts are concerned.

A final general rule is that both axes should be correctly labeled and that the units of these axes should be clearly designated. Consider the various interpretations which might have been placed on the data previously shown in Figures 3.1 and 3.2 had this rule not been followed. Omission of any of this essential information renders the graph meaningless and therefore worthless.

GRAPHS INDICATING FREQUENCY OR AMOUNT

Histograms

With these few guide lines, let us construct a graph indicating frequency. Suppose that we have determined the IQs of 77 children in the second grade of a local public school and we wish to graphically display these scores in a meaningful manner. The data collected might look something like that given in Table 3.2. These scores are listed in the order in which the children were tested. Notice that the same confusion about interpretations from a mass of data exists here as it does with the 2560 scores that were collected from the visual-brightness study designed in Chapter 2.

As a first step in bringing some order to these IQ scores, one might simply arrange them sequentially from lowest to highest score as has been done in Table 3.3. A number of the individual scores have been combined where two or more people received the same measured IQ. This is shown in the column labeled f (Frequency). For example, beside

TABLE 3.2.   IQ scores for 77 school-age children

103	98	102	100
100	101	100	104
97	111	110	97
106	105	95	102
109	107	104	96
104	95	98	106
107	100	113	92
111	110	107	103
101	88	111	117
94	104	91	101
86	99	103	99
105	93	108	100
110	106	115	109
114	94	92	88
104	109	106	104
112	105	96	96
93	112	90	116
108	108	99	107
103	98	119	114
			105

the IQ score of 101 is an f value of 3. This indicates that three people had a measured IQ of 101. The first IQ score listed, 86, has an f value of 1 and indicates that only one individual had a measured IQ of 86.

Although this sequential listing clarifies the data somewhat, there are still too many individual scores to be comprehended easily. Perhaps further grouping will alleviate this problem. Some individual judgment must be used in such grouping. For example, should one use 8 groups or 20 groups? Obviously, if there are only 4 or 5 scores to begin with, it would be ridiculous to insist on 10 groups. As a general rule, however, if there are over 50 measurements, somewhere between 10 and 20 groups should be used. From 10 to 12 groups should be used for relatively small sets of data, expanding to 18, 19, or 20 groups for those studies involving large amounts of data.

In situations where 50 or more measurements are available for analysis, one suggested way to proceed is as follows:

1. Subtract the lowest score from the highest score of the set. This gives the total range of the scores available.

TABLE 3.3. Simple sequential arrangement of the IQ scores of 77 school-age children

IQ SCORE	f FREQUENCY
86	1
87	0
88	2
89	0
90	1
91	1
92	2
93	2
94	2
95	2
96	3
97	2
98	3
99	3
100	5
101	3
102	2
103	4
104	6
105	4
106	4
107	4
108	3
109	3
110	3
111	3
112	2
113	1
114	2
115	1
116	1
117	1
118	0
119	1

2. Divide this total range by some number between 10 and 20 that yields a whole number. As an example, if the range were 145, one might divide this total range either into 20, 16, or 13 parts, depending upon how many scores were available for analysis. This would yield an interval width (the number of units in each group) of 7 for the 20 categories, 9 for 16 intervals, or 11 for 13 intervals.

3. Arrange the interval width so that it is an odd value whenever possible. In the preceding example the widths were 7, 9, or 11—odd numbers. The reason for this step will become apparent when we actually construct the graphs.

Now let us apply these steps to the 77 IQ scores collected. Note that the lowest IQ score reported for this grade is 86. The highest score is 119. Thus our total range is 33 IQ units (119 − 86). In this particular case, a good choice for the number of class intervals seems to be 11. This gives us the three-unit class interval that we have previously suggested as a desirable goal (i.e., an odd value of the class width).

Since our lowest score is 86 we may wish to begin our grouping into intervals at an IQ value of 85. The first class interval would include the scores 85, 86, and 87. The working limits of this interval are 85 to 87. For our second class interval we would include the scores 88, 89, and 90. The working class limits here are 88 to 90. These are called working limits because they are defined in terms of the actual integer values with which we must work—85, 86, 87, etc.

If we had constructed a bar graph using these working intervals, we might be tempted to extend one of the bars from the point representing 85 IQ to that representing 87 IQ. If such a procedure was followed, the next bar would begin at the point indicating 88 IQ and a space would be left between the 87 and 88 IQs. This is obviously incorrect, for we wish to indicate that we have measured the total range of IQs. Theoretically, at least, it would be possible for us to obtain an IQ falling somewhere between 87 and 88. An additional problem with the working limits is that they tend to give us the wrong interval width. In the example given above, we include scores of 85, 86, and 87 in the working interval from 85 to 87. Thus, this interval is actually three IQ units wide. If we subtract 85 from 87, however, we get the impression that the interval is only two units wide.

To correct for both of these deficiencies in the working interval, designate the "actual limits" of the intervals. It may be assumed, since all of our scores were reported in whole numbers, that the examiners rounded all actual scores to the nearest even digit. Consequently, a reported score of 86 actually means that the individual tested somewhere between 85.5 and 86.5. By extension, then, the first interval for our data has actual class limits of 84.5 to 87.5 instead of 85 to 87.

One should note that this designation of actual class limits remedies both of the deficiencies of the working interval. If graphed, the categories have contiguous boundaries; and the width of the class interval may be determined by subtraction ($87.5 - 84.5 = 3$). In most of our work, we will use the actual class limits instead of working limits. For convenience, these class limits may be listed on a separate sheet of paper and a tally made of the number of times a score falls into each of the class limits. Thus we avoid listing each of the IQs separately.

In our first interval we have only one score—86. In the second interval we have three scores. Successive intervals have 5, 7, 8, 10, 14, 11, 9, 5, 3, and 1 scores respectively. A sequential arrangement of the actual class limits and the number of individuals scoring within each interval is presented in Table 3.4.

The construction of our graph from this point is relatively simple. The horizontal axis must be divided to include the range from 84.5 (lower boundary of our first class interval) to 120.5 (upper boundary

TABLE 3.4.   Grouped distribution of the IQ scores of 77 school-age children

| ACTUAL CLASS LIMITS | | MIDPOINT | f (FREQUENCY) |
LOWER	UPPER		
81.5	84.5	83	0
84.5	87.5	86	1
87.5	90.5	89	3
90.5	93.5	92	5
93.5	96.5	95	7
96.5	99.5	98	8
99.5	102.5	101	10
102.5	105.5	104	14
105.5	108.5	107	11
108.5	111.5	110	9
111.5	114.5	113	5
114.5	117.5	116	3
117.5	120.5	119	1
120.5	123.5	122	0

of our last class interval). Once this length has been established, the Y axis will be constructed to have approximately 14 parts, as 14 is the number of cases in our most populous category.

To construct a histogram (bar graph) from these data, we draw a line one unit high at a score value of 84.5 to indicate one individual in the range from 84.5 to 87.5. At 87.5, another line one unit high is drawn, and a horizontal line is drawn connecting these two points. This indicates a single individual in the first class interval. At 87.5 we also extend the line to a three unit height. The upper bound of this category is at 90.5. A vertical line three units tall is drawn at this point and a horizontal line is drawn connecting these two. This process continues until all categories have been exhausted. Note that 12 categories are used in the final construction shown in Figure 3.3.

Although our actual range was 33 units, the graph extends 36 units $(120.5 - 84.5)$. Inclusion of an additional category is normal, because

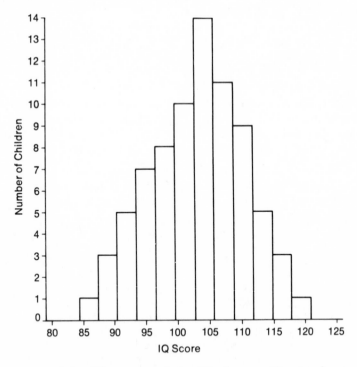

FIGURE 3.3. Histogram of the IQ data on 77 school-age children previously presented in Table 3.4.

we typically begin our graph below the lowest score and extend it beyond the highest score.

As a final point in the construction of the histogram we should label both axes. The horizontal axis would be labeled "IQ" or "Intelligence Quotient." The vertical axis would be labeled "Number of Subjects." This labeling prevents confusion in interpretation.

Frequency Polygons

The same data may also be presented as a frequency polygon or line graph. In the construction of a frequency polygon, each step is identical to that previously discussed for the histogram, with two exceptions. First, the frequency polygon is a line drawing and is plotted from the midpoints rather than from either class limit. The second distinction is that one additional class interval (midpoint) is plotted on either end of the data to complete the line drawing so that it intersects the horizontal axis.

Since the frequency polygon uses lines instead of bars, we must condense all of the information given in a particular category into a single point. The most logical point to use, assuming that an equal number of scores lie on each side, is the center of the interval—thus, the rationale behind using the midpoint to indicate the center of a given category. To determine a midpoint, first determine the interval width, divide the result by two, and add it to the lower actual limit. The midpoint for the first interval of the data previously listed in Table 3.4 would be: $3 \div 2 + 84.5 = 86$. This example illustrates another reason for using odd values as interval widths—all midpoints will be integer values.

To construct a frequency polygon from the data presented in Table 3.4, we would first determine the variables to be represented by both the horizontal and vertical axes. We design the graph to conform to the 60 to 80 percent rule for length of the Y axis. The number and the width of the class intervals are then determined, e.g., based on the range and approximate number of intervals required. The data for each class interval would then be tallied exactly as for the histogram.

Because of the need for an additional class interval in the frequency polygon, our first class interval (instead of 84.5 to 87.5) would be 81.5 to 84.5. Since none of the IQs fall within this range, the frequency is zero. Also, rather than the highest class interval being 117.5 to 120.5, an additional class interval of 120.5 to 123.5 would be included. Again, since no subjects have IQs within this range, the frequency would be zero.

Each class midpoint is then determined. For the first class interval (81.5 to 84.5) the midpoint is 83.0; the midpoint for the second interval is 86.0, the third 89.0, etc. The midpoint of the final interval (120.5 to 123.5) is 122.0. In the frequency polygon, each of the frequencies is plotted as a point above the class midpoint. Consequently, at an IQ value of 83, a point is plotted at a frequency value of 0; and at an IQ value of 86, we would plot a point at a frequency value of 1. This would continue until all categories were exhausted. Finally, we connect all of these points by straight lines to obtain the frequency polygon presented in Figure 3.4.

The reason that the two extra class intervals are included is apparent from inspection of this figure. Notice that inclusion of the extra class intervals results in a closed figure. Had we started at a frequency of 1

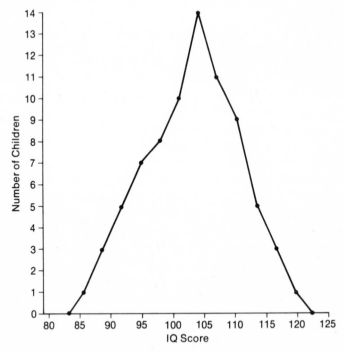

FIGURE 3.4. Frequency polygon of the IQ data on 77 school-age children previously presented in Table 3.4.

for the class interval 84.5 to 87.5, the graph would have started at a frequency of 1 rather than at 0 point. The final point on the graph would be at an IQ value of 119 with a frequency of 1. This would leave some question in the mind of the person who interprets the results as to whether there might have been additional scores which were not included in the graph. The inclusion of the extra two intervals with their zero-frequency units gives a neat closed appearance to the graph and indicates that all values fall within the designated limits.

The particular graphic display that an experimenter uses is a matter of preference; each type has both advantages and disadvantages. One of the primary advantages of the histogram, or bar graph, is that the area beneath a given point is easily seen to be proportional to the number of subjects who have obtained that particular score. The frequency polygon, on the other hand, does make much clearer our assumption that all of the scores in a given class interval fall at the midpoint—an interpretation which is sometimes overlooked with the histogram. One difficulty with the histogram is that we seem to imply some discontinuity between groups. That is, it appears that there is a sudden break at the class interval. The lines of the frequency polygon seem to indicate a flowing or continuous process. Which of these considerations is more important to the experimenter may determine the method of graphic display to be used.

GRAPHS INDICATING VARIABILITY

The Sample Study

All of the graphs constructed thus far have been displays of information following an experiment or survey. We have previously indicated that graphs may also be used for the analysis of data from experiments. Consequently, it is tempting to turn directly to analysis of the data collected in our experiment on visual discrimination. However, in all of the foregoing examples, each subject has had but a single score, e.g., an IQ of 101; while in the study of visual discrimination, we must analyze 64 scores for each subject. If there were some graphic method of deriving a single index of brightness for each subject, then summary graphs could be made either in the form of histograms or frequency polygons. Perhaps a review of the general area of thresholds will indicate the proper steps for graphically deriving such an index.

Each subject in our discrimination experiment was required to adjust, as precisely as possible, a variable light so that it appeared identical in brightness to another light. As you tested the subjects, you probably noticed that some individuals had a systematic tendency to set the variable light higher than the constant, while others tended to set the variable light lower than the constant. The average of one individual's settings is called the *point of subjective equality* (PSE) because it indicates what setting of the variable light is accepted by that individual as being equal in brightness to the constant.

In the review of the literature conducted prior to initiating this study, we found that this point of subjective equality varies from individual to individual and reflects different motivational characteristics of the subjects. For example, one person may have been exceedingly cautious as he approached the point of equivalence. Rather than risk the error of going beyond the point of exact equality, he may have had a systematic tendency to stop too soon. A second individual may have refused to quit turning the dial until he was certain that he had reached the actual point of equality. This would tend to give him settings which were consistently lower (on descending trials) than the matching or constant stimulus. The former type of error is known as an *error of anticipation;* the latter type as an *error of habituation.*

It is the variability of the settings, however, rather than these constant errors, that indicates the subject's power of discrimination. If there is a wide range of settings which the individual considers approximately equal, then his power of discrimination is relatively poor. If only a very narrow range of settings is accepted as equal, then his power of discrimination is relatively good. For example, if the constant light is at a setting of 150, one subject might make two settings of the variable light at 100 and 200. His point of subjective equality is thus 150, but discrimination is poor. If another individual makes settings of 149 and 151, his point of subjective equality is also 150. His power of discrimination, though, is much better than that of the first subject. Thus, discrimination is indicated not by the point of subjective equality, but by the range of errors about this point. It is the relationship between the variability of a subject's errors and what is known as the normal, or bell-shaped, curve that gives the rationale for the graphic determination of an index of brightness discrimination.

In your introductory psychology course, you have undoubtedly seen data represented in graphs by a bell-shaped curve. The function illustrated in these graphs is known as the normal curve and describes many of the kinds of data that are collected in psychology. In the IQ graphs previously constructed, few people had very low scores or very high scores. Most of the individuals tested had scores near 100. As a consequence, the graphs tended to approximate the normal curve. Had all possible IQs been tested and the intervals been very small, a normal curve would have resulted.

These distributions, however, are distributions of scores. What should be the relationship between sets of errors and the normal curve? As an illustration, we might have people estimate the length of a room. If the actual length of that room is 18 feet, differences in judgments could possibly reflect temporary states on the part of the individual. If a subject temporarily thinks of distances in an auditorium, he may underestimate the length of the room. Perhaps another individual has just finished some project in which extremely small measurements were taken and will tend to drastically overestimate the length of the room. This variability in judgments would be an error variability. However, most of the subjects would tend to estimate the length of the room within 2 or 3 feet of the 18-foot mark. If we recorded the estimates of the distance, we would find many judgments near 18 feet, with progressively fewer judgments farther away on either side of 18 feet. Thus, we would tend to obtain a normal distribution of judged room lengths. We find that discrimination is poor with respect to judged room length, and as a consequence, the range of the judgments is wide.

Let us take a second example. Suppose that we have another group of people measure this same room with a steel tape measure. Once again we would find a range of errors because some people would stretch even a steel tape measure to a greater degree than others. There may be misreading errors or errors in holding the tape tightly against the wall. Again, we would get values of the length of the room which would vary around the true 18-foot mark. This, obviously, is another error distribution. Since the amount of tape stretch or misreading would vary from person to person, we would again tend to get some normal distribution of these readings though we would seldom get readings which would fluctuate as much as 3 inches from the 18-foot mark. We would thus have a normal distribution of errors, but the range of these errors would be small and the discrimination would be good in comparison to the judged room lengths illustrated above.

Similarly, in the study that we have designed, a particular subject who has good discrimination will tend to set the variable light at very nearly the same point each time and the range of his errors will be small. If he has relatively poor discrimination, the range of his judgments will tend to be large. Thus, we see that a subject's power of discrimination varies in direct proportion to the range of his errors. This is the rationale for using the variability of his judgments as an index of his power of discrimination.

You should note that the graphs we have previously constructed do indicate, to some extent, the variability of scores. For example, the graphs of IQs showed that the IQs ranged from 86 to 119 for the sample that was tested. Had we tested a group of children who had been grouped on the basis of ability, we might have had an IQ range of only 95 to 105. This would be indicated by the graph as a reduction in the range—a reduction in the variability of the IQ scores for that class as compared with the class originally tested.

It is this property of graphs (the indication of variability) that early workers in the area of psychophysics used as an instrument for the analysis of their results. The histogram and the frequency polygon were not used, however, because of the difficulty of accurately determining an index of variability from such graphs. For example, would it be possible for you to accurately determine the range of IQs centering on the overall class average which includes 50 percent of all individuals tested? Yet this range is what early workers in psychophysics used as an index of discrimination.

Since most of the settings of an individual tend to cluster somewhere near his point of subjective equality, it seems appropriate to use the stimulus values that include the middle 50 percent of his responses as an index of the differential threshold. The 25 percent of his responses to either side of this middle range are not used because they may reflect special or temporary states of the individual which are unusual and not connected with the experiment. Dividing by two the range of stimulus values that include this central 50 percent of all responses approximates the measure that has been recognized in the psychophysical literature as the *differential threshold* (DL). For example, if 50 percent of an individual's responses were found in the range from 145 to 155, his DL would be $(155 - 145)/2 = 5$. Although we are concerned primarily with the indices of brightness discrimination of the subjects, our study may have much wider utilization and generalization if we convert to an index approximating the DL.

The Ogive

We have seen, however, that an accurate determination of this value would be difficult to obtain from either the histogram or frequency polygon. We would, instead, graph the cumulative proportions of responses. Consider what a normal or bell-shaped curve would look like if graphed in the form of cumulative proportions. Again using the example of judged room lengths, we would find that very few—say only 1 percent of all people—would make judgments of 10 feet or less. An additional 10 percent might have judgments of between 10 feet and 15 feet, for a total of 11 percent of all people who make judgments of less than 15 feet. As we continue toward the 18-foot judgment, we would find more and more judgments within each grouping and, consequently, an increasing proportion. As we move beyond this point we would find increasingly fewer judgments the further we go. This would give us smaller and smaller increments in the cumulative proportions until we reached 100 percent of all judgments. If these proportions were plotted in graphic form, they should look something like Figure 3.5.

The smooth S curve shown in this figure is known as the ogive and is simply the transformation of a normal curve into cumulative proportions. The advantage of the ogive is that it permits a very rapid estimate of the variability of a distribution. One need only refer to the

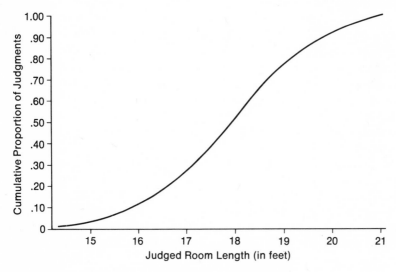

FIGURE 3.5. Cumulative proportion of judgments of the length of an 18-foot room. Note that relatively few individuals make judgments less than 15 feet or greater than 21 feet. This is reflected in the flatter slope of the ogive.

vertical axis for the desired proportion, refer across to the line graph, and drop to the horizontal axis for the appropriate stimulus value. For example, in Figure 3.5 one may begin at the 75 percent point on the vertical axis, draw a straight line from that point until it intersects the ogive, and then project a straight line downward until it intersects the horizontal axis. The value of 19.0 feet is the stimulus value corresponding to the 75 percent cumulative percentage of judgments. A similar procedure for the *Y*-axis value of 25 percent yields a stimulus value of 17.0 feet. Subtraction $(19.0 - 17.0)$ gives the range of stimulus values including the middle 50 percent of judgments (2 feet).

From this point we may proceed directly to the determination of the differential-brightness thresholds (DL) for each of our subjects. A portion of the data we might have collected for three subjects is presented in Table 3.5. As the data are still arranged in counterbalanced

TABLE 3.5.   A sample portion of the recorded scores of three subjects

SUBJECT NO. 1		SUBJECT NO. 2		SUBJECT NO. 3	
TRIAL*	SCORE	TRIAL	SCORE	TRIAL	SCORE
A	129	A	131	A	118
D	142	D	172	D	161
D	132	D	125	D	169
A	147	A	132	A	163
D	118	D	133	D	.
A	165	A	160	A	.
A	144	A	175	A	.
D	164	D	145	D	.
D	164	D	145	D	.
A	148	A	153	A	.
A	141	A	190	A	.
D	130	D	135	D	.
A	145	.	.	.	.
D	177	.	.	.	.
D	142	.	.	.	.
A	160	.	.	.	.
.	.	.	.	.	.
.	.	.	.	.	.
.	.	.	.	.	.
.	.	.	.	.	.

* The symbol *A* represents an ascending trial and the symbol *D* represents a descending trial.

order, the first step is to restructure these data, grouping the ascending and the descending trials sequentially from high to low for each individual.

The ascending trials for Subject No. 1 are rearranged into an ordered set in Table 3.6. Since only 32 scores are available for analysis, these scores have not been grouped. The variability of the subject's settings is readily apparent in this table. It is also apparent that this subject tends to have a setting of the point of subjective equality somewhere near 140. This, in an ascending series (since the constant value was set at 150), would be the error of anticipation previously discussed. The power of discrimination of this subject is reflected in the variability of his settings about this point of subjective equality.

Since we wish to construct an approximation of the ogive, we must

TABLE 3.6.   Ordered arrangement of Subject No. 1's ascending scores

ACTUAL STIMULUS VALUES	CUMULATIVE NUMBER OF RESPONSES	CUMULATIVE PROPORTION
110	1	.031
122	2	.063
126	3	.094
128	4	.125
129	5	.156
130	6	.188
132	7	.219
133	8	.250
134	9	.281
138	10	.313
140, 140, 140	13	.406
141	14	.438
142, 142, 142, 142	18	.562
144	19	.594
145, 145	21	.656
147, 147	23	.719
148	24	.750
151	25	.781
152	26	.813
154	27	.844
156, 156	29	.906
160, 160	31	.969
165	32	1.000

convert the responses of this subject to cumulative proportions of his total responses. He has had 32 ascending trials, so each trial is about .031 of the total. Beginning with the lowest stimulus value to which a response is made, we successively determine how many of the responses are at or below each particular stimulus point. These cumulative proportions are listed in the right hand section of Table 3.6. To determine the cumulative proportion of responses for any given level, count the number of responses to that stimulus level and divide by 32 (the total number of responses). For example, consider the number of responses at or below a setting of 142. We count 18 responses either at a setting of 142 or lower. To determine the cumulative proportion of responses, divide 18 (the number of responses to this point) by 32 (the total number of responses). This yields a cumulative proportion of approximately .562. The remaining values listed in the right hand side of Table 3.6 were determined in a similar fashion.

From the entries in Table 3.6, note that the range of scores for the X axis should probably be from about 100 to 175. In the same table, cumulative proportions range from .000 (no responses) to 1.000 (all of the responses) and specify the range of values required for the Y axis.

Figure 3.6 shows the completed graph of the data given in Table 3.6. Both axes of this graph are correctly labeled to minimize the possibility of error in its interpretation. In this figure, each of the cumulative percentages is plotted as a single point. The intersection of a Y axis cumulative-proportion value of .031 and an X axis stimulus value of 110 is a point which represents the lowest response of the subject. Similarly, the point of intersection of a Y axis value of .562 and X axis stimulus value of 142 represents the 18 responses of the subject at or below a stimulus value of 142.

One could connect these points to derive a graph, as represented by the dotted lines in Figure 3.6. If we were presenting actual summary data of an experiment in a journal report, the graph might actually be drawn in this manner. More often, however, one makes some assumption about the underlying function of the data. In this particular case it seems that there is some general curve of the responses. The curve that we assume the responses should actually fit is the ogive. The best-fitting ogive to these data is presented in the solid line in Figure 3.6. The rationale behind the use of this solid line (which actually intersects very few of the sampled data points) stems from psychophysics. One assumes that a judgment at any one time is a "random fluctuation" from some central point. As a consequence, judgments should form a

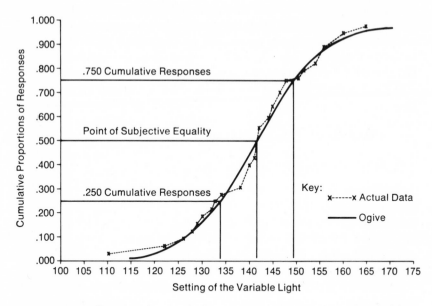

FIGURE 3.6. Graph of cumulative response proportions for Subject No. 1's ascending scores. Note that the actual data matches the theoretical ogive rather well.

normal curve. Since we are graphing cumulative proportions, and may assume that the errors in discrimination are normally distributed, then the best-fitting curve for the data should be the ogive—the curve which best fits cumulative normally distributed data.

When plotting cumulative proportions, we assume that errors are normally distributed and fit by inspection some general S-shaped curve which seems to go near a majority of the points plotted. From this smooth curve, we may determine the DL from the .250 and .750 as an index of both variability and discrimination. For this subject, we note that the 25 percent level, as represented by the solid-line figure, occurs at a stimulus setting of approximately 133.5. The 75 percent level in this figure occurs at a stimulus setting of approximately 149.5. To convert these values to an approximation of the differential threshold, subtract the 25 percent level from the 75 percent level and divide by two. For this subject, the range (the difference between a setting of 133.5 and a setting of 149.5) is 16 units and the differential threshold is approximately 8.0. A further simplification is possible in view of the symmetry of the ogive about the .500 cumulative response proportion point. One determines both the point of subjective equality (the stimulus value corresponding to .500 on the ogive) and the stimulus value corresponding to .750. Subtraction of these two values gives the DL directly. For example, the PSE shown in Figure 3.6 is 141.5, the .750 point is 149.5, and the DL is 8.0.

ANALYSIS OF EXPERIMENTAL DATA

Graphic Presentation of Experimental Results

This graphic solution of the differential threshold has reduced the quantity of data that we must consider. We have replaced the 64 original scores for this subject with two DL scores, one for the ascending and one for the descending series. For the study as a whole, instead of the 2560 scores originally collected we now have only 80 scores— the ascending and descending DL's for each of 40 subjects.

These data are listed by ascending–descending order for each subject in Table 3.7. The solid line across the center of the table differentiates those subjects who participated in the "light" condition from those who participated in the "dark" condition. It is extremely difficult to tell by visual inspection of the data whether or not the background had some effect on the behavior of the subjects. Some subjects who participated in the "light" condition have DL's as high as 34.0, while some subjects in the "dark" condition have DL's as low as 10.0. For these two groups there exists a definite overlap in computed differential thresholds.

To further simplify these data, it is necessary to summarize them by constructing either histograms or frequency polygons. Since it is often a matter of choice which of these graphs one uses, let us select the frequency polygon as a method of illustrating our results. The procedures for constructing the frequency polygons have already been explained (see pp. 63–65).

Since differences may exist between the ascending and descending DL's, four graphs have been constructed—two for each of these conditions. These are presented in Figure 3.7. The upper two graphs are distributions of the DL's for the "dark" condition; the lower two are for the "light" condition. In each pair of graphs, the first graph given is for the ascending DL and the second is for the descending DL.

What conclusions may we now draw regarding the outcome of our

TABLE 3.7. DL's graphically computed: brightness-discrimination study

EXPERIMENTAL GROUP	SUBJECT NO.	ASCENDING DL	DESCENDING DL
	1	8.0	10.5
	2	13.5	12.0
	3	12.0	12.0
	4	7.0	9.0
	5	17.0	13.0
	6	15.0	24.0
	7	17.0	9.0
	8	11.0	10.0
	9	17.5	34.0
"Light"	10	21.5	14.5
	11	8.0	19.0
	12	10.5	14.0
	13	11.5	12.5
	14	14.0	12.0
	15	26.0	22.0
	16	13.5	13.5
	17	16.0	20.5
	18	10.0	17.5
	19	12.5	10.0
	20	15.0	9.5
	21	12.5	21.0
	22	14.0	15.0
	23	13.0	13.0
	24	21.5	23.0
	25	11.0	16.0
	26	12.5	19.0
	27	21.0	25.0
	28	19.0	27.0
	29	14.0	13.0
"Dark"	30	16.0	17.0
	31	25.0	20.5
	32	18.0	18.5
	33	13.0	21.5
	34	20.0	21.0
	35	24.0	28.5
	36	17.0	11.0
	37	25.0	24.0
	38	10.0	15.0
	39	18.0	17.0
	40	17.0	15.5

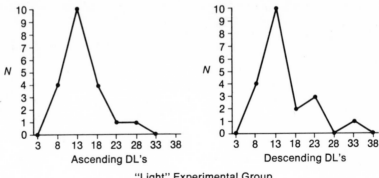

"Light" Experimental Group

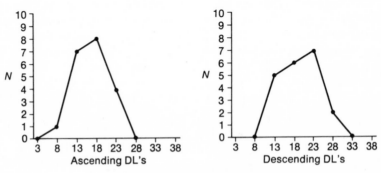

"Dark" Experimental Group

FIGURE 3.7. Frequency polygons illustrating the DL's computed for the study of brightness discrimination as a function of background illumination. These graphs use a 5-interval width for grouping.

experiment? The question that we wish to answer is whether visual discrimination is better when the background is dark than it is when the background is light. From simple inspection of the four graphs, the DL's collected under the "dark" condition appear higher than the DL's collected under the "light" condition. This relationship seems to hold for both the ascending and descending trials, and we may conclude that visual discrimination is enhanced by light adaptation.

Significance of Experimental Results

Suppose, however, that we rephrase the question, adding the word "significantly." We are now asking, "Is brightness discrimination significantly better in a light background than in a dark background?" The word "significantly" has a somewhat different meaning in statistics than it has in common usage. In everyday usage, a significant difference is one which is of practical import. A significant difference in statistical terms implies a difference that is unlikely to have occurred by chance alone. Although we must consider both of these meanings when we interpret an experiment, the statistical meaning has precedence. Consequently, our question becomes: "Under light-background conditions, are the differential-brightness thresholds as determined by the method of graphic analysis so much lower than those for conditions of dark background that they are unlikely to have happened by chance alone?"

Our present state of sophistication regarding statistical analysis is inadequate to answer this question. Our graphs do not contain enough information to determine whether or not our experiment was a success. Several factors might be involved in our results. Perhaps we inadvertently selected those subjects with good visual discrimination to participate in the "light" group. Possibly the two graphs in the lower part of Figure 3.7 seem to indicate a better discrimination under "light" conditions simply as a consequence of this chance event. We need to know the probability that our results could be obtained from such chance assignment of subjects. Also, we note that some of the subjects in the "light" group actually have poorer discrimination than some of the subjects in the "dark" group. Only for the groups as a whole does there seem to be any difference. Possibly the difference between our two groups is relatively small with respect to those differences that occur between individuals.

We note that there also exists possibility for error in the analysis of the data from this experiment. Although each of the subject's settings was recorded to the nearest unit on our apparatus, some room for error was present in the construction of the graph. Two persons might draw slightly different ogives, even though both were working from the same data. Thus a possibility exists that the DL's which we have calculated are unreliable. Would it be possible that all of the DL's calculated for the "dark" group could have been misjudged on the high side, while all of the DL's for the "light" group were misjudged on the low side? Again we would like to know the possibility of the difference between the two groups having occurred as a result of such a chance factor.

A third point that we should consider in relation to the results of our experiment is concerned with the validity of the experiment itself. In the very process of constructing the best-fitting ogive to each subject's data, it was necessary to assume that the various settings of each subject were random, normally distributed errors about his point of subjective equality. If this assumption was in error, then our method of determining the differential threshold was in error. A second assumption was that the DL is, in fact, a measure of discriminability. If our measure is not a measure of discriminability, but of some other function, any conclusion that we draw may be in error. It might be possible for the two groups to differ significantly, i.e., exhibit results which are not due to chance alone, but on a measure which is unknown to the experimenter. Such results would, of course, yield meaningless conclusions.

Finally, recalling the effects of experimenter bias, is it possible that we are "just looking at it that way" rather than actually noting a true difference between the two sets of frequency polygons? That is, is it possible that the shapes of the graphs shown in Figure 3.7 are leading us to some conclusion not actually supported by the data?

The solution to several of our problems lies with the statistical methods to be introduced in future chapters. We will learn in the next chapter, for example, that it is possible to manipulate the scores mathematically to determine points of subjective equality and DL's which will be reliable across individuals. This will eliminate much of the subjective bias involved in the construction of the normal ogive. Use of these same mathematical procedures will also yield a meaningful estimate of the true differences between the two groups. Only after we have thoroughly investigated probability and its relationship to our data will we be able to state that our results are either "this way" or "that way."

SUMMARY

Graphs can be used for both the analysis and the display of large masses of data, thus simplifying interpretation of the data. The two main types of graphs are those which show relationships between two or more variables, and those which indicate relative frequencies of occurrence of values for a single variable. Certain general rules should be followed in using either type of graph: (1) the height of the Y or vertical axis should be approximately 60 to 80 percent of the X or horizontal axis; (2) the independent and dependent variable should be displayed on the X and Y axes respectively; (3) it is necessary to use an origin which indicates a meaningful relationship where frequencies or amounts are concerned; (4) both axes should be correctly labeled and the units clearly designated.

The graphs most commonly used to display and/or analyze frequency data are histograms (bar graphs) and frequency polygons (line graphs). A typical procedure for constructing either graph is: (1) determine the range by subtracting the lowest score from the highest; (2) divide the range into an appropriate number of odd-value interval widths; and (3) group the data into these intervals.

The histogram is constructed by using bars which encompass the actual class intervals, usually one-half unit larger and smaller than the working interval. The frequency polygon is constructed by joining the points indicating frequency at the midpoint of each class interval. One additional midpoint above and below the grouped data is plotted to provide a neat closed appearance to the frequency polygon.

For greater ease in determining an estimate of variability, a graph of cumulative proportions was used for the analysis of the data from the differential-brightness threshold study. In order to construct these graphs, several assumptions had to be made: (1) that the subject's errors were normally distributed; (2) that the range from the PSE to the .750 point was a valid measure of brightness discrimination; and (3) that this measure approximated the differential brightness threshold. Based on these assumptions, ogives were constructed on each graph and DL's were computed from these ogives. Visual inspection of summary graphs of these DL's seemed to support our original hypothesis but valid conclusions concerning the significance of our data could not be made. Although the procedural difficulties associated with the free-hand sketch were seen as reducing the reliability of the DL, the most important limitation of the graphic method was the lack of sufficient statistical knowledge to evaluate the validity of our assumptions.

4. Descriptive Statistics

MEASURES OF CENTRAL TENDENCY

The Mean

So far we are unable to reach any satisfactory conclusion regarding the outcome of our experiment, an undesirable state of affairs. Let us see how we may determine a DL which is more reliable than that obtained graphically. Recall that our first step, following the actual construction of the graph, was determination of the point of subjective equality. This point is simply an average setting for the subject and may reflect motivational differences, individual biases, and so forth. You have probably been using averages for many years in your day-to-day living. For example, if you want to know the average weight of a group of apples, you first weigh all of them. To find the average you divide the sum of all the individual apple weights by the number of apples weighed. A mathematical formulation for this operation would be:

Average apple weight = Sum of all individual apple weights ÷
Number of apples.

It should be apparent that we can determine a point of subjective equality in a similar manner. That is, we should be able to sum all of our individual judgments, divide by the number of judgments, and determine mathematically the point of subjective equality. In formula style this would be:

PSE = Sum of all individual settings ÷ Total number of settings.

In psychology, this arithmetic average is called a *mean*.

In statement form this formula for the point of subjective equality would read: The mean setting on the brightness discrimination apparatus is equal to the sum of all of the individual settings divided by the total number of settings. This formulation is, however, somewhat cumbersome. Consequently, to save both time and space, psychologists have developed a shorthand, or symbolic form for writing formulas. Although the particular symbols used may vary from one text to another, the following are widely accepted and shall be used in this text:

SYMBOL	MEANING
X	any individual score
$\bar{X}$	mean of all the individual scores
Σ	take the sum of all
N	the total number of individual scores

Our previous formula can now be expressed:

$$\bar{X} = \frac{\Sigma X}{N}$$

Note that this formula is indiscriminate with respect to the specific mean being computed. One might determine the mean height of all men in the United States. Here X would represent the height of any particular individual and ΣX would represent the sum of all men's heights in the United States. N would be the total number of men in the United States, and, finally, $\bar{X}$ would be the mean height of all men in the United States.

For our discrimination experiment, if X represents any particular setting of a given individual, then ΣX represents the sum of all of that individual's settings under a particular condition. N is the total number of trials, and $\bar{X}$ will be the point of subjective equality, or mean setting.

Let us apply this formula to the data presented in Table 3.5 in the previous chapter and reprinted in Table 4.1. The data presented are the ascending scores of Subject No. 1. Here, X is any of the individual response settings, i.e., 110, 122, 126, etc. At the bottom of this table the sum of all of these individual settings (4541) is designated as ΣX. Computation of the point of subjective equality is also shown at the bottom of this table. Since we have 32 settings, $N = 32$. To determine the point of subjective equality, the sum of all the individual response settings (4541) is divided by the total number of response settings (32). This mean setting of 141.91 differs from the point of subjective

TABLE 4.1.   Mathematical computation of the ascending PSE for Subject No. 1.

ACTUAL STIMULUS VALUE (X)		
110	140	145
122	140	147
126	140	147
128	141	148
129	142	151
130	142	152
132	142	154
133	142	156
134	144	156
138	145	160
		160
		165
		$\Sigma X = \overline{4541}$
		$N = 32$

$$\bar{X} = \frac{\Sigma X}{N} = \frac{4541}{32} = 141.90625$$

equality determined graphically in Figure 3.2. There, using the graphic method, the point of subjective equality was estimated as 141.5—a difference of .41 stimulus units.

There are several advantages to the use of a mathematical formula instead of the graphic method for determination of the point of subjective equality: The scores may be analyzed without sequentially arranging them; the procedures are commonly used; and the requirement for drawing a graph is eliminated. We previously noted that each point of subjective equality might be somewhat in error depending upon the person who sketched the freehand ogive. Use of a mathematical computation of the point of subjective equality minimizes the possibility of error; the only mistakes likely to occur are those in simple addition and division. The probability of such errors seems small in comparison with the possible error inherent in the sketching of the freehand ogive. Thus, use of this mathematically formulated **PSE** (point of subjective equality) should increase the reliability of our data.

The Mode and the Median

Before we proceed to mathematical determinations of the DL, we should note that the arithmetic mean may sometimes yield misleading conclusions. For example, consider the data presented in Table 4.2,

TABLE 4.2. Incomes for seven individuals selected at random

INDIVIDUAL	INCOME (X)
1	$\$\quad 0$
2	0
3	0
4	5,000
5	8,000
6	9,000
7	1,000,000
	$\Sigma X = \$1,022,000$
	$N = 7$

$$\bar{X} = \frac{\Sigma X}{N} + \frac{1,022,000}{7} = 146,000$$

which lists the incomes of seven individuals selected at random from the United States. The three with zero dollars income are probably children. These scores are followed by three individuals who have typical incomes—$5000, $8000, $9000. The last person listed is an aberrant individual (with respect to income) who has an income of $1,000,000. The computation of the mean income for this group of seven persons is shown at the bottom of Table 4.2. The sum of all 7 of these incomes is $1,022,000. Since we have 7 individuals, our mean income is $146,000—hardly a typical American income.

Studying these data, three different investigators might arrive at completely different conclusions regarding the average income of people in the United States. Someone critical of the United States, for example, could state that the average income in the United States is zero dollars. The statement would be based on what we term the *modal* income—the most frequent income. The data presented in Table 4.2 lists three individuals with zero income. Possibly, as noted earlier, these are children. However, it is a fact that more people in this sample have zero incomes than any other single income. Thus, one may cite the modal income as the average income for the United States.

A person who wished to glorify the virtues of the free-enterprise system might use the *mean* income previously computed. Thus, he would report the average income in the United States as $146,000.

A third individual might use yet another method of determining the average income in the United States, designating as average that score which falls at the exact middle, i.e., the one with as many incomes above it as there are below it. This middle score is known as the *median*. For the data listed in this example, the middle, or median, income is $5000. We see that it is important to specify what operation we are using—the mean, the mode, or the median—when we say that a given score is the average score.

The relative positions of these measures of central tendency (mean, median, and mode) differ with the shape of the distribution. The fictitious income data may be described as having positive skewness. That is, if we made a histogram of the income data, we would find that the tail of the distribution would stretch far to the right of our graph. It is also possible for data to be negatively skewed. In such a case the long tail of the graph would stretch far to the left. Between these extremes, the distribution of data gives a normal curve that is not skewed. Examples of these three types of curves are shown in Figure 4.1. Note the relationship of the mode, the median, and the mean for

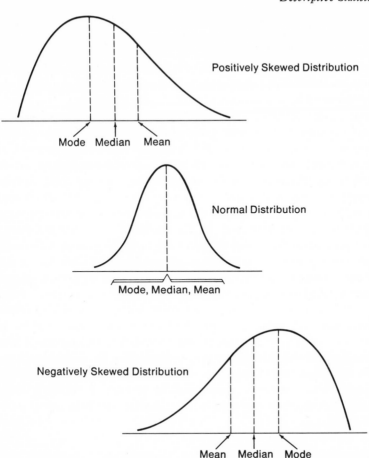

FIGURE 4.1. An illustration of the relative positions of the mean, median, and mode in three types of distributions. These relative placements have been exaggerated for illustrative purposes.

these three cases. For the positively skewed curve, the mode is the lowest, the median falls between the mode and the mean, and the mean is the highest score of the three averages. For the negatively skewed curve, the converse is true. Only in nonskewed curves are the three averages identical. As a consequence, it is only when a particular distribution is normal that the mode, the median, and the mean may all be used as the representative or average score.

The point of subjective equality which was determined by the graphic method is, in effect, a median. That is, the point of subjective equality determined graphically was at the 50 percent point of the cumulative responses. Consequently, half of the scores are above this point, and half of the scores are below it. This is our definition of the median.

For us to regard our mean as being the same as the point of subjective equality determined graphically, we must necessarily assume some symmetrical or nonskewed distribution. In our particular case, we have previously assumed that these scores are random-error deviations from the point of subjective equality and that they do form a normal distribution. Thus, the mean we computed arithmetically should be approximately equal to the median we computed graphically.

Let us continue with each of the points of subjective equality that were previously determined graphically. One divides each of the subjects' settings into ascending and descending trials, sums the 32 scores for each condition, and divides by 32 to determine a point of subjective equality. With the aid of a calculator it will be relatively easy to determine the points of subjective equality for both ascending and descending trials of the "dark"-condition and "light"-condition subjects. Most calculators will sum the scores and record N simultaneously. Determination of the ascending and descending PSE's for each subject under each condition would, however, be only half of the graphic analysis completed in the earlier chapters. The primary problem is still the determination of the differential threshold about these points of subjective equality.

MEASURES OF VARIABILITY

Deviations from the Mean

We have noted earlier that an index of discrimination should be determined from the range or spread of settings about the point of subjective equality. One possible index of discrimination might be computed by using the deviations from the mean of all settings. Consider the data given in Table 4.3, listing the deviation of each individual setting from Subject No. 1's mean setting of 142. It might be satisfactory to simply sum these scores and derive a mean deviation. When we complete this process, however, we see that the sum of the deviations from

TABLE 4.3. Deviations, absolute deviations, and squared deviations of response settings (Subject No. 1)

DEVIATION (x)	ABSOLUTE DEVIATION $(/x/)$	SQUARED DEVIATION (x^2)
−32	32	1024
−20	20	400
−16	16	256
−14	14	196
−13	13	169
−12	12	144
−10	10	100
− 9	9	81
− 8	8	64
− 4	4	16
− 2	2	4
− 2	2	4
− 2	2	4
− 1	1	1
0	0	0
0	0	0
0	0	0
0	0	0
+ 2	2	4
+ 3	3	9
+ 3	3	9
+ 5	5	25
+ 5	5	25
+ 6	6	36
+ 9	9	81
+10	10	100
+12	12	144
+14	14	196
+14	14	196
+18	18	324
+18	18	324
+23	23	529
$\Sigma x = -3$	$\Sigma /x/ = 287$	$\Sigma x^2 = 4465$

$$\text{Mean Deviation} = \frac{\Sigma x}{N} = \frac{-3}{32} = -.09$$

$$\text{Mean Absolute Deviation (Average Deviation)} = \frac{\Sigma /x/}{N} = \frac{287}{32} = 8.97$$

$$\text{Mean Squared Deviation (Variance)} = \frac{\Sigma x^2}{N} = \frac{4465}{32} = 139.53$$

$$\text{Standard Deviation} = \sqrt{\frac{\Sigma x^2}{N}} = \sqrt{\frac{4465}{32}} = 11.81$$

the mean is approximately zero. This would be true for all computations of deviations from the point of subjective equality. As a matter of fact, this serves as a check on our computation of the mean. If we have computed accurately, the sum of all deviations from the mean will be zero. This property leads to a physical definition of the mean as a sort of center of gravity of the distribution. Given the normal curve illustrated in Figure 4.1, you may see that if we were able to "suspend" the normal curve from the mean, it would balance. This property of the mean explains why you will sometimes hear it referred to as "the first moment" of the distribution—the center of gravity.

The sum of the deviations listed in Table 4.3 is not exactly zero because we have used 142 as an approximate rather than the true mean. Had we used the exact mean of 141.90625 we would have found the sum of the deviations to be exactly zero.

How may we, then, arrive at some meaningful estimate of the variability of a subject's scores about his point of subjective equality? One possible solution would be to ignore the minus signs in Table 4.3. If we ignore these minus signs, we could then sum the absolute deviations and derive a mean absolute deviation. This is an appropriate statistical technique and is called the *average deviation*. This computation is shown in the second column of Table 4.3. Such a solution, however, is not satisfying in that we are arbitrarily changing the signs of our scores.

Variance

A more acceptable way to eliminate these minus signs is to square each of the scores. As you remember from high-school algebra, a negative score multiplied by a negative score yields a positive score. So, if we square each of the deviations in the first column, we obtain the positive values listed in the third column of Table 4.3. Again, the figures listed here are only approximate, since the mean was rounded to 142. With only positive numbers in this third column, it is possible to sum all of these squared deviations and thus determine a mean squared deviation.

Let us examine a few of the properties of this mean squared deviation. First, rather than mean squared deviation, we usually refer to it as *variance*. In our study, variance is a measure of the variability of the subject's settings about his point of subjective equality. Variance, then, may be a satisfactory measure of the differential threshold. But we should also consider a second point. When the mean squared deviation is derived, the variability is stated in square units. That is, if each of the scores originally analyzed was recorded in inches (e.g., heights of men in the United States), each squared deviation from the mean would be recorded in square inches. Similarly, the mean squared deviation or variance would be given in square inches.

Standard Deviation

This creates some problems. Our index of discrimination should be in the same units as the DL's that were previously derived by the graphic method. The simplest method of accomplishing this is to find the square root of our mean squared deviation. This returns our estimate of variability to the original units of measurement. This square root of the mean squared deviation is called the *standard deviation* (σ).

One advantage to the use of the standard deviation rather than the average deviation is that the former has a physical meaning similar to that of the mean. That is, the standard deviation is the second moment of a normal distribution, or the center of gravity of a normal distribution which has been folded on itself at the mean. Many statistical tables are scaled in terms of the standard deviation, which has come to have universal meaning among psychologists.

Parameters

Let us examine some of the properties of both the mean and the standard deviation as they relate to one another. The statistics we will be using throughout most of this text are termed parametric statistics. The term *parameter* means a variable determining a function. In psychology, for example, we may speak about the parameters of behavior. Some of the parameters of bar pressing in the rat are hours of deprivation, amount of reward, and previous training trials. That is, these variables act so that they in part determine how many bar presses an animal will make. One finds that up to a certain point increases in the deprivation time of an animal will lead to more bar presses per minute (17). Similarly, with a given deprivation time, the rate of bar pressing will be a function of the amount of reward. Unfortunately, in most of psychology, we are unaware of all of the parameters that influence behavior.

The normal curve is a mathematical concept and is defined by only two parameters—the mean and the standard deviation. That is, knowing these two values, one can construct the normal distribution. In describing the distribution we find that these two parameters (the mean and the standard deviation) are independent parameters of the normal curve. Thus we may have changes in the mean of a distribution which are independent of changes in the variability and conversely we may have changes in variability which are independent of changes in the mean. Consider, in this respect, the data of our experiment. We might find two individuals who have basically the same powers of discrimination. That is, one individual may have approximately the same variability in his settings as another. This does not mean that the two must have the same point of subjective equality. Possibly one of these subjects is extremely cautious and will have an error of anticipation, while the other is overcompensating and will have an error of habituation. These errors would be independent of the basic powers of discrimination of the two subjects. This is an illustration of the statement that changes in the mean may occur independently in relation to the standard deviation.

As a second example, we might test two individuals who exhibit an error of anticipation. One of these individuals may accept only a very narrow range of settings as being equal to the constant light. The other individual may have a very wide range of settings which he accepts as being equal to the constant light; yet their points of subjective equality, or mean performances, might be equal. Thus, it does not follow that two individuals having the same point of subjective equality will also have the same power of discrimination. This is equivalent to permitting changes in the standard deviation which are independent of changes in the mean.

It was previously stated that the mean and the standard deviation are the only parameters of a normal curve. That is, given the mean and the standard deviation, it should be possible to determine the exact shape of the distribution. If we are able to determine this shape, then it follows that we know exactly how many people or how many observations are included in each portion of the distribution.

It is possible to convert this to a percentage basis. For example, consider the theoretical distribution of intelligence quotients. If we know that the mean IQ is 100 and the standard deviation is 16, then we are able to state that approximately 68 percent of all individuals tested will have IQs between 84 and 116. This area is illustrated in Figure 4.2. As illustrated in that figure, about 34 percent of all IQs are found in the score range between the mean (100) and the mean plus 1 standard

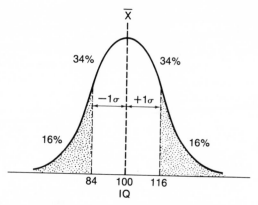

FIGURE 4.2. A normal distribution of IQ scores. Note that approximately 68 percent of all individuals tested will have IQs between plus and minus one standard deviation from the mean (84 → 116).

deviation (100 + 16 = 116). Similarly, approximately 34 percent of all IQs will be in the score range from the mean minus 1 σ (100 − 16 = 84) to the mean (100). Simple addition, then, resulted in the previous statement that 68 percent of all individuals tested will have IQ scores between 84 and 116.

Although we have chosen even units in this example, it is possible to choose any fraction of a standard deviation unit as well as whole numbers. As an illustration, one might want to know approximately what percentage of all of the people tested should be expected to exhibit IQs between 68.64 and 131.36—both of which are 1.96 standard deviations from the mean (100 − 1.96 × 16 = 68.64 and 100 + 1.96 × 16 = 131.36). The distribution of IQ scores that we might expect to find is illustrated in Figure 4.3. Notice that approximately 47.5 percent of all scores are to be found in the range from $\bar{X}$ − 1.96σ to $\bar{X}$. A similar situation exists for the range from $\bar{X}$ to $\bar{X}$ + 1.96σ. Thus, within this particular score range we would expect to find approximately 95 percent of all of the people tested. Recalling that the normal curve is symmetrical about the mean, we can see from this that approximately 2.5 percent have IQs above 131.36 and approximately 2.5 percent have scores less than 68.64.

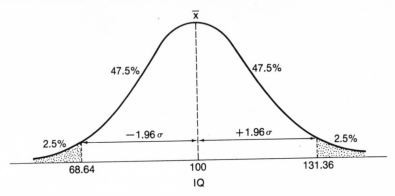

FIGURE 4.3. An IQ-score distribution illustrating the 95 percent included between -1.96σ and $+1.96\sigma$. Thus, only 2.5 percent of the population tested have IQs above 131.36, and only 2.5 percent received scores blow 68.64.

Standard Scores

Notice that in both examples the scores were expressed as a specific number of standard deviation units from the mean. These are standard scores and reflect the fact that only the independent parameters of the mean and standard deviation are required to completely describe a normal distribution.

The use of such standard scores has the advantage of reducing the number of tables we need. If such units were not used, it would be necessary to have one table describing the percentages of IQs falling between certain limits, another table describing the percentages of people whose heights fall within certain limits, another for weights, etc. One can hardly visualize the overstuffed look of our textbooks if such tables were required. Fortunately, use of these standard score equivalents permits us to have a single table which completely describes all normal curves, provided one knows the mean and the standard deviation.

Such a table is given in Appendix B (p. 282). The first column of this table is listed as x/σ. The symbol in the numerator of this fraction, lower-case x, represents a deviation score. Since we have used a capital X to represent a score, it seems appropriate to use the lower-case x to symbolize the deviation of a given score from the mean. In the previous example, the IQ score of 84 is a deviation of 16 units from the mean of

100. Thus, the score of 84 can also be represented as an x score of -16. The minus sign indicates that this deviation is below the mean. As you note in Appendix B, no minus scores are given. However, since the normal curve is symmetrical about the mean, the same number of σ units on either side of the mean will represent an equivalent number of cases. This property of the normal curve has been illustrated in both Figures 4.2 and 4.3. Consequently, we determine only the direction from the minus sign. Similarly, the score of 116 also has an x or deviation score of $+16$. The plus sign shows that this score is to the right-hand side of the mean.

The second symbol used in this table is that of the lower-case Greek letter sigma (σ). This lower-case sigma represents the standard deviation. The original use of the sigma follows from the first letter of the term itself: S. Since we have previously used the capital Greek letter sigma (Σ) to stand for "sum of," the standard deviation uses the lower-case form of the letter as its symbol.

The heading in Appendix B indicates that one divides the deviation from the mean (x) by the standard deviation (σ) to provide an entry. In the first example (the scores between 84 and 116) we found that an IQ score of 84 is a deviation score of -16. If the standard deviation is also 16, then the value of x/σ is $-16/16$ or -1.00. Reading down the outside column of Appendix B, we find the figure of 34.13 corresponding to a x/σ value of 1.00. This is the percent of the area under the normal curve between the mean and our x/σ value of -1.00. Similarly, the x/σ value for a score of 116 is $+1.00$ ($x/\sigma = +16/16 = +1.00$). As a consequence, 34.13 percent of the total area of the normal curve is between the mean (100) and a score of 116. If we know that 34.13 percent of all people have IQ scores between 84 and 100, and that 34.13 percent of all people have IQ scores between 100 and 116, we must sum to determine how many have scores between 84 and 116. Summing these two values indicates that 68.26 percent of all people have IQ scores between 84 and 116.

In the example illustrated in Figure 4.3, we wished to know what percentage of the population should have IQ scores between 68.64 and 131.36. Although we suspect that it will be impossible to measure IQs to two decimal places, the problem is still interesting from a mathematical point of view. Again, we must first determine the deviation of each of these scores from the mean. For the lower score we obtain a deviation value of -31.36 ($68.64 - 100 = -31.36$). The upper score is a deviation score of $+31.36$ ($131.36 - 100 = +31.36$). If the standard deviation is 16, we find that the x/σ value for both of these scores is 1.96. Again, note that the plus or minus sign indicates only the direction from the mean. In Appendix B, the value corresponding to a x/σ score of 1.96 is 47.50. Thus, 47.50 percent of all of the people should have IQ scores between 68.64 and 100. Additionally, 47.50 percent of the people should have scores between 100 and 131.36. Summing these two values gives us 95.00 percent of all of the people—and supports our original statement that approximately 95 percent of all people should have IQ scores between these two limits. The second statement concerning these two scores was that approximately 2.5 percent of the population should have scores above the upper limit, and 2.5 percent of the population should have scores below the lower limit. Thus, we are able to specify in detail the types of scores we might expect.

We find some possibility for developing inferences about data based on these x/σ values. For example, imagine that you reach into someone's personnel file without knowing anything about the individual himself. In this personnel file are a large number of scores from various tests. Suppose that you draw a slip of paper reporting a test score of 68. Immediately you are able to make some inference about this score, for example, "I don't know what this score is, but it's not an IQ score." Of course you run some risk of error. Perhaps this is one of the 2.5 percent of the individuals who have IQ scores below 68.64. The risk of such an error, though, is minimal. Since you are taking some chance of error, the statement should be, "I don't know what this is, but it *probably* is not an IQ score." Thus, we see that we are able to make some inferential statements about data without having any knowledge of that data other than the mean and the standard deviation of the population from which it is assumed to have been drawn.

At this point we can return to our primary concern—establishing a differential-brightness threshold for the subjects. We determined the differential threshold by use of the point of subjective equality and the stimulus value corresponding to the .75 cumulative-response proportion. The mean, or point of subjective equality, is the 50 percent point previously marked in our graphic analysis. The .75 cumulative-response proportion is 25 percent above the mean. Reading from the body of the table to the sides in Appendix B, we find that 25 percent of the area of a normal curve is included within approximately .67 x/σ units from the mean. Had our table been more detailed, we would have found that approximately .6745 x/σ units from the mean would include 25 percent of all cases. Since the score range from the PSE ($\bar{X} = 0[x/\sigma]$

units) to the .75 cumulative-proportion point ($\bar{X} + .6745[x/\sigma]$) is a measure of the DL, we are able to determine our standard deviation, and multiply it by .6745 to obtain an estimate of the differential threshold. Note that direct subtraction is required in theory, but is unnecessary in practice:

$$\left(\bar{X} + .6745\,\frac{x}{\sigma} \right) - \bar{X} = .6745\,\frac{x}{\sigma}$$

For the ascending trials of Subject No. 1, we find that the DL is approximately 7.967 (i.e., .6745 × 11.81 = 7.967). The computation of this standard deviation was illustrated in Table 4.3. You should note that this DL is relatively close to the value of 8.0 as determined by the graphic method (see Figure 3.6).

Computational Formula for the Standard Deviation

Perhaps on reviewing the computation of σ in Table 4.3 you recall that the actual mean was 141.90625 rather than the value of 142 which was used there for purposes of simplification. For the response value of 141, we have listed the square as 1. If, however, we squared the true deviation from the mean (.90625), the result would be .8212890625. Thus it is apparent that we make some errors when we round the mean. It is for this reason that we did not, in our original discussion, give a formula for the standard deviation based on x deviations. The following formula is, in every respect, exactly equal to a deviation formula but simplifies the process for calculation. Additionally, this formula gives us an exact value, so rounding errors are minimized. The formula is:

$$\sigma = \sqrt{\dfrac{\Sigma X^2 - \dfrac{(\Sigma X)^2}{N}}{N}}$$

The numerator of the fraction inside the radical is the sum of the squared deviations from the mean—often shortened to "sum of squares." The denominator (N) converts this sum of the squared deviations to a mean squared deviation or "mean square." Finally, the square root of this variance is the standard deviation. Later, when we investigate the technique of analysis of variance, we shall explore these two terms, sum of squares and mean square, in greater detail.

One advantage of using this formula is its computational simplicity when working with a calculating machine. Almost all calculators have operations for cumulative multiplying or squaring, and can directly compute ΣX^2 and ΣX. The first term of this formula (ΣX^2) indicates that we are to sum the individual squared scores. The ΣX in the second term simply means to sum all of our individual observations. The indicated operation is to first sum all of the scores, then square the sum.

The Sample Study

To determine the σ of the ascending settings for Subject No. 1, square each of the scores and then sum the squares. Thus, we would square 110, square 122, square 126, etc.; then sum the results. Note that this is something quite different from squaring the sum of all of the scores. In this example, the sum of all of the squared scores is 648,861, whereas the square of the sum of all of the scores is $(4,541)^2$ or 20,620,681. The difference between these two figures is considerable. When the standard deviation for Subject No. 1's ascending trials (computed by use of the above formula) is multiplied by .6745, we once again find a DL of 7.967. The required computations are shown in Table 4.4.

Note that it is not necessary to sequentially order the subject's

TABLE 4.4. Computation of DL for Subject No. 1's ascending trials

$$\Sigma X = 4541$$
$$\Sigma X^2 = 648{,}861$$
$$N = 32$$
$$\bar{X} = \frac{\Sigma X}{N} = \frac{4541}{32} = 141.90625$$

$$\sigma = \sqrt{\frac{\Sigma X^2 - (\Sigma X)^2/N}{N}} = \sqrt{\frac{648.861 - (4541)^2/32}{32}}$$

$$= \sqrt{\frac{4464.72}{32}} = \sqrt{139.5225}$$

$$= 11.812$$

$$DL = .6745\sigma = .6745 \times 11.812 = 7.967$$

settings. The particular order of the settings does not affect the computation of the σ. In Table 4.4, since ΣX was available, we have computed the mean or point of subjective equality even though this quantity was not required for calculation of the DL.

A similar computation would be completed for the settings of each subject's ascending trials and for his descending trials. When all of these computations are completed, we again have 40 estimates of the DL available for analysis. It seems appropriate in this case to analyze these DL's by using the same method employed in the computation of the individual DL's. That is, rather than visually inspecting the four graphs to determine whether or not differences exist, we might compute means and standard deviations for each distribution of DL's.

We have found that computation of the point of subjective equality and DL by a mathematical approach can eliminate much of the subjective bias of the graphic analysis. Similarly, we should expect that computation of means and standard deviations for the distributions would also improve the accuracy of any conclusions that we might draw. The procedure for computing these means and standard deviations is the same as that previously used for computation of the DL except that we are no longer interested in determining the 25 percent interval and will not multiply σ by .6745.

A sample computation of the mean and standard deviation on one of these groups of data is given in Table 4.5. These summary figures were made directly on a calculator. In this case the Xs, or individual scores, are the DL's for each individual and N has changed from 32 trials per subject to an N of 20 subjects. Use of the formula for the mean ($\bar{X} = \Sigma X / N$) yields a mean DL for this group of 13.287. Use of the computational formula

$$\sigma = \sqrt{\frac{\Sigma X^2 - \dfrac{(\Sigma X)^2}{N}}{N}}$$

yields a standard deviation of 4.165. A similar computation would be completed for each of the other three groups.

This procedure has reduced even further the amount of data that we must comprehend. Six intervals of data were included in each of the separate graphs previously shown in Figure 3.7. For the four groups, then, 24 pieces of data had to be integrated to derive an estimate of the differences between our groups. When a mathematical

TABLE 4.5. Computation of $\bar{X}$ and σ of the ascending trials' DL of subjects participating in the "light" condition

SUBJECT NO.	DL	SUBJECT NO.	DL
1	7.967	11	7.954
2	13.427	12	10.650
3	12.362	13	11.444
4	6.966	14	14.342
5	11.311	15	26.158
6	14.512	16	13.437
7	16.943	17	15.966
8	10.795	18	10.038
9	17.615	19	12.770
10	15.994	20	15.091

$$\Sigma X = 265.742$$

$$X^2 = 3,877.958 \qquad N = 20$$

$$\bar{X} = \frac{\Sigma X}{N} = \frac{265.742}{20} = 13.287$$

$$\sigma = \sqrt{\frac{\Sigma X^2 - \dfrac{(\Sigma X)^2}{N}}{N}} = \sqrt{\frac{3,877.958 - \dfrac{70,618.811}{20}}{20}}$$

$$= \sqrt{\frac{3,877.958 - 3,530.941}{20}} = \sqrt{\frac{347.017}{20}} = \sqrt{17.351}$$

$$= 4.165$$

approach is used there are only four separate means, and the complexity of the task is reduced. These four means, with their respective standard deviations, are listed in Table 4.6.

We may now repeat our original question: "Are the differential-brightness thresholds as determined from standard deviations under conditions of dark adaptation so much higher than those determined under conditions of bright adaptation that they are unlikely to have happened by chance alone?" Any conclusion that we might reach at this point should be a much more stable one than was available at the end of the previous chapter. One of the criticisms in that chapter was that it might have been possible for one person to draw one ogive while

TABLE 4.6. Comparison of ascending and descending trials for both "dark" and "light" test conditions

CONDITION	$\bar{X}$	σ
Ascending "Dark"	17.043	4.501
Descending "Dark"	19.051	4.683
Ascending "Light"	13.287	4.165
Descending "Light"	15.152	6.669

another might draw a slightly different ogive, even though both were working from identical data. Thus a chance existed for unreliability in the DL's calculated.

For the present data, however, assuming that no arithmetic mistakes have been made, the DL's mathematically computed by one experimenter should be identical to those calculated by another. Thus the reliability of the DL's has gone sharply upward. Also, we have eliminated possible errors in surveying differences between our graphs. In the data reported in Table 4.6, we may directly compare the means and standard deviations. This should eliminate most of the effects of experimenter bias that are often present in judgments made from graphs.

We should note, though, that some of the major problems outlined in the previous chapter are still unresolved. For example, when we selected subjects for our two groups, possibly some mischance of selection placed subjects with good visual discrimination in the "light" group and subjects with poor visual discrimination in the "dark" group.

Once again, we are unable to determine whether the results obtained are due to the experimental variable or to an extraneous variable such as a chance misplacement of subjects. One method for resolving this question has been briefly hinted at in this chapter. Recall that when we were discussing the random selection of a single score from a person's personnel file we found that we could state with some degree of probability that the low score drawn was not an IQ score. In light of the probabilistic interpretation of data discussed in the first chapter, this seems to be a reasonable conclusion. Thus we should be able to use a computation of variability to help us determine the probability of our experimental results having occurred by chance alone.

SUMMARY

This chapter has presented methods for determining the two parameters of a normal distribution—the mean and the standard deviation. The formula for the computation of a mean is:

$$\bar{X} = \frac{\Sigma X}{N}$$

where: X = any individual score
$\bar{X}$ = mean
Σ = sum of all
N = number of scores

The mean is thus an arithmetic average. Other measures sometimes used to describe data are the mode (most frequently occurring score) and the median (middle score in a sequentially arranged distribution of scores). A PSE computed graphically (a median) is equal to one computed arithmetically (a mean) only if the distribution of scores is normal.

The second parameter of a normal distribution is the standard deviation and may be computed by the formula:

$$\sigma = \sqrt{\frac{\Sigma X^2 - \frac{(\Sigma X)^2}{N}}{N}}$$

where:

σ = standard deviation
X^2 = square of an individual score

Since $\bar{X}$ and σ are independent parameters of a normal distribution, variations in one parameter may occur independently of variations in the other parameter. As they are the only two factors determining the shape of a normal curve, one may utilize a standard score ($[X - \bar{X}]/\sigma$) to compute percentages of individuals falling within any particular score range.

Application of these descriptive statistics to the data of the sample study was seen to increase the reliability of the mathematically derived PSE's and DL's compared to those computed graphically.

5. Variability of Means

POPULATION VS. SAMPLE

In the previous chapter, the mean and the standard deviation were used to describe the distribution of individual scores for a subject. This was termed parametric statistics because it assumed the parameters of the normal distribution. Use of such parametric statistics permits an experimenter to make some inferences about a particular score. That is, given a score of 68 from a person's personnel file, one could say with some degree of confidence that this was not an IQ score.

It may seem to you that the same types of statements could be made about the means of a distribution. For example, the various points of subjective equality (means) which we computed were not all identical, i.e., all individuals did not have the same point of subjective equality. Since these means themselves form a distribution, one may refer to the variability of a distribution of sample means.

To eliminate possible confusion in our discussion, let us define the terms *population* and *sample*. Population refers to all of the scores about which we wish to generalize. For example, if we wish to discuss IQ scores in the United States, the population of IQ scores includes the IQ of every individual in the United States. If the IQ test has been accurately constructed, then this population should have a mean IQ of 100. Had we tested every individual in the United States, summed the individual IQ scores, and divided by the total number of people in the United States, the result should be a mean IQ of 100.

A sample, on the other hand, refers to a limited portion of any given population. Suppose that we select every one-thousandth name on the census list of the United States. This would represent a sample drawn from the total population of the United States. If we measure the IQs of these individuals, they should have a mean IQ of approximately 100. This mean, which is usually fairly close to the population mean, is called a sample mean.

Note that we can never be sure that the mean of the sample drawn will be exactly that of the whole population. If we were to draw several samples from the census list, we might expect the various sample means to differ somewhat from each other and from the true population mean. Thus we may speak about the variability of a group of sample means. The population mean has no variability because it includes every possible case.

Let us look at this variability of the sample mean in our own experiment. Theoretically, it may be assumed that the characteristics of anticipation (an undershoot) and habituation (an overshoot) are equally present in people. That is, if our constant-stimulus light is at a setting of 150, some individuals may exhibit either errors of anticipation or of habituation in their settings of the variable light. In an ascending series, one individual might stop consistently at 145—an error of anticipation. Another individual might consistently stop at 155—an error of habituation. If we were able to measure every individual in the population, we might expect to find that the errors of anticipation would cancel, over all individuals, the errors of habituation.

For the population as a whole, the point of subjective equality would be at a setting of 150. This chain of assumptions may be incorrect. But in the absence of data to the contrary, this is the best guess we can make.

In a particular experiment, however, we cannot measure all of the individuals in the population. Rather, we select at random some number of individuals from this population. It is possible that in this small random sample most of the individuals would, in fact, exhibit an error of anticipation. That is, out of 20 individuals selected, 15 might exhibit the error of anticipation. The mean for this small sample would thus be lower than 150. Had we chosen another group it is possible that most of this second group of subjects would exhibit the error of habituation. Consequently, the overall mean for the second group would be greater than 150. We must, therefore, speak of the variability of a sample mean.

STANDARD ERROR OF A MEAN

What factors influence this variability of the sample mean? Fortunately there are methods by which we may directly determine the expected variability of any sample mean. Let us examine two fictitious examples. Suppose that we wish to determine the mean IQ of students attending Flunkout U. Our population is the IQ scores of all students attending Flunkout U. Notice that the limits of the population are specified. We may decide, however, that even to measure the IQ of every individual at Flunkout U. would be much too difficult a task. As a consequence, we decide to sample this population.

To insure that we have a truly random sample, we go to the total list of student names. From this list of student names we choose three students and measure their IQ scores. In this sample, it is possible that we have chosen at random three individuals on the probation list of the school. These three individuals are represented by the small squares in Figure 5.1. The normal curve illustrated here is a distribution of all of the IQ scores at Flunkout U. At the top of this distribution is the mean of that population. The dotted line through the small squares represents the mean of the first sample drawn ($\bar{X}_1$).

Note that we are considerably in error if we use this estimate as the mean of the population. Had we chosen a second set of three individuals we might have drawn three students on the Dean's list, with

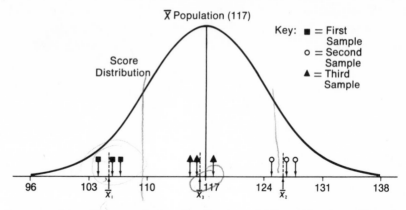

FIGURE 5.1. The population distribution of IQs at Flunkout U. and three possible samples of size three that might be obtained. The data points are plotted inside the curve to indicate relative probabilities for sampling such scores.

IQ scores such as those shown by the o symbols in Figure 5.1. The mean of this sample is also a dotted line and is designated $\bar{X}_2$. Again, we are considerably in error if we estimate the population mean from this sample. Perhaps a third sample might be drawn, designated by the small triangles in Figure 5.1. Here, by a happy chance of sampling, we get three individuals whose mean $(\bar{X}_3)$ is relatively close to that of the population we are attempting to measure.

Thus, successive samples from the population of students at Flunkout U. have yielded widely varying sample means. Had we chosen many, many samples of size three from this population, we would be able to describe the distribution of sample means. An example is shown in Figure 5.2. Had we taken *all possible* combinations of three students each, we would have obtained a normal distribution of sample means. The mean of this distribution of means would be the population mean.

The three examples previously discussed are designated by arrows in Figure 5.2. The means of our first two samples are, in fact, unlikely to have been determined by chance alone. Since we have a normal distribution of sample means, it is possible to compute a standard deviation of this distribution. The width of one standard deviation is shown in Figure 5.2.

You should especially note that this distribution is a distribution of means, not of scores. We designate the standard deviation of this dis-

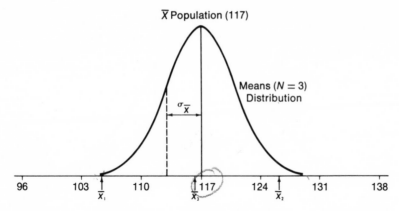

FIGURE 5.2. Distribution of all possible sample means of size three that could be drawn from the population of IQs at Flunkout U. The standard error of the mean is approximately 4 units.

tribution of means by $\sigma_{\bar{x}}$ in which the subscript $\bar{x}$ indicates that the standard deviation is of sample means rather than of scores. The standard deviation is a measure of the amount of error that we might expect in estimating the population means from a sample of size three and is usually referred to as a standard error. The proper term for the sigma with the subscript $\bar{x}$ is "standard error of a mean."

Sample Size and $\sigma_{\bar{x}}$

In Figure 5.2, the standard error of a sample mean is rather large. To reduce the possibility of error, we might decide to choose more than three subjects for our sample. Let us see how enlarging the sample will affect the standard error of the mean. We return to the list of student names at Flunkout U. and choose ten students instead of three. These ten individual IQ scores are shown as small squares in Figure 5.3. Again we get some scores from the probation list, far to the left of the IQ range. However, when we choose as large a sample as ten, it becomes much less probable that all ten individuals will be on the probation list. The mean of these ten scores is designated by the dotted line labeled $\bar{X}_1$.

Another sample of size ten that we might have drawn is shown by the small circles in Figure 5.3. Although we may get some individuals who are on the Dean's list, it is highly improbable that ten individuals

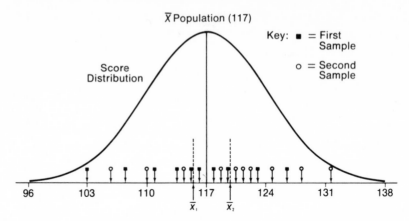

FIGURE 5.3. The population distribution of IQs at Flunkout U. and two possible samples of size 10 that might be obtained.

drawn at random from the student list will all be on the Dean's list. The mean of this sample is designated $\bar{X}_2$.

If we continued drawing samples of size ten and computing the means, we would get another normal distribution of means similar to that shown in Figure 5.4. Once again the distribution of the means from *all possible* combinations of ten individuals chosen at random from our

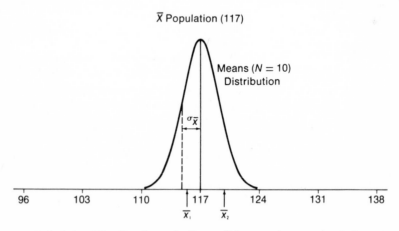

FIGURE 5.4. Distribution of all possible sample means of size 10 that could be drawn from the population of IQs at Flunkout U. The standard error of the mean is approximately 2 units.

population would have a mean equal to the population mean. The distribution, however, is quite different from the distribution of means based on an *N* of 3. The standard deviation of this distribution of means, or the standard error of the mean, is rather small. This reflects the fact that in any particular sample we are extremely unlikely to obtain individuals who are all either very high or very low.

We can compare the distribution shown in Figure 5.2 with that in Figure 5.4, since both samples were drawn from the same population of students' IQ scores. Note that the distributions of means differ according to the size of the sample chosen. As we increase the number of people in any given sample we decrease the standard error of the mean, i.e., we stand less chance of error in our estimate of the population mean if we test a larger proportion of the individuals in that population. A comparison of these two figures indicates that one of the factors affecting the variability of a distribution of sample means is that of sample size. The relationship is an inverse one, for $\sigma_{\bar{x}}$ decreases as the sample size increases.

Population σ and $\sigma_{\bar{x}}$

There is a second factor which contributes to the variability of a sample mean. We have discussed the judgments that might be made of the length of an 18-foot room. One distribution of judged room

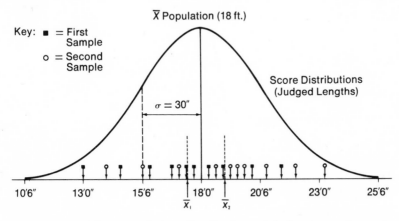

FIGURE 5.5. The population distribution of judgments of an 18-foot room with two possible samples of size 10 that might be randomly selected.

lengths that might be obtained is shown in Figure 5.5. Note here that the mean is 18 feet, with the typical judgments spread over a range from 12 to 24 feet.

Suppose that we select 10 people at random, from the population of the United States, and ask them to estimate the length of an 18-foot room. These scores ($N = 10$) are shown as small squares in Figure 5.5. The mean of these ten judgments ($\bar{X}_1$) is just slightly more than 17 feet; i.e., this particular sample tends to underestimate the length of the room.

Had we chosen a second group of ten people, their scores might have resembled the o sample in Figure 5.5. This mean ($\bar{X}_2$) is slightly less than 19 feet, i.e., a general overestimation of the room. If we took many samples of size ten and computed the means, the distribution of means might resemble the distribution shown in Figure 5.6. The overall mean is again 18. Very rarely would we expect to sample ten consecutive people whose average judgment would be less than 16 feet or over 20 feet.

The standard deviation of this distribution of means ($\sigma_{\bar{x}}$) is approximately 9½ inches. You will recall that a standard error of the mean ($\sigma_{\bar{x}}$) is a standard deviation of a distribution of means. Following the logic developed in the previous chapter, we find that 68 percent of the time the mean judgment of 10 randomly selected individuals will fall

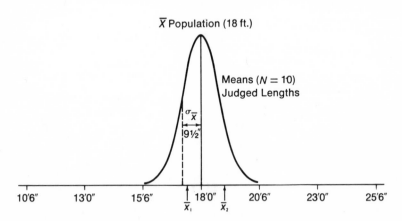

FIGURE 5.6 Distribution of all possible sample means of size 10 that could be drawn from the population of judgments of an 18-foot room. The standard error of the mean is approximately 9½ inches.

within a range of from 17 feet 2½ inches ($\bar{X}$ minus one $\sigma_{\bar{x}}$) to 18 feet 9½ inches ($\bar{X}$ plus one $\sigma_{\bar{x}}$). Consequently, 68 percent of the time we would expect the mean judgment of 10 people to fall between 17 feet 2½ inches and 18 feet 9½ inches.

We might easily improve the accuracy of each individual's estimate of the room length by allowing him to use a steel tape measure calibrated to the nearest one-hundredth of an inch. A distribution of measured lengths using this tape might resemble that shown in Figure 5.7. The overall mean is again 18 feet, with some variability about this point. Some individuals have a tendency to bend the tape measure when placing it against the wall and so measure the room as longer than 18 feet. Other individuals tend to place the tape measure slightly away from the wall, obtaining measurements of less than 18 feet. The total variability of the measured judgments will be much less than that of the visually judged lengths. That is, the standard deviation of the score distribution in Figure 5.5 is much greater than the standard deviation of the score distribution in Figure 5.7.

Let us see how this difference in the basic variability of the population affects the standard error of the sample mean. We have again designated by small squares the ten possible scores that we might obtain, and the mean is designated $\bar{X}_1$. Note that most of the first group

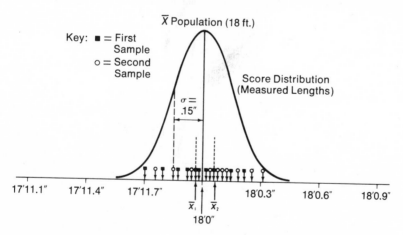

FIGURE 5.7. Distribution of the population of measurements of an 18-foot room and two samples of size 10 that might be randomly drawn. (X axis plotted to 100χ scale given for Figures 5.5 and 5.6.)

tend to make errors which result in measured room lengths of less than 18 feet. By chance alone, another group of individuals (shown as o's) might tend to have errors in the opposite direction resulting in measurements of the room greater than 18 feet. The mean of this second group of measurements is designated as $\bar{X}_2$.

A distribution of measured mean room lengths, based on the computed means of many size-ten samples, is shown in Figure 5.8. Once again we have a normal distribution. The mean of this distribution of means is 18 feet, the actual room length. The variability in this case, however, is very much smaller than that for judged room lengths. When we compute the standard deviation ($\sigma_{\bar{x}}$) of this distribution, the value is approximately .05 inches.

Again following the logic derived in the previous chapter, we find that 68 percent of the time we would expect the mean to be between 17.95 feet ($\bar{X}$ minus one $\sigma_{\bar{x}}$) and 18.05 ($\bar{X}$ plus one $\sigma_{\bar{x}}$). Compare the distribution of means in Figure 5.8 with that of Figure 5.6. In both instances we have chosen ten people at random and plotted their means with respect to determined room lengths. In Figure 5.6, however, these room lengths were estimated or judged lengths. In Figure 5.8 we recorded measured room length. For the first set of means, the

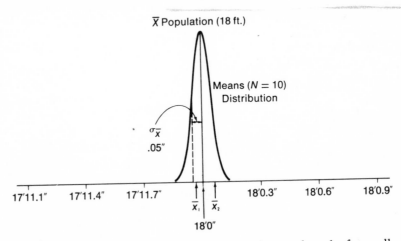

FIGURE 5.8. Distribution of mean measured room lengths from all possible samples of size 10 from the population of measurements of an 18-foot room. The standard error of the mean is approximately .05 inches. (X axis plotted to 100χ scale given for Figures 5.5 and 5.6.)

standard error of the mean was 9½ inches; for the second set, the standard error of the mean was .05 inches.

Since we have chosen $N = 10$ in both instances, the only difference between the two is the variability of the two populations of scores from which these judgments arise. That is, the standard deviations of the score distributions presented in Figures 5.6 and 5.8 are different. A relatively wide standard deviation of the score distribution exists for the data in Figure 5.6, while the data in Figure 5.8 reflects a relatively narrow range of measured lengths, i.e., a very small standard deviation.

Thus the second factor which influences the standard error of the mean is the standard deviation of the population of scores from which the sample was drawn. This relationship is a direct one: as the standard deviation of the population increases, the $\sigma_{\bar{x}}$ also increases. The relationship between $\sigma_{\bar{x}}$ and the other factor influencing it (sample size) is more complex. We have seen that as the number of subjects is increased, the variability of the mean will decrease. This decrease in variability is not a linear one; the standard error of a mean decreases as $\sqrt{N}$ increases.

If we may assume that we are sampling from a population of normally distributed scores, then these two parameters (the population σ and the number of scores in the sample) are the only variables influencing the standard error of the mean. It then becomes possible to generate the following formula:

$$\sigma_{\bar{x}} = \frac{\sigma}{\sqrt{N}}$$

Inferences Based on $\sigma_{\bar{x}}$

Your reaction at this point might be "So what does this have to do with our experiment? Since we have not taken all possible samples, how can we compute a standard error of the mean?" Let us examine in detail each part of this question. First, what has this to do with our experiment? We have stated that, theoretically, the errors of habituation and the errors of anticipation should cancel one another. The general statement is that the true population mean of all points of subjective equality would be 150, the setting of our constant stimulus. It is possible for us to examine the validity of this statement.

Assume that for the 20 individuals selected, the sample mean was 145. For the ascending series, this would indicate an error of anticipation. If we knew that the standard error of the mean was two units, we would be able to compute the probability of obtaining such a result by chance alone. We found in the previous chapter that a deviation of plus and minus one standard deviation from the mean included 68 percent of all cases. If, in our experiment, the true population mean is 150 we would expect 68 percent of all of our sample means to fall between 148 and 152.

In another example, we found that approximately 95 percent of all cases lie within ± 1.96 standard deviations from the mean. If our population mean is 150, then we would expect approximately 95 percent of the sample means to fall within the range from 146.08 $(150 - [1.96 \times 2])$ to 153.92 $(150 + [1.96 \times 2])$.

Here we must employ one other computation. Based on the x/σ units of Appendix B, we see that 99 percent of all the cases would fall within ± 2.58 sigma units from the mean. Thus if the true population mean is 150 and $\sigma_{\bar{x}}$ is 2, then 99 percent of all of the means that we might obtain should be in the range from 144.84 $[150 - (2.58 \times 2)]$ to 155.16 $[150 + (2.58 \times 2)]$. Although these computations refer to sample means rather than to raw scores, we are able to use the standard error of the mean exactly as we would use a standard deviation. As has been pointed out before, $\sigma_{\bar{x}}$ is simply the σ of the distribution of means.

Let us return to the hypothetical mean of 145 that occurred in our sample. Based on the computations described above, we find that a deviation of five points $(145 - 150 = -5)$ should occur less than 5 percent of the time, and only slightly more than 1 percent of the time by chance alone. We may thus state that it is highly unlikely that the sample mean of 145 was obtained as a chance deviation from a mean of 150. Thus we suspect that the true population mean of such settings is not 150. One possible explanation is that there exists, in the population as a whole, a significant error of anticipation. If we accept this explanation, then the experimental results obtained are simply some chance deviation from this overall error of anticipation.

We can restate this in slightly different terms. We have found that the deviation of -5 points exhibited by our sample mean of 145 is not likely to have occurred by *chance alone*. If it is not likely that our results happened by chance alone, then some factor other than chance must be involved. A reasonable explanation is that there is a true deviation, in the population as a whole, from the assumed mean of 150. Finding an error of anticipation for our sample leads us to assume that there may be, for the population as a whole, an error of anticipation.

THE NULL HYPOTHESIS

Note that we have actually determined the probability of our results having occurred as a result of chance alone. In other words, we have asserted that there are no actual differences between a sample mean and the population mean, and have then proceeded to determine the probable accuracy of this assertion. The statement that there are no true differences between the population $\bar{X}$ and the sample $\bar{X}$ is known as a *null hypothesis*. Use of the null hypothesis provides a single point that we may test, i.e., the true difference between a sample mean and the population mean is zero.

In the hypothetical results of our study, we find that the actual difference of five is an unlikely event to have occurred by chance alone. Thus, we are able to reject the null hypothesis of no difference and conclude that some true difference probably does exist.

Let us choose a slightly different example. The theory underlying IQ tests is that the population as a whole has a mean IQ of 100 with a σ of 16. Possibly, however, the intelligence of the population as a whole has been rising since the tests were originally developed. To test this possibility we first draw a random sample of 25 people from the census list. We then measure the IQ of each individual selected and determine a mean IQ for the group as a whole.

Suppose that the mean IQ for these 25 people is 110. The null hypothesis states that there are no *true* differences between this sample mean and our theoretical population mean of 100, i.e., such differences as do exist are a function of sampling errors alone. The test of this hypothesis involves the standard error of the mean for the sample ($N = 25$) and the population standard deviation ($\sigma = 16$). In this particular case we would find that the deviations of 10 or more should happen less than 1 percent of the time by chance alone. As a consequence, we say that the probability that we will obtain a mean of 110 when the population mean is 100 merely by chance, if there are no *true* differences between our sample mean and the assumed mean, is .01.

If the probability that the null hypothesis is true is less than .01, then we may, with only minimal chance of error (1 percent), reject it. It is much more probable that our sample mean does reflect a real difference in IQ. The direction of the difference indicates that the non-chance factor involved may be one of increased intelligence over the original standardization data.

In our study, we have asked whether or not there were significant differences between the discrimination thresholds determined under light background conditions and those determined under dark background conditions. If we could determine the standard error of the means for each condition, we should be able to tell whether our results might have happened by chance alone or whether there exists a true difference in performance.

We have found that the standard error of the mean is determined by testing all possible combinations from our population, finding the mean for each combination, and then computing the standard deviation of the means. In our experiment, we have only one sample of people with ascending DL's determined under light background conditions. How may we determine the standard error of the mean from a single mean?

A partial answer lies in the formulation of the parameters which affect the standard error of the mean. We have noted previously that this formula is:

$$\sigma_{\bar{x}} = \frac{\sigma}{\sqrt{N}}$$

This defines the standard deviation of the distribution of means, given all possible combinations which could be drawn from the total population. If we know the standard deviation of the population we may simply insert it into this formula and, by use of the sample size, determine the standard error of the mean had such operation been carried out.

THE z TEST

In the example of IQ scores, we stated that the standard deviation of the population of IQ scores was 16. Since the size of the sample of students was 25, the standard error of the mean for this sample size would be:

$$\sigma_{\bar{x}} = \frac{\sigma}{\sqrt{N}} = \frac{16}{\sqrt{25}} = \frac{16}{5} = 3.2$$

We may now determine a x/σ value for the difference between our sample mean (110) and our assumed population mean (100). This

114

process is known as a z test. The formula for the z test follows that of x/σ and is written:

$$z = \frac{\bar{X}_{\text{sample}} - \bar{X}_{\text{population}}}{\sigma_{\bar{x}}}$$

Completing this z test for the data previously given, we find:

$$z = \frac{\bar{X}_{\text{sample}} - \bar{X}_{\text{population}}}{\sigma_{\bar{x}}} = \frac{110 - 100}{3.2} = \frac{10}{3.2} = 3.125$$

As may be noted from this example, the z test differs from x/σ only in that a sample $\bar{X}$ is tested instead of an individual score. This sample $\bar{X}$ is tested against its expected variability ($\sigma_{\bar{x}}$) in the same manner that a single score is tested against its variability (σ). Consequently, if we wish to know how frequently so large a deviation from the true population mean of 100 might have occurred by chance alone, we consult the x/σ table in Appendix B. The logic of the determination of the area outside of plus and minus 3.125 z units is identical with that previously presented.

p-VALUES

In psychology, however, we are usually not interested in the exact probability of occurrence of a particular event. Custom has dictated that we may claim significant results if our data could have happened by chance alone either less than five times in one hundred ($p = .05$) or less than one time in one hundred ($p = .01$). Thus, only two of the values listed in Appendix B are of particular importance in our analysis of the data. We find that results which would occur only five times in one hundred by chance alone correspond to a z value of 1.96. Results that would occur by chance alone no more than one time in one hundred correspond to a z value of ·2.58. Note that these two z values remain constant for all data.

The two p values corresponding to the z values of 1.96 and 2.58 indicate the probability (p) that the null hypothesis is true. Consequently, they also indicate the probable error that one might make if he rejects the null hypothesis as being false. If the stated p value is .05, then one time in twenty an experimenter might be in error by concluding that the sample mean differs from the assumed population mean.

For the $p = .01$ level, this possibility of error is reduced to one in a hundred but with an increased chance of not detecting a true difference when it is actually present.

Which of these two levels of p to require in order to state that an observed value is significantly different from an assumed value is a decision left to the experimenter. Although this decision may often appear to be a function of the personality of the experimenter, some logical grounds for choice do exist. When studying a relatively unexplored area of psychology, an experimenter may decide to report his results only when he is fairly certain that a true difference exists and that his conclusions would be confirmed if the experiment were replicated. In such a case, the experimenter might not wish to attribute significance to his data unless $p = .01$ or lower. A replication or extension of a previous experiment might be judged significant at the $p = .05$ level when results are obtained which confirm the conclusions of the original experiment. If, however, conflicting or contradictory results are to be reported after a replication of an earlier experiment, a $p = .01$ or lower may be desirable.

The particular value of p chosen for a given experiment might also be related to factors involved with the ultimate use of the findings. If significant findings indicate radical or costly changes in some procedure, then the more strict value of $p = .01$ would probably be used to interpret the results. Findings which suggest the necessity for further research in areas related to human welfare (such as preliminary drug reports) may be reported as significant if the p value is .05.

You should note that the various factors entering into the decision of which p value to use in interpreting the results of a study are all available to the experimenter prior to beginning the analysis of the data. Strictly speaking, this decision should be made before analysis of the data and then the significance of the results should be assigned on the basis of that decision. For the IQ data just discussed, it seems appropriate to accept the $p = .05$ level as a decision point. When the z-test results are interpreted, we find that our value of z (3.125) is larger even than the 2.58 required at the .01 level. Consequently, we may say that the probability that the null hypothesis is true is less than .01. That is, there is less than one chance in one hundred that we would get a mean IQ of 110 for 25 subjects from chance factors alone. We are able to reject the null hypothesis and state that a true difference from the original standardization data probably exists in the population as a whole.

THE *t* TEST

Estimating the Population Standard Deviation

One limitation must be observed in using the *z* test. As outlined here, the *z* test is appropriate *only* where the population standard deviation is known. When the population standard deviation is not known we must use a slightly different technique.

We can logically deduce this variation in technique. If the population standard deviation is unknown, it should be possible to use the standard deviation of our sample in the formula in place of the standard deviation of the population. For example, in Figure 5.5, the two samples represented would have a much larger standard deviation than those depicted in Figure 5.7. Thus, our sample standard deviation should match rather closely that of the population standard deviation. In Figure 5.5, the population standard deviation is comparatively broad—indicating a wide variability in the individual judgments of room length. For the data shown in Figure 5.7, the population standard deviation is quite small—indicating that the measurements of room lengths have, comparatively, much less variability. When we look at the two samples drawn from this data we find a much wider range of variability of judged lengths than is evident in the sample of measured room lengths. Consequently, the sample standard deviation should be a fairly close estimate of the population standard deviation; and, from pragmatic studies, we find that this is true.

Consider, however, the three samples previously illustrated in Figure 5.1. In this particular case we have only three individuals. It seems fairly obvious that any three individuals' scores will probably not encompass the same range as we find in our population. As a consequence, the standard deviation computed on these three individuals would tend to be much smaller than the population standard deviation. When we choose as many as ten individuals (see Figure 5.3) we find that the samples more nearly encompass the same range as that of the population.

Consequently, as we increase our sample size, the standard deviation of the sample becomes a better estimate of the population standard deviation. In very small sample sizes, the population standard deviation may tend to be greatly underestimated. As the sample size increases, the discrepancy between the population standard deviation and the sample standard deviation becomes smaller, i.e., they more nearly match.

There is a way to minimize this discrepancy when we use the sample standard deviation instead of the population standard deviation in our z test. The formula used to compute either a population standard deviation or a sample standard deviation for descriptive purposes is:

$$\sigma = \sqrt{\dfrac{\Sigma X^2 - \dfrac{(\Sigma X)^2}{N}}{N}}$$

To change this to an appropriate formula when using a sample standard deviation as an estimator of the population statistic, divide the numerator by $N - 1$ (termed *degrees of freedom, df*) for the sample. With this substitution, the appropriate formula becomes:

$$s = \sqrt{\dfrac{\Sigma X^2 - \dfrac{(\Sigma X)^2}{N}}{\text{degrees of freedom or } (N - 1)}}$$

Note that the sample value of the standard deviation, when used to estimate the population σ, is designated by the symbol s. Similarly, an estimate of the population σ^2 based on sample data would be designated by the symbol s^2. The computational difference, in both cases, is that the sum of squared deviations from the mean is divided by N for the population value but is divided by $N - 1$ or degrees of freedom (df) for the estimated value.

Degrees of Freedom

To understand the concept of degrees of freedom, consider the 5 scores listed in Table 5.1A. The sum of these scores is 15 and the mean is 3. How many scores could be selected at random and placed in a similar table to yield a mean of 3, i.e., how many scores are free choices given the mean of 3? The mean is the parameter to be tested and may result from many different combinations of scores. In the second table, 5.1B, the first score drawn at random is 156. The second score drawn at random is −47, the third is 34, and the fourth is −87. May we then choose another number at random? No, the final number in this series is fixed if we state that the mean of this set of 5 numbers must be 3. Some simple computation indicates that our last number *must*

TABLE 5.1A. Basic distribution of size 5 and mean of 3

SCORE (X)	COMPUTATION
3	
4	
2	
1	$\bar{X} = \dfrac{\Sigma X}{N} = \dfrac{15}{5} = 3$
5	
$\Sigma X = 15$	
$N = 5$	

TABLE 5.1B. Distribution with 4 numbers chosen at random retaining mean of 3

RANDOM NUMBERS	COMPUTATION
156	
−47	
34	
−87	
Forced Choice: −41	$\bar{X} = \dfrac{\Sigma X}{N} = \dfrac{15}{5} = 3$
$\Sigma X = 15$	
$N = 5$	

be −41. If we then sum these 5 numbers, we again get a sum of 15 and a mean of 3.

Thus, with any set of 5 numbers having a given mean, we are free to randomly select only 4 of them. The fifth number will be determined by the particular mean. In Table 5.1 we have four degrees of freedom, i.e., degrees of freedom indicate how many of the scores are free to vary. In general, given N scores with a specified $\bar{X}$, only $N − 1$ scores are free to vary.

How does this relate to the formula for a standard deviation when used as an estimator? Recall that the numerator of the formula for the standard deviation is the sum of squared deviations *from the mean*. If the population mean were known, we could determine the sum of the squared deviations of the sample scores from that mean. In our sample, however, we must find the sum of squared deviations *from the sample mean*.

Given any particular sample mean, one of the scores in the sample is not free to vary. Had the population mean been known, all of the sample scores could have varied at random about that mean. The sum of squared deviations from a sample mean will tend to be smaller than the sum of squared deviations from a population mean. Therefore, the appropriate correction factor is to divide by $N - 1$ (or df) instead of dividing by N. The formula for a sample s used as an estimate of the population σ is:

$$s = \sqrt{\frac{\Sigma X^2 - \dfrac{(\Sigma X)^2}{N}}{N - 1}}$$

The t Test: Formulae and Example

Even this correction factor, however, is not absolutely accurate. Sometimes, by chance alone, the sample will contain scores that are much closer together than typical scores drawn from that distribution. This, in turn, would result in a much smaller sample standard deviation—so much smaller that the correction factor alone would not be able to make it approach the value of the population standard deviation. Clearly, this chance factor must also be taken into account. The final correction is accomplished in the interpretation of the t test.

Let us examine the logical development of a t test. We have seen that the z test (where the population standard deviation is known) is:

$$z = \frac{\bar{X}_{sample} - \bar{X}_{population}}{\sigma_{\bar{x}}}$$

The $\sigma_{\bar{x}}$ was determined by the formula:

$$\sigma_{\bar{x}} = \frac{\sigma_{population}}{\sqrt{N}}$$

If we now use the standard deviation of the sample, instead of the population standard deviation, we find that the standard error of the mean may be too small. That is, given a population standard deviation of 10, with a sample size of 25, the standard error of the mean would be:

$$\sigma_{\bar{x}} = \frac{\sigma}{\sqrt{N}} = \frac{10}{\sqrt{25}} = \frac{10}{5} = 2$$

If we use the sample standard deviation in this formula, by chance alone we might find it to be somewhat smaller than the standard deviation of the population. For example, if the standard deviation of our sample is 9, the standard error of the computed mean would be:

$$s_{\bar{x}} = \frac{s}{\sqrt{N}} = \frac{9}{\sqrt{25}} = \frac{9}{5} = 1.8$$

where

$s_{\bar{x}}$ = estimated standard error of the mean based on s
s = estimate of population σ using sample data
N = sample size

The standard error of the mean computed using this particular sample standard deviation is, by chance alone, somewhat smaller than that based on the standard deviation of the population.

For example, assume that the mean of some specified population is 109, and the mean of the sample tested is 118. Computing a z test on the results listed above, we would find:

$$z = \frac{\bar{X}_{sample} - \bar{X}_{population}}{\sigma_{\bar{x}}} = \frac{118 - 109}{2} = \frac{9}{2} = 4.5$$

Redesignating these same operations as t and using the standard deviation of the sample, we would have:

$$t = \frac{\bar{X}_{sample} - \bar{X}_{population}}{s_{\bar{x}}} = \frac{118 - 109}{1.8} = \frac{9}{1.8} = 5$$

The use of this sample standard deviation yields a higher t value than we would obtain had we used the z value and the population standard deviation. This larger factor is "made up" in the t table given in Appendix C. One evaluates the t ratio by computing the degrees of freedom (df) and determining the corresponding values in Appendix C. When determining the significance of a difference between a sample mean and a population mean, the degrees of freedom will always equal the number of observations in the sample minus one. The logic follows that previously discussed and illustrated in Table 5.1. Note that for very small sample sizes, where we might obtain a much smaller sample standard deviation than population standard deviation, a very large value of t is required to reach the .05 level. You should compare this value with the 1.96 required at the .05 level for the z test. As N

increases, the value of t required at the .05 level approaches closer and closer to the 1.96 level required of the z test. For values of df larger than 30, we may use 1.96 and 2.58 as values of t significant at the .05 and .01 levels.

The Sample Study

We can apply this t technique to the data of our experiment. If there were no systematic errors of anticipation or habituation in our study, the true population mean of the points of subjective equality should be 150 (the setting of the constant light). That is, by chance alone, we should test as many people whose point of subjective equality is above 150 as those below 150. The actual data for the ascending series for the "dark" group are shown in Table 5.2. As we do not know the population standard deviation for points of subjective equality, we must use the sample standard deviation. The necessary computations are shown in the lower portion of Table 5.2. The mean point of subjective equality for these 20 subjects in this condition is 145.7. The sample standard deviation used as an estimator for these 20 settings is:

$$s = \sqrt{\frac{\Sigma X^2 - \dfrac{(\Sigma X)^2}{N}}{N-1}} = 5.141$$

The standard error of the mean using this estimate of our population standard deviation is:

$$s_{\bar{x}} = \frac{s}{\sqrt{N}} = \frac{5.141}{4.472} = 1.148$$

The t ratio that we compute is:

$$t = \frac{\bar{X}_{\text{sample}} - \bar{X}_{\text{population}}}{s_{\bar{x}}} = \frac{145.7 - 150}{1.148} = \frac{4.3}{1.148} = 3.749$$

The degrees of freedom associated with this t value are:

$$df = N - 1 = 20 - 1 = 19$$

In this example, we might randomly select 19 numbers. The twentieth number, however, must be fixed since we have predetermined that the 20 numbers as a whole must have a mean of 145.7.

In Appendix C, we read down the column labeled degrees of free-

TABLE 5.2.   Points of subjective equality for subjects participating in the ascending "dark" condition

SUBJECT NO.	PSE (X)	SUBJECT NO.	PSE (X)
1	145	11	152
2	150	12	135
3	139	13	146
4	149	14	144
5	147	15	154
6	146	16	145
7	138	17	148
8	151	18	137
9	145	19	151
10	147	20	145
		$N = 20$ $\Sigma X =$	2914
		$\Sigma X^2 =$	425,072

$$\bar{X} = \frac{\Sigma X}{N} = \frac{2914}{20} = 145.7$$

$$s = \sqrt{\frac{\Sigma X^2 - (\Sigma X)^2/N}{N-1}} = \sqrt{\frac{425,072 - 8,491,396/20}{20-1}} =$$

$$\sqrt{\frac{425,072 - 424,569,8}{19}} = \sqrt{26.43} = 5.141$$

$$s_{\bar{x}} = \frac{s}{\sqrt{N}} = \frac{5.141}{\sqrt{20}} = \frac{5.141}{4.472} = 1.148$$

dom until we reach 19. We then read across the tabled .05 and .01 levels and find that a t value of 2.093 is required at the .05 level, and a t value of 2.861 is required at the .01 level. Since our obtained t is larger than that value required at the .01 level, we say that the probability is less than .01. This is usually abbreviated as $p < .01$. According to the t value that we have just computed, the probability is less than one in one hundred that the null hypothesis is true.

Here the null hypothesis states that there is no true difference between our sample mean and the population mean of 150, and that the differences we observe are a function of chance or random error alone. We reject this null hypothesis, and state that it is improbable that these differences have occurred as a function of chance alone. It is much more probable that our sample mean does reflect a true difference between this group and the assumed population value of 150.

Interpreting a t Value

This is as far as the *t* value goes. To indicate the direction of the probable true difference we must look at the direction of the difference between our sample mean and the assumed population mean. Since our sample mean is less than the population mean, we may assume that a true error of anticipation does exist for our group.

Failure to note the direction of differences is one of the most common errors made by beginning students in statistics. Suppose, for example, that the working hypothesis had stated that people would tend to exhibit an error of habituation when making discriminations. The analysis of these data might be similar to that in Table 5.2. Many students would look at the results of the *t* test, determine that the probability was less than .01 that the null hypothesis was true, and decide that their working hypothesis was confirmed. However, in order to confirm a working hypothesis, both significance and direction must confirm the hypothesis. In this particular instance, although the results are significant, the working hypothesis is disconfirmed in that anticipation rather than habituation is shown.

Other mistakes typically made in interpretation of the *t* test are those which violate the basic assumptions of the test: (1) One must assume that the sample drawn is derived from a normal distribution of scores. If the sample does not come from a normal population of scores, then all computations of means, standard deviations, and standard errors of the means may be in error. (2) We must also assume that the individuals have been randomly selected from the population. If, for example, we select subjects on some nonrandom basis which admits only those from the upper end of our distribution, then the standard deviation computed on such scores will be much lower than the population standard deviation. In this case, we are not even sure what correction needs to be made, and conclusions based on the *t* test are meaningless.

In actual practice, we almost never obtain data that are precisely normally distributed. This does not mean that we may never use the *t* test for data analysis. As a matter of fact, the *t* test is relatively insensitive to minor deviations from normality (12). Only when the data are obviously not normal from visual inspection does one need to give some thought to possible misleading conclusions.

At this point, you may want to test whether or not the difference between the means we have determined for the "dark" and the "light" condition could have arisen by chance alone. While we have discussed one method for determining whether or not a mean could have arisen by chance alone, the question that we wish to test in our experiment involves two sample means—those for the "dark" and those for the "light" sample. This particular *t* test is not designed to test two sample means. It is appropriate only for those situations where we have one sample mean and a known population mean. The more advanced techniques required for analyzing the difference between two sample means are introduced in the next chapter.

DESIGN CONSIDERATIONS

Although the *z* test and the *t* test are not appropriate techniques for analyzing the data from our experiment, they are valid statistical techniques and have a definite place among the tools at the disposal of an experimental psychologist. The range of studies in which they may be used is wide indeed.

Basically, these tests are appropriate in any situation where: (1) the population mean is known, or a theoretical value may be assumed; (2) the underlying population of scores from which the sample is drawn may be assumed to be normally distributed; (3) each score in the sample is randomly selected from the population; and (4) either the population σ is known or may be estimated from the sample data. If the experimental question to be answered meets these qualifications, the data may be analyzed either by use of the *z* test or the *t* test, depending upon whether the population σ is known or must be estimated from sample data.

A prime consideration in the design of studies to be analyzed by one of these two techniques is the number of subjects to be tested. Since the standard error of the mean decreases as a function of N, the inclusion of additional subjects increases the possibility of finding a true but small difference between the population $\bar{X}$ and the sample $\bar{X}$. This is especially true for the *t* test, where not only the standard error of the mean, but also subsequent interpretation (by degrees of freedom) is affected by sample size.

At the same time, it must be recalled that the standard error of the mean does not decrease directly with N. The $\sigma_{\bar{x}}$ for a sample of 120 subjects is not one-fourth the size of the $\sigma_{\bar{x}}$ for a sample of 30 subjects but is only one-half that size. The additional reduction, then, may be very costly both in time and money. You should also note that very little advantage is gained in the t table by increasing df beyond certain values.

SUMMARY

In this chapter, we have seen that sample means, like test scores, may vary. The standard deviation of a distribution of sample means was identified as the standard error of a mean, $\sigma_{\bar{x}}$. The defining formula was:

$$\sigma_{\bar{x}} = \frac{\sigma}{\sqrt{N}}$$

where: σ = the population standard deviation

N = number of scores included in the mean

Since the standard error of a mean functions as a standard deviation, it is possible to determine whether or not a particular sample mean differs significantly from a given population mean. When the population standard deviation is known, the z test is used. The correct formula is:

$$z = \frac{\bar{X}_{\text{sample}} - \bar{X}_{\text{population}}}{\sigma_{\bar{x}}}$$

If the value of z exceeds ± 1.96 or ± 2.58, the results are statistically significant at the .05 and .01 levels, respectively.

If a sample standard deviation is used as an estimator of the population standard deviation, one must compute that sample standard deviation by the formula:

$$s = \sqrt{\frac{\Sigma X^2 - \frac{(\Sigma X)^2}{N}}{N - 1}}$$

The $s_{\bar{x}}$ is then computed according to:

$$s_{\bar{x}} = \frac{s}{\sqrt{N}}$$

The appropriate test is the t test, determined by:

$$t = \frac{\bar{X}_{sample} - \bar{X}_{population}}{s_{\bar{x}}}$$

The computed value of t is judged for significance in the t table by utilizing degrees of freedom (df). In this particular case:

$$df = N - 1$$

These two tests are appropriate only as a test of a single sample mean and therefore were not applicable to the data collected from the study originally designed in Chapter 2.

6. Analysis of Variance

LOGICAL DEVELOPMENT OF ANALYSIS OF VARIANCE

None of the methods of analysis so far developed has been appropriate for analyzing the data collected in our sample study. Yet each has helped to build the statistical background required to understand a technique which is generally applicable to such data—analysis of variance. As you recall, variance is a mathematical way of describing the variability between scores in a distribution. Its relationship to the standard deviation (s) is shown by the symbol s^2, indicating that it is simply the square of the standard deviation. Our new technique, then, is a method of analyzing this variance.

The theory of analysis of variance is based on a single fact: If we have two estimates of the variance of a single population, they should be approximately equal. From our previous discussion of IQs, recall that the standard deviation was 16. If we measure the IQ of every even-numbered thousandth person on the census list we should get a variance estimate of approximately 256 (i.e., 16^2). If we then measure the IQ of every odd-numbered thousandth person on the census list, we should again get a variance estimate of approximately 256. Thus, two estimates of the variance of the same population should be approximately equal. If we divide one sample variance into the other, the ratio should be approximately 1.00. In the example above, 256 ÷ 256 = 1.00. This ratio of two estimates of the population variance is called the F ratio.

It is important to remember that sample variances, like sample means, will not necessarily stay the same from one test situation to another. That is, estimates of the variance tend to fluctuate from one sample to the next. For example, if one were to test a group of 20 individuals on a verbal learning task, the variance might be 9. In a replication with a different sample of subjects, the variance might be 10. Thus, any two variance estimates that we compute may not necessarily be exactly equal.

If we computed many estimates of the variance of a single population, we would tend to get a range of values. If these variance estimates were paired and an F ratio determined for each pair by dividing one estimate into its pair member, we would tend to get a range of F values. This range of F values based on random sampling alone is known as the F distribution.

One note of caution should be observed. The two estimates of the population variance that are used to determine an F ratio must be independent of one another. That is, the selection of individuals for one estimate of the population variance should not influence in any way the selection of the second group of individuals.

Our problem, then, becomes one of deriving two independent estimates of the population variance. The first of these estimates follows directly from our previous discussions of standard deviations and variance of a sample. If we have the scores of any one sample, then the mean squared deviation (MS) from the mean of the sample is one estimate of the population variance. If we have two or more samples, the *MS* of each sample would be an estimate of the population variance. In such a situation, the best overall estimate would be a combination of the mean squared deviations within each sample.

The selection of this as our best estimate is related to the concept of degrees of freedom. The *MS* for a single sample of size 20 would have $N - 1$, or 19 degrees of freedom. Had we taken 3 such samples, computed the mean square within each sample, and then combined these to derive a single estimate we would have had a total of 57 degrees of freedom ($19 + 19 + 19$). As you recall from our previous discussion, the larger the number of degrees of freedom, the more accurate will be our estimate of the population variance. To summarize, we may say that our best estimate of the population variance will be derived through a knowledge of the variability within each of the samples tested.

To use the analysis of variance technique, it is necessary to derive a second estimate of the population variance which is independent of that previously obtained. Since we have used *MS* within each sample once, we may not use it again. To do so would violate the principle that the two estimates of the population variability must be independent.

The resolution of this problem follows from the fact that the mean and the standard deviation of a sample are independent parameters of that sample distribution. We may, therefore, have variations between sample means without variations in the standard deviations of these samples and vice versa. Since we used the *MS* within each sample as our first estimate of the population variance, we must use differences between sample means for our second estimate.

If we have two or more means available for analysis, we may compute a standard deviation of these means. The standard deviation of a group of means was termed the standard error of the mean ($s_{\bar{x}}$) in the previous chapter. Let us see how we may derive an estimate of the population variance from this standard error of the mean. If we multiply the *MS* of the means ($s_{\bar{x}}^2$) by N, we get a second estimate of the population variance:

$$s_{\bar{x}} = \frac{s}{\sqrt{N}}$$

$$\text{Squaring:} \quad s_{\bar{x}}^2 = \frac{s^2}{N}$$

$$\text{Multiplying by } N: \quad (N)s_{\bar{x}}^2 = s^2$$

Note here that the number of degrees of freedom differs from the degrees of freedom computed within each group. That is, if we have three means from which to compute the between-groups *MS*, the degrees of freedom for this estimate of the population variance will be two. By using the variance estimate based upon sample means, we have met the requirement for independent estimates of the population variance for our *F* ratio. Since means of the groups can vary independently of their respective standard deviations, this between-groups estimate of the population variance is not related to the within-groups *MS* derived earlier.

If we have taken random samples from a single population, the distribution of the ratios of the between-groups-variance estimates (based on sample means) to the within-groups-variance estimates (based on the variance within each sample) is the *F* distribution. In some cases, we should expect the between-groups-variance estimate to be larger than the within-groups-variance estimate, and vice versa. However, the typical value of this ratio should be approximately 1.00. That is, over many samples the between-groups variance should be approximately equal to the within-groups variance.

Let us suppose that we have conducted an experiment in which the experimental treatment has produced true differences in the performance scores obtained. For example, the mean of the experimental group might be 20 points higher than the mean of the control group. If we caused a true change in performance scores, these means are not random samples but reflect the true difference. Therefore, the difference between our means should be larger than would be expected by chance alone. In turn, the between-groups-variance estimate, based on these means, would also be much larger than the within-groups estimate. Finally, the ratio of the between-groups-variance estimate to the within-groups-variance estimate would tend to be greater than 1.00. A true difference between means, then, is reflected by an *F* ratio of more than 1.00.

However, we would occasionally expect to obtain, by chance alone, a larger between-groups variance than within-groups variance. How may we determine whether the larger *F* ratio we obtained is due to a true experimental difference or merely to random chance? Once again we must rely upon our probabilistic view of truth. If the *F* ratio determined is larger than that which would *probably* occur by chance alone, then we say that our means are significantly different.

The *F* values that we expect to occur by chance alone, either .05 or .01 proportion of the time, have been determined. A table of these

F values is given in Appendix D. This table lists *df* for the numerator along the horizontal axis and *df* for the denominator along the vertical axis. If we recall our discussion of degrees of freedom for both the within-groups and the between-groups estimates of the variance, the table seems logically arranged.

Had we tested three groups of subjects, we would have obtained three means. Associated with these three means would be two degrees of freedom in the computation of the between-groups *MS*. Since the between-groups *MS* is used as the numerator of our F ratio:

$$F = \frac{\text{numerator } MS}{\text{denominator } MS} = \frac{\text{between } MS}{\text{within } MS}$$

we see that we have two degrees of freedom in this numerator. If each of these three groups contains five subjects, the mean squared deviation within any one group would have four degrees of freedom associated with it. Combining the *MS* within all groups, we would have 12 degrees of freedom (four from each of the three groups) for the within groups estimate of the variance. As this is the denominator of the F ratio, we have 12 denominator degrees of freedom for this particular experiment. Refer to the top of Appendix D (under *df* for numerator) for the heading "2" and to the side of the table for "12" (under *df* for denominator). At the junction of these two entries are two figures. The first, 3.88, is the value of F that would occur only 5 times out of 100 on the basis of chance alone. The second entry, 6.93, is that value which would occur by chance alone only one time in 100. If, for this example, the observed value of the F ratio is greater than 3.88, we may say that there is a significant difference between our means—$p < .05$. It is highly unlikely that this difference could have occurred by chance alone.

COMPUTATIONAL PROCEDURES FOR ANALYSIS OF VARIANCE

The following example illustrates the method for computing an F ratio. Suppose that an experimenter is interested in determining whether or not variations in instructions effect performance in a verbal learning task. The experimenter, in this hypothetical example, might decide to test the effect of 3 different sets of instructions on the performance of 15 subjects, with 5 subjects given each of the sets. A recording of the errors made by each of the subjects is presented in Table 6.1. We note

TABLE 6.1. Number of errors made by 5 subjects on a verbal learning task following 3 sets of instructions

INSTRUCTION SET NO. 1	INSTRUCTION SET NO. 2	INSTRUCTION SET NO. 3		
4	6	7		
2	1	3		
1	7	3		
3	2	7		
5	4	5		
$\Sigma X_1 = 15$	$\Sigma X_2 = 20$	$\Sigma X_3 = 25$	$\Sigma\Sigma X = 60$	
$\bar{X}_1 = 3$	$\bar{X}_2 = 4$	$\bar{X}_3 = 5$		
$N_1 = 5$	$N_2 = 5$	$N_3 = 5$	$N_{1+2+3} = 15$	

that the lowest number of errors is made when using instruction set no. 1 ($\bar{X}_1 = 3$ errors). Instruction set no. 2 produces the next fewest errors ($\bar{X}_2 = 4$ errors), and instruction set number three produces the most errors ($\bar{X}_3 = 5$ errors). We wish to know whether the variations of these three means are likely to have occurred by chance (are due to sampling errors alone) or represent a true difference arising from the experimental treatments.

The formula for variance (using sample data as an estimator of the population parameter) is:

$$s^2 = \frac{\Sigma X^2 - \dfrac{(\Sigma X)^2}{N}}{N - 1}$$

The numerator of this formula for variance $\left(\Sigma X^2 - \dfrac{[\Sigma X]^2}{N}\right)$ is the sum of the squared deviations from the mean. We are able to take advantage of one mathematical quality of this "sum of squares" in our computation of variance estimates for between groups and within groups. The sum of the squared deviations for any particular set or group is always additive, i.e., a sum of squares computed within groups plus a sum of squares computed between groups must always add to the total sum of squares for the set or group.

To illustrate this point, consider all 15 scores in Table 6.1 as constituting a single distribution. These 15 scores sum to 60. A computation of a sum of squares for this total distribution of 15 scores is shown in Table 6.2. In this table we have abbreviated the total sum of squared deviations from the mean as *TSS*, as defined by the formula previously given. This formula states that we must find the sum of all of the scores individually squared and then subtract from this sum the square of the sum of the scores divided by *N*. The computation shown in Table 6.2 yields a *TSS* of 62. This sum of squares is the result obtained when all 15 scores are regarded as constituting a single distribution.

In our development of the logical basis for analysis of variance, we found that our best estimate of the population variance would be derived by summing the variance within each group. Similarly, we may sum the squared deviations from each group to obtain a within-groups sum of squares. This is abbreviated as *WSS* in Table 6.2. Note that we again square each of the individual scores in each set, but subtract from these the mean squared sum for that individual set. That is, to obtain a partial result for instruction set no. 1, we square each of those 5 individual scores (4, 2, 1, 3, 5). From this we subtract the sum of those 5 scores squared, divided by the number of scores in that group $15^2/5$. A similar computation would be made for instruction set no. 2

TABLE 6.2. Computation of the sum of squares for a total distribution of 15 scores from 3 groups

$$TSS = \Sigma X^2 - \frac{(\Sigma\Sigma X)^2}{N_{1+2+3}}$$

$$= 4^2 + 2^2 + 1^2 + 3^2 + 5^2 + 6^2 + 1^2 + 7^2 + 2^2 + 4^2 + 7^2 + 3^2 + 3^2 +$$

$$7^2 + 5^2 - \frac{(60)^2}{15} = 302 - 240 = 62$$

$$WSS = \left(4^2 + 2^2 + 1^2 + 3^2 + 5^2 - \frac{15^2}{5}\right) + \left(6^2 + 1^2 + 7^2 + 2^2 + 4^2 - \frac{20^2}{5}\right) +$$

$$\left(7^2 + 3^2 + 3^2 + 7^2 + 5^2 - \frac{25^2}{5}\right) = (55 - 45) + (106 - 80) +$$

$$(141 - 125) = 10 + 26 + 16 = 52$$

$$BSS = \frac{(\Sigma X_1)^2}{N_1} + \frac{(\Sigma X_2)^2}{N_2} + \frac{(\Sigma X_3)^2}{N_3} - \frac{(\Sigma\Sigma X)^2}{N_{1+2+3}}$$

$$= \frac{15^2}{5} + \frac{20^2}{5} + \frac{25^2}{5} - \frac{60^2}{15} = 250 - 240 = 10$$

and for instruction set no. 3. The sum of these three within-group sums of squares constitutes the *WSS* in the table.

The final computation shown in Table 6.2 is the between-groups sum of squares (*BSS*). Since the differences between our groups are indicated by the means of each group, it is appropriate to determine the sum of the squared deviations by substituting the mean of a group for each score within that group. This is equivalent to multiplying the *MS* of the means by a factor of N as was indicated by the formula for developing a variance estimate from sample means. Thus, for instruction set no. 1, we would substitute the score 3 (the mean of that group) for each of the 5 scores in that group. Our between-groups sum of squares would then involve squaring these 5 means and summing them. The actual procedure to be used is somewhat simpler because of the relationship between the mean, the sum, and the number of scores. In our particular example, the sum of the squares of the substituted means would be:

Squared scores between groups (instruction set no. 1)

$$= 3^2 + 3^2 + 3^2 + 3^2 + 3^2$$
$$= 9 + 9 + 9 + 9 + 9$$
$$= 45$$

We obtain the same answer by dividing the square of the group sum ($15^2 = 225$) by the number of scores in that group (5). In general, the derivation is:

$$\bar{X} = \frac{\Sigma X}{N}$$

$$\text{Squaring: } \bar{X}^2 = \frac{(\Sigma X)^2}{N^2}$$

$$\text{Multiplying by } N: N\bar{X}^2 = \frac{N(\Sigma X)^2}{N^2} = \frac{(\Sigma X)^2}{N}$$

Instead of squaring each of the means and then multiplying by N, we are able to square each of the sums for the group and divide by the number of scores in that group. This computation is shown in Table 6.2.

$$BSS = \frac{15^2}{5} + \frac{20^2}{5} + \frac{25^2}{5} - \frac{60^2}{15} = 45 + 80 + 125 - 240 = 250 - 240 = 10$$

These computations illustrate the additivity of sums of squares, i.e., TSS (62) $= WSS$ (52) $+ BSS$ (10). As a general rule, we may say that the total sum of squares equals the between sum of squares plus the within sum of squares for any set of data. As a final simplification for computations in the analysis of variance, we most often compute only TSS and BSS (which usually involve only integers and which may be easily determined with the aid of a calculator). To derive WSS from these two figures, it is necessary only to subtract, i.e., $WSS = TSS - BSS$. However, it may be wise to check by computing the WSS directly.

Computation of the sum of squares is only the first step in analysis of variance. We must recall that sums of squares are not variance estimates. To convert these figures to estimates of the population variance, it is necessary to divide by some factor of N. For the within sum of squares, it is apparent that we have placed restrictions upon the value computed, i.e., each variation was computed as a deviation from its own column (group) mean and not from the grand mean. As a consequence, the appropriate factor of N required to convert the WSS to an estimate of the population variance is the degrees of freedom associated with that sum of squares.

Since each instruction-set group contains 5 individuals, there are 4 degrees of freedom associated with each instruction set. For the 3 sets combined, then, we have 12 degrees of freedom. Division of the WSS (52) by its appropriate degrees of freedom (12) gives a within mean square of 4.33. This computation is shown in the fourth column of Table 6.3.

Table 6.3 is called a Summary Table because it summarizes in logical form all of the computations required for an analysis of variance. The first column is labeled "Source" and refers to the sources of the variation of scores in the experiment. In this simple analysis of variance, there are only two independent sources of variation—within-groups variation and between-groups variation. These sum to equal the total variation in the table.

TABLE 6.3. Summary table

SOURCE	SS	df	MS	F	p
Between	10	2	5.00	1.15	NS
Within	52	12	4.33		
Total	62	14			

The second column is labeled "*SS*" for sum of squares and simply lists the results of the computations made earlier. Again note the general additivity of sums of squares. The third column in the Summary Table (*df*) is degrees of freedom. These have previously been computed as 2 for between-groups variation and 12 for within-groups variation. Note that the *total df* equals the sum of between- and within-groups *df*. That is, if we were to consider the original table as a single distribution of 15 scores, there would be (12 + 2 =) 14 degrees of freedom associated with it. This is a check on the accuracy of the determination of our between and within *df*.

The fourth column of Table 6.3 is labeled "*MS*" for mean square. As you recall, a mean squared deviation from the mean is an estimate of the population variance. In this fourth column, we have one estimate of the population variance which has been derived from between-groups variations. We also have a second, and independent, estimate of the population variance, derived from our within-groups variations. The ratio of these two estimates of the population variance is the *F* ratio, which is given in the fifth column of Table 6.3. Division of the between *MS* (5) by the within *MS* (4.33) yields an *F* ratio of approximately 1.15.

Upon inspection of the table for *F* listed in Appendix D, we find that *F* ratios of 3.88 are expected to occur by chance alone 5 times out of 100. Since our computed *F* ratio (1.15) is less than the $p = .05$ value listed in Appendix D, we must conclude that we do not have significant differences between our means. That is, although the between *MS* to within *MS* ratio is greater than 1, it is a value that might frequently occur by chance variation of *F* ratios alone. Thus, the differences between our means (Table 6.1) cannot confidently be attributed to our experimental treatments. We have, therefore, indicated in the right-hand column that the probability (*p*) value is so high ($> .05$) that the *F* ratio is considered not significant (NS), or not significantly different from 1.

We should note that the *F* ratio compares the variability of all of the means in a study, not the differences between any pair of means. For example, let us say that the means of a drug study indicate that the lowest dosage of the drug affects behavior least. An increasingly detrimental effect on behavior becomes apparent as dosage is increased through several levels. Even with a significant *F* value, we are not justified in stating that the greatest dosage of the drug produces significantly more decrement in performance than does the least dosage. The *F* ratio simply tells us that the total distribution of these means is an unlikely chance occurrence. The only exception to this general rule occurs when only two groups are compared by analysis of variance. Clearly, if the F ratio indicates that the difference between these two means is unlikely to have happened by chance alone, then the two means may be considered significantly different.

A second computational example will illustrate this point and further demonstrate the procedures used in an analysis of variance. Suppose that an administrator of a small college is concerned about both the quality of instruction and the demands made upon the instructors' time. He has heard that discussion and lecture promote greater learning than lecture alone. However, to provide discussion sections as well as lectures will require greater time from instructors. As a consequence, he does not wish to initiate lecture plus discussion unless he is certain that a significant improvement in performance can be demonstrated. The administrator selects 12 students at random from the college and assigns 7 of these to attend only the lecture portion of a class. He assigns the remaining five to attend the lecture and a discussion section. At the first midterm, a 30-point multiple choice examination is administered to all 12 students. Their scores are presented in Table 6.4.

The administrator must determine whether the five students in the lecture-plus-discussion section have a significantly higher mean score than the seven students who attended only the lectures. The appropriate analysis of this data is shown in Table 6.5. First, the total sum

TABLE 6.4.   Individual scores on a 30-point multiple-choice test

LECTURE GROUP	LECTURE + DISCUSSION GROUP
9	
12	
13	22
10	25
11	26
14	23
15	24
$\Sigma X_1 = 84$	$\Sigma X_2 = 120$
$N_1 = 7$	$N_2 = 5$
$\bar{X}_1 = 12$	$\bar{X}_2 = 24$
$\Sigma\Sigma X = 204$	
$N_{1+2} = 12$	

TABLE 6.5.   Computation of the significance of the difference between two groups

$$TSS = 9^2 + 12^2 + \ldots + 15^2 + 22^2 + 25^2 + \ldots + 24^2 - \frac{204^2}{12} = 3926 -$$

$$3468 = 458$$

$$BSS = \frac{84^2}{7} + \frac{120^2}{5} - \frac{204^2}{12} = 1008 + 2880 - 3468 = 420$$

$$WSS = 458 - 420 = 38$$

SOURCE	SS	df	MS	F	p
Between	420	1	420	110.5	<.01
Within	38	10	3.8		
Total	458	11			

of squares is computed by squaring each of the individual scores, summing these squares, and subtracting from this sum the square of the sum of all scores divided by 12. This total sum of squares is 458. To compute *BSS:* square each subgroup sum and divide each by its *N;* sum the resulting scores; from this total, subtract the square of the overall sum divided by total *N*. As noted in Table 6.5, *BSS* equals 420. The final sum of squares computation follows from the previous discussion. Since the total sum of squares equals the between sum of squares plus the within sum of squares, one may determine *WSS* by simple subtraction of *BSS* from *TSS* (458 − 420 = 38).

Following these basic computations, the administrator would devise a summary table similar to that shown in the lower portion of Table 6.5. Note that since there are only two means, we have one degree of freedom associated with between *SS*. Since we have 7 people in the lecture group, we have 6 degrees of freedom associated with the within *SS* for that group. The 5 students in the lecture-plus-discussion group contribute 4 degrees of freedom to within *SS* and, consequently, the within *SS* degrees of freedom is 10. If we consider the total table as a single distribution of 12 scores, we have 11 degrees of freedom. Thus the degrees of freedom between groups and within groups sums to the total.

The *MS* listed in the fourth column of the summary table is simply the division of each *SS* by its *df*. Finally, *F* is the ratio of these two estimates of the population variance to each other. In this particular case, we obtain an F ratio of 110.5. When we refer to the F table in Appendix D, we find that this value of F greatly exceeds even that value required for significance at the .01 level. Consequently, in the sixth column of the summary table, the p value is reported as $< .01$.

We should note in this special case that the analysis indicates a significant difference between the two groups, i.e., one group did significantly better than the other group. This, however, is all that our analysis of variance shows. To determine the actual direction of this difference we must once again consult the figures given in Table 6.4. The mean for the lecture group is 12, whereas the mean for the lecture-plus-discussion group is 24. The significance of this difference is given by the F table, and the direction of this difference by the actual means.

We may, therefore, say that, as measured by test performance, the lecture-plus-discussion group has a significantly higher mean than the lecture group. Only when we have determined both the significance and the direction of the difference may we state that our working hypothesis is confirmed. Possibly, we might have obtained a significant p value with the lecture group being significantly higher than the lecture-plus-discussion group. In such an instance, although we would have obtained significant results, they would not have confirmed our working hypothesis. Indeed, such results would have indicated that the addition of the discussion to the lecture tends to decrease performance.

Type I and Type II Errors

From these two computational examples, it should be apparent that one risks two types of errors when he states conclusions based on an analysis of variance. The first, or Type I error, may be demonstrated by our second example. It might be possible that the differences between our groups could, in fact, happen by chance alone. That is, although we randomly assigned the students to these two groups, some mischance of selection may have assigned "A" students to the lecture-plus-discussion groups and "D" students to the lecture–only group. Note that the probability of a Type I error is given by the p value reported in the summary table. Since the p value reported for the lecture mean versus lecture-plus-discussion mean is less than .01, we say that the probability of having made a Type I error is less than .01.

The second type of error, Type II, may be demonstrated by the data regarding instructional sets. A Type II error is one of omission rather than of commission, i.e., perhaps the F ratio of 1.15 has occurred as a consequence of the differences between our treatments. In our test situation, however, additional factors may have masked the small effect that was indeed present so that we are unable to detect this by means of the analysis of variance. Possibly a true effect does exist due to instructional sets, but this effect is so small with respect to the variation between subjects that we are unable to detect it with analysis of variance.

We see then that there are two possible errors one can make in formulating a conclusion based on experimental data. A Type I error involves stating that a significant difference exists when in fact the results are due to chance. The Type II error results in stating that there is no significant difference between means when a true difference does exist. We may reduce the possibility of a Type I error by refusing to report results as significant unless they reach certain stated p values. Methods of reducing Type II errors are more complex. However, in an analysis of variance design, we may state as a general rule that an increase in the number of subjects tested in each of our groups will tend to decrease the possibility of a Type II error. An increase in the number of people in each of our samples also increases the degrees of freedom associated with the within MS. Consequently the F value required for significance decreases, as may be seen in the table in Appendix C. Thus, as we increase the N in our sample, a smaller overall effect is more likely to be detected.

ANALYSIS OF VARIANCE COMPARED TO t TEST

Before proceeding directly to an analysis of the data from the study developed in Chapter 2, let us answer one question that may arise concerning analysis of variance. In the previous chapter, we used the t test to determine the significance of a difference between a sample mean and a population mean. Is there not some variation of this t test which can be used when we wish to determine the significance of a difference of two sample means? There is such a technique, and it is often used to analyze experimental data. Remember, however, that this t test is appropriate only when we have two sample means. If we have more than two, the t test cannot be used as a test between all possible combinations of those means, even taken two at a time. Analysis of variance is a more general technique in that it may be used to analyze two or more sample means.

Further, the t test, if computed step by step in its logical development, would require that we take five square roots. This increases the probability of rounding errors in our results. Thus, the analysis of variance is a simpler technique, as well as being more generally applicable.

As a final point, the two techniques give identical results with respect to *p* values, as one may convert a *t* value to an *F* value by squaring it. Therefore, a *t* test of two sample means reported in the literature may be regarded as a special case of analysis of variance.

ANALYSIS OF THE SAMPLE STUDY

Now, let us turn to an analysis of the data from the differential-brightness study. It might seem appropriate to complete an analysis of variance between the four distributions of DL's—"brighter" ascending and

TABLE 6.6.   Mean DL's for "dark" and "light" conditions in the brightness-discrimination experiment

EXPERIMENTAL GROUP	SUBJECT NO.	ASCENDING DL	DESCENDING DL	AVERAGE DL
	1	7.967	10.575	9.271
	2	13.427	12.279	12.853
	3	12.362	12.107	12.234
	4	6.966	8.899	7.933
	5	11.311	13.180	12.245
	6	14.512	23.861	19.187
	7	16.943	9.070	13.006
	8	10.795	9.950	10.372
	9	17.615	37.440	27.528
"Light"	10	15.994	14.441	15.217
	11	7.954	18.742	13.348
	12	10.650	13.770	12.210
	13	11.444	12.782	12.113
	14	14.342	12.358	13.350
	15	26.158	22.264	24.211
	16	13.437	13.675	13.556
	17	15.966	20.598	18.282
	18	10.038	17.297	13.669
	19	12.770	10.193	11.481
	20	15.091	9.572	12.332

$$\Sigma X = 284.398$$
$$\bar{X} = 14.2199$$

TABLE 6.6.   (*Continued*)

EXPERIMENTAL GROUP	SUBJECT NO.	ASCENDING DL	DESCENDING DL	AVERAGE DL
	21	12.544	20.779	16.662
	22	13.990	14.654	14.322
	23	12.925	13.366	13.145
	24	21.575	23.050	22.313
	25	10.763	16.267	13.515
	26	12.405	19.142	15.774
	27	20.773	24.927	22.850
	28	19.073	26.737	22.905
	29	13.825	13.355	13.590
"Dark"	30	15.746	16.884	16.315
	31	24.833	20.504	22.668
	32	18.133	18.339	18.236
	33	12.987	21.594	17.291
	34	19.936	20.808	20.372
	35	23.873	28.631	26.252
	36	17.118	10.961	14.040
	37	25.126	23.949	24.537
	38	10.161	14.828	12.495
	39	18.066	16.898	17.482
	40	17.016	15.356	16.186

$$\Sigma X = 360.950$$
$$\bar{X} = 18.0475$$

descending DL's, and "darker" ascending and descending DL's. Note, however, that this procedure would violate one of the assumptions made at the beginning of this chapter: that selection of the individuals for any one estimate of the population variance does not influence in any way the selection of a second group of individuals. For simple analysis of variance, our scores are assumed to be independent samples from the population. Since the ascending and descending DL's for either group are obtained from the same individuals, it must be assumed that these two scores are not independent of each other. It is therefore necessary to combine these scores if the data to be analyzed are to represent independent samples.

The simplest way to obtain independent scores for this analysis is to average, for each S independently, his ascending and descending DL.

TABLE 6.7.   Analysis of variance computations—sample study

$$TSS = \Sigma X^2 - \frac{(\Sigma \Sigma X)^2}{N_{1+2}}$$

$$= 9.271^2 + 12.853^2 + 12.234^2 + \ldots + 16.186^2 - \frac{(645.348)^2}{40} =$$

$$11,329.999 - 10,411.851 = 918.148$$

$$BSS = \frac{(\Sigma X_1)^2}{N_1} + \frac{(\Sigma X_2)^2}{N_2} - \frac{(\Sigma \Sigma X)^2}{N_{1+2}}$$

$$= \frac{(284.398)^2}{20} + \frac{(360.950)^2}{20} - \frac{(645.348)^2}{(40)} = 4,044.111 + 6,514.245 -$$

$$10,411.851 = 10,558.356 - 10,441.851 = 146.505$$

$$WSS = TSS - BSS = 918.148 - 146.505 = 771.643$$

SOURCE	SS	df	MS	F	p
Between	146.505	1	146.505	7.215	$< .05$
Within	771.643	38	20.306		
Total	918.148	39			

The 20 averaged DL's for the "light" experimental condition can then be compared with the 20 averaged DL's for the "dark" experimental condition to determine whether the average DL's for the two groups are significently different. These scores are reported in Table 6.6. By averaging these scores we have reduced the final analysis to one similar to the lecture versus lecture-plus-discussion example presented earlier.

The calculations required for determining the sums of squares are presented in Table 6.7, in the lower portion of which is the summary table for this analysis. Of primary importance to us is the fact that the final p value associated with this analysis of variance is less than .05. By referring again to the means in Table 6.6, we see that the "dark" experimental group has a mean DL which is significantly higher than the DL of the "light" experimental group. The results are significant and are in the direction predicted by the original working hypothesis. We may thereby conclude that our working hypothesis has been confirmed.

Since we have only two groups, we may state that average DL's obtained under conditions of dark-background lighting are significantly higher than DL's obtained with bright-background illumination. Because we have directly manipulated values of the independent variable, the research qualified as an experiment rather than a study of preexisting groups. Consequently, if we may assume that all other conditions were identical for our two groups, we may make a causal statement: Differences in background illumination caused the differences observed in our experiment. From a scientific viewpoint, our experiment has been a success.

It is appropriate to review the steps that led to this success. Following the initial idea for the study, a thorough review of the literature revealed that the study had not been done before. Our literature review also acquainted us with approaches used by others and indicated some of the extraneous variables to be controlled. An experimental study was designed to incorporate these findings, and procedures were developed for testing subjects. A pilot study was completed to assure that no detail had been forgotten. The collection of data and its appropriate analysis then led directly to the conclusion stated above. Had any of these steps been eliminated, the study could possibly have been unsuccessful. Having attended to these necessary steps this study should make a contribution to scientific knowledge when it is reported in the literature.

DESIGN CONSIDERATIONS

The introduction of the technique of simple analysis of variance opened many areas of investigation that previously had been closed. With this technique, it is possible to design experiments which are much more complex than were the simple experimental group: control group designs upon which many earlier findings in the research literature were based. A review of current research literature indicates that a majority of these experiments use some form of analysis of variance as the method of data reduction.

Simple analysis of variance is an appropriate test of significance in any situation where: (1) the underlying population of scores from which the samples are drawn may be assumed to be normally distributed; (2) the treatment effects are assumed to be linear and additive (and thus the only changes between samples are those of mean differences, while the sample variances remain approximately equal); and (3) the scores are randomly and independently drawn from the population.

These assumptions must be carefully considered by the experimenter in designing a study. For example, one might possibly use either of two different measures of the dependent variable for a particular experiment. Other considerations being equal, the test which has in the past yielded normal distributions of scores would be preferred. Similarly, one should consider the possible effects of the treatment variable on the distribution of scores collected. If it appears that the treatment is likely to be perceived in widely varying ways by different subjects, then it is possible that the variances within each sample may not be approximately equal. Often this effect can be minimized by minor changes in treatments or instructions.

Finally, in considering what number of subjects to test in a given experiment, one should consult the F table under the anticipated df. If a relatively high value of F is required for significance, it is often possible to test more subjects and thereby increase the within df and decrease the value of F required for significance.

SUMMARY

In this chapter, we have presented analysis of variance as a method for analyzing the differences between two or more sample means. This technique is based on the fact that independent estimates of the variance of a single population should be approximately equal. The distribution of the ratios of two such estimates, known as the F distribution, is used to interpret the analysis of variance.

The two independent estimates of the population variance required for this analysis are: (1) an estimate of variance due to within-groups variations, and (2) an estimate of variance due to between-groups variations. In the typical computation, one first derives a total sum of squared deviations from the overall mean (TSS):

$$TSS = X_1{}^2 + X_2{}^2 + \ldots + X_N{}^2 - \frac{(\Sigma\Sigma X)^2}{N_T}$$

where $X_1, X_2, \ldots X_N$ are all of the individual scores in the total distribution, $\Sigma\Sigma X$ is the sum of all of the individual scores, and N_T is the total number of scores available for analysis.

The sum of squared deviations due to between-groups variations (BSS) is next computed by the formula.

$$BSS = \frac{(\Sigma X_A)^2}{N_A} + \frac{(\Sigma X_B)^2}{N_B} + \ldots + \frac{(\Sigma X_N)}{N_N} - \frac{(\Sigma\Sigma X)^2}{N_T}$$

where $\Sigma X_A, \Sigma X_B, \ldots \Sigma X_N$ are sums of individual scores for each group, and $N_A, N_B, \ldots N_N$ are the number of individual scores in each of the separate groups.

The sum of squared deviations due to within-group variations (*WSS*) may then be found by subtraction:

$$WSS = TSS - BSS$$

The remaining steps in the analysis of variance are illustrated by the summary table below.

SOURCE	SS	df	MS	F	p
Between	BSS	No. Groups $-$ 1	Divide SS by df	$\dfrac{\text{Between } MS}{\text{Within } MS}$	
Within	WSS	$(N_A - 1) + (N_B - 1)$ $+ \ldots + (N_N - 1)$			
Total	TSS	$N_T - 1$			

The same form may be followed for listing the results of an analysis of variance in a report.

These mean squared deviations (*MS*) from the overall mean are estimates of the population variance. The observed *F* ratio is tested by referring to a table of critical *F* values. Proper entry to this table requires that one use the values shown at the intersection of the *df* for the numerator (between *df*) and the *df* for the denominator (within *df*).

In the interpretation of the final *p* value, it should be recognized that analysis of variance is a test of the overall distribution of group means. As a consequence, one may not claim significant differences between any isolated pair of means within this distribution unless there were only two groups represented in the original data.

Further, it was seen that two possible errors exist: (1) claiming differences between groups when no true difference exists—a Type I error; and (2) finding no differences between groups when a true difference does exist—a Type II error.

An analysis of variance must be based on the assumption that the data were randomly drawn from a population of normally distributed scores. Although the F test is relatively insensitive to minor deviations from this assumption, one should at least visually scan the data to insure that no major deviations are present.

Finally, the analysis of variance technique was applied to the study originally designed in Chapter 2. Significant results were found to support the original working hypothesis. The overall success of the experiment was attributed to the careful planning, design, and execution of this study.

7. The Research Report

COMMUNICATION AND VERBAL EXTRANEOUS VARIABLES

The study we began in Chapter 2 has now been analyzed and has been found to yield significant results. At this point however, these results are still a part of the private world of the investigator. The results must be communicated to others to be integrated into the world of science, for science can expand only through the accumulation and interpretation of such data. You will recall from Chapter 2 our discussion of replication, range extension, conflict resolution, and theory testing—all experimental methods having their origin in the literature of the field. Until the results we have obtained become a part of that literature, none of these methods of extension can be applied to our particular study. Further, we saw in our review of the literature that no comparable study existed; the report of our results in the literature may save another investigator the time and effort of repeating this same study. The final step in an experiment, then, is the communication of the results of that experiment to others in the field.

Before beginning the writing of our scientific report, let us investigate some of the factors affecting the reliability of communication. The use of the word "reliability" in reference to the writing of a scientific report is intended to emphasize the similarity between the experiment itself and its verbal expression. We know that an experiment must be reliable, or any interpretation of the data becomes meaningless. Similarly, any communication or report of the experiment should be reliable to avoid giving false or misleading impressions to the reader. That is, one should anticipate the same basic interpretations of the report from one reader to the next. Reliability of verbal expression is, however, very difficult to assess.

We have learned that the presence of extraneous variables contributes to the lack of reliability in an experiment. These unwanted variables may be at least partially controlled by such techniques as elimination, constancy of conditions, balancing, counterbalancing, randomization, etc. If we consider those factors which inhibit the communication of the "truth" of an experiment to be another group of extraneous variables, perhaps we shall find suitable methods for their control.

One such group of verbal extraneous variables was discussed early in the seventeenth century by Francis Bacon, the father of the philosophy of science. In his essay "Novum Organum," Bacon (1) listed several factors that he felt must eventually limit the applicability of science. Of primary importance to this discussion was his statement that the very methods used in communicating experimental results often obstruct rather than enhance the progress of science. He writes, "For it is by discourse that men associate; and words are imposed according to the apprehension of the vulgar. And therefore the ill and unfit choice of words wonderfully obstructs the understanding."

It must be recognized that man has but a limited vocabulary with which to express all of his thoughts, feelings, and impressions; and verbal communication becomes, at best, only an approximation of the speaker's intent. Some classes of words convey a much clearer idea of the message than do others. For example, the following two statements might be found in a psychology textbook: "The ego is considered to be the first differentiation of the id," and "The rat was placed at the end of the maze." The first of these sentences refers to a basically subjective conclusion; the second defines an objective state of affairs. We typically find greater agreement between individuals regarding objective rather than subjective statements. For maximum agreement, then, the scientific report should strive for objectivity, eliminating as many references to thoughts, emotional states, opinions, and other non-observable phenomena as possible.

Another opportunity for verbal extraneous variables to affect the scientific report occurs as the individual reader attaches meaning to specific words. Suppose two people should read that Mr. X had, without success, submitted the same proposed municipal ordinance to the city council each year for the past 14 years. Although both readers have read exactly the same material, one might describe the aspiring lawmaker as "pigheaded and stubborn" while the other characterizes him as "true to his own ideals." Clearly, there is some difference in the mental picture communicated to these two individuals.

The converse may also be true, as when two individuals use the same word to connote entirely different meanings. As one example, what one person believes to be anxiety might not agree with another's interpretation of the concept of anxiety. If we report our results using terms which have two or more possible meanings, some opportunity for misinterpretation exists. The use of operational definitions can compensate to some extent for this semantic difficulty. Perhaps we do not agree that the best definition of an anxious person is "one threatened with shock" but at least we understand the intent of the author. Even with the operational definition, one must eventually rely on some set of basic terms which have a degree of universal agreement. It is extremely unlikely that scientists will develop universal agreement for any term that is not immediately demonstrable. The operational definition is only a partial balance for the unreliability caused by different interpretations of the same word.

In addition to these possible misinterpretations, Hayakawa (13) has shown that the use of emotionally laden terms also inhibits communication of fact. The statement, "He is the greatest statesman who ever lived," is simply a reflection of the fact that the individual speaker respects the object of that statement very, very much. The statement, "He was the author of the XY plan for foreign aid, the AB plan for domestic welfare relief and the LM plan for conservation," tells us of the basis on which such judgment was made. In a similar fashion, the statement, "He's a dirty rotten fink," only indicates to us that the author of the statement dislikes the referent of the remark very, very much. A more precise way to communicate the basis for this statement might be, "He is alleged to have beaten his mother, stolen candy from small children, and kicked his favorite dog." In report writing, the reliability of communication is improved by replacing judgmental statements with facts.

This discussion has listed some of the verbal extraneous variables which tend to reduce the reliability of a scientific report. Since man has a limited vocabulary, the scientist can only approximately communicate his thoughts. This deficiency may be minimized by the use of objective rather than subjective statements. A second extraneous variable arises from the fact that people may use different words to describe the same concept or may use the same word to describe different concepts. This variable is partially controlled through the use of operational definitions. Finally, we have seen that the use of emotionally laden terms reduces the reliability of communication. Thus, factual rather than judgmental statements should predominate in scientific writing. With these general concepts in mind, let us turn directly to the basic format of a typical research report.

APA RESEARCH REPORT FORMAT

The American Psychological Association has developed a standardized format which is generally applicable to most types of research reports and is preferred by many of our psychological journals. We will use this format, outlined in the *APA Publication Manual*, in writing our sample report.

The typical research report includes the following sections: (1) Abstract, (2) Introduction, (3) Method, (4) Results, (5) Discussion, and (6) References. You may have noted in your literature review how much this standardized format aided your search, allowing simple location of the pertinent information in any given report.

The abstract of an article found in your literature review was printed in *Psychological Abstracts* and was probably your first reference source to the journal article itself. Many times it is possible to tell whether or not a particular article is of value to your study by simply reading the abstract. In an article which appeared to be of interest it may only have been necessary to read one of the sections. For example, if you were interested in the purpose of the study and its theoretical background, you would consult the introduction section of the report.

If the study was of only tangential value to your own but you wished to know what variables had been controlled, you would turn to the methods section. This section often causes an additional problem in communication—that of selecting what to report and what to omit. For example, one would not normally report the subjects' names in an experiment, but certainly would report how many subjects were used. There is a very simple guide to the selection of items to report and to omit. This is replication. If another investigator could not replicate your basic study, then your report is incomplete. Any additional information beyond that required for replication is usually excess material and probably should be omitted. This selection is a judgmental process and should reflect those variables that you have considered important in the study. In most cases, these will be variables for which you have controls. For example, you would probably include the statement that all subjects were given a standardized set of instructions because you believe that instructions are an important variable and one for which control is necessary. However, you would probably not give the actual instructions themselves in the research report unless they had specific meaning to the study.

Following the methods section are the results. This section outlines the type of data, the analyses that were made, and the statistical outcome of the study. Here, one has the problem of determining the content of the section and must also consider whether or not the data have been correctly analyzed. The study we have been following throughout the text was deliberately designed so that many different kinds of analyses are possible (correlation, factorial design analysis of variance with randomly assigned subjects, correlated-scores analysis of variance, etc.). As we progress through the remainder of the text you should note what changes would occur in your report had these analyses been made. The practical issue involved is that of retaining the data from your experiment. When someone else reads this report he may want to complete the analyses that seem to be most appropriate. In all probability, you will not list the raw data of your study in the research report, but it should be made available upon request.

The discussion section of the report gives the author's interpretation of what happened in the experiment. Each reader may, after scanning the data, reach his own conclusions about the outcome of the study, which may or may not agree with those of the author. This is why conclusions are not included directly with the results. Also in this section are suggestions for further research. These are sometimes of inestimable value in generating new research proposals.

The discussion is probably the most difficult section for the new experimenter to write. Most of the verbal extraneous variables discussed earlier are more difficult to control in this portion of the report. The initial section of the report should be factual but in the discussion or conclusions section one must generalize his results beyond the specific conclusions warranted by his data, including some statements of opinion. Here one must "stick his neck out," and like the turtle will make no progress unless he does so. Too many student reports end with a simple statement that "The hypothesis was confirmed." It is usually possible to draw some further implications from the data.

According to some writers, the process of science consists in actually seeing the same data in different ways. For example, Kuhn (22, pp. 117–118) illustrated this point with the basic idea of the pendulum— Aristotle saw the pendulum swinging as "constrained fall" whereas Galileo saw the same pendulum swinging as "periodic motion." From this one observation there evolved two entire systems of scientific thought. Similarly, in your report you can perhaps integrate your own data with that from other reports and generate some new method of regarding the data. Much of the real creativity of science arises at this point, for by seeing things from a new perspective one may open up new theoretical concepts.

The last section of a report includes all references specifically mentioned in the body of the report itself. As you noted in your own literature review, this reference section sometimes simplifies greatly the task of surveying the field. Accuracy and completeness are of primary importance in this section.

Manuscript Preparation

Because the format recommended by the American Psychological Association has proven itself as an aid to precise and efficient communication, it is used as a model for report writing in many introductory experimental psychology courses, and has been adopted for use in this text. Although many of the rules may seem to be somewhat arbitrary, they are specifically formulated to ease the transition from a typed manuscript to an actual published report. For example, the APA requirement that articles be as short as possible and still be consistent with maximum reliability is based on actual journal page limitations due to high publication costs.

You should also note that manuscript style is somewhat different from the final style of the printed article. For example, the abstract must be on a separate page in a manuscript because it is printed in smaller type at the beginning of the final article. This abstract will be forwarded, as is, to *Psychological Abstracts*.

Footnotes, when used, are also typed on a separate page. This is because your typed pages may not correspond to page length in the article itself. The article will be set in type with the footnotes cut in as required.

For a similar reason tables and figures are prepared separately. It may not be possible to place these tables and figures exactly where you wish them to be in the printed article. In the manuscript, then, we place the notation:

- -

Insert Figure XX about here

- -

This indicates to the printer that you would like Figure XX to be placed as closely as possible to that paragraph of the report.

When your manuscript is actually set in type the printer will copy it slavishly. This sometimes leads to difficulty. For example, we may underline a word for emphasis. Underlining to a printer, however, means to set the word or words in italics. A dash indicates to the printer that he is to include a dash at that point. Your manuscript should avoid hyphenations at the end of a line unless you wish the hyphenation sign to appear in the final printed article. If a mistake has slipped by both yourself and the editor it will appear in the report.

There is also the possibility of pages from your article being lost or confused with pages from another article. To prevent this your name and the page number should be printed on each page. It is also wise to print a short title, especially if you have more than one article submitted to a particular journal.

These are only a few of the precautionary measures which must be observed when preparing a manuscript. Rather than attempting to give all of these in this text, it is recommended that the experimenter make a careful study of the most recent American Psychological Association *Publication Manual*. All of the various requirements for a research report are listed in that manual.

SAMPLE REPORT

To acquaint you with the basic structure of the American Psychological Association form, portions from a sample report are included in this chapter. You should note that this is actually only the barest indication of what each section of a research report should contain. The comments to the left of the page are those pertaining to the schematic report; to the right is the report itself. Dashes completely across the page indicate the end of one page and the beginning of the next.

PUBLICATION OF A REPORT

For most students, the exercise in writing a report in APA format will be one more course requirement to be fulfilled. A few students, however, do complete original research studies and submit them for publication while still undergraduates. If your report is intended for publication, several additional steps must be followed after the original manuscript has been completed. First, after your manuscript has been carefully edited it is well to let your colleagues criticize it for errors in content or construction, typographical errors, etc. At this time it is also wise to consider the choice of a particular journal in which you wish your article to appear. Each of the more than 500 journals reviewed by *Psychological Abstracts* has a specialized area of psychology from which its articles are drawn. It is to your advantage to attempt to match the content of your manuscript to the usual contents of a specific journal. The editor of a journal which is not publishing in the area of your report will be likely to return the manuscript with the suggestion that you submit it elsewhere. Also, a specific journal is usually read by those in the field who are most conversant with the area studied and therefore interested in the results of your study.

(No short identifi-
cation on Abstract
page)

(Descriptive title)

DIFFERENTIAL-BRIGHTNESS

THRESHOLDS AS A FUNCTION OF

BACKGROUND ILLUMINATION

(Author)

John H. Doe

(Affiliation)

Amy Baker College

(Abstract gives hy-
pothesis, design, re-
sults, and conclusions
in 120 words or less.
Abbreviations first
given in full, except
S for Subject.)

Abstract

On the basis of Hecht's

(1934) work on visual acuity,

it could be predicted that the

differential brightness

threshold (DL) should vary

inversely with ambient

illumination. DL's were

computed for 40 Ss tested under

conditions of either low or

high background illumination.

The results affirmed the

hypothesis based on Hecht's

results. These results were

seen as supporting Pirenne's

(1945) suggestion that an

increase in illumination

results in an increase in the

number of active receptor

elements and, therefore, a

finer functional visual mosaic.

- -

(Begin on new page
with no short iden-
tification)

(Descriptive title)

DIFFERENTIAL-BRIGHTNESS

THRESHOLDS AS A FUNCTION OF

BACKGROUND ILLUMINATION

(Author)

John H. Doe

(Affiliation)

Amy Baker College

(Introduction   not
labeled; note refer-
ence style; give rel-
evant literature with
rationale for hypoth-
esis tested.)

Seemingly incompatible

conclusions regarding the

differential-brightness

threshold (DL) may be made from

Kohlrausch's (1931, pp.

1499-1594) findings that

retinal sensitivity increases

as a function of adaptation and

from Hecht's (1934, pp. 704-828)

findings that visual acuity

increases as a function of

illumination. Since the DL is,

like visual acuity, essentially

a discrimination task, Hecht

should predict a decrease in

the DL as illumination is

increased. The current study

is designed as a partial test

of this prediction.

Method

(Include number, source, and any special characteristics of subjects. Underline indicates italics.)

Subjects.--Twenty male and 20

female introductory psychology

students at Flunkout University

volunteered as Ss for the study.

All were naive with respect to

the specific experimental task

and had normal color vision.

- -

(Short identification and page number)

Doe, DL's & Background

Page 2.

(Apparatus section should give all information required for replication of study; designate settings so others may extend range of study.)

Apparatus.--All settings of the DL were made on Lafayette Instrument Company's Model 701 Differential Brightness Apparatus. The constant light was kept at a numerical setting of 150 (corresponding to 0.382 ftc. 3/16 in. from the source). The variable light at settings of 100 and 200 corresponded to 0.163 and 1.10 ftc. respectively, 3/16 in. from the source.

Results

(Again, criterion of replication should be used for selection of material; note use of plural and possessive forms of abbreviation for subject; numbers less than ten written out, ten or more in Arabic numerals; common items such as inches, minutes, etc. are abbreviated.)

Procedure.--Ss were randomly assigned to participate in either the light background or dark background condition with the restriction that each group contain 10 males and 10 females. Prior to each S's

participation, room lighting
was adjusted by means of a
potentiometer so that
illumination at S's eye level
measured either 10 μl. (dark)
or 100 μl. (light). During the
15-min. adaptation period the
method of adjustment was
demonstrated. Special emphasis
was placed on the fact that
retracing was not permitted.
This was followed by a series
of eight practice trials. At
the conclusion of the adaptation
period a series of 64 trials
counterbalanced between
ascending and descending
settings were recorded to the
nearest numerical unit.

Results

(Results section con-
tains not only final
analysis but also all
manipulations of data;
statistics such as *t*, *z*,
and *p* are marked for
italics; degrees of
freedom are shown in
parentheses following
statistical symbol; fig-
ures and tables are
not included in text
but their approximate
position is indicated
as shown.)

The 64 settings from each $\underline{S}$

were separated into ascending

or descending trials and the

standard deviations computed.

DL's for each $\underline{S}$ for each set of

trials were computed from the

formula: DL = .6745 standard

deviation. As a final index of

brightness discrimination for

each $\underline{S}$, his ascending and

descending DL's were averaged.

The final indices were analyzed

by simple analysis of variance

and significant differences

between the dark and light

background groups were found,

$\underline{F}$ (1, 28) = 7.215; $\underline{p}$ < .05.

The magnitude and direction of

these differences are shown

in Figure 1.

- - - - - - - - - - - - - - - -
Insert Figure 1 about here
- - - - - - - - - - - - - -

- -

Doe, DL's & Background

Page 3.

As noted here, the group

participating in the light

background-illumination

condition exhibited lower DL's

than did the group tested under

dark background illumination.

Discussion

(Discussion includes whether or not hypothesis was confirmed, implications and generalizations of results, and suggestions for further research; not a place for excuses for study poorly planned or executed.)

Significantly lower DL's were

obtained with increased

background illumination,

confirming the prediction made

on the basis of Hecht's results

on visual acuity. It would

appear that Pirenne's (1945)

model relating the number of

active retinal receptor

— —

Doe, DL's & Background

Page 4.

elements to total illumination

(as illumination increases,

more receptor elements become

active and thus provide a finer

functional mosaic) seems an

appropriate explanation for

these results. Further studies

of the DL, however, are

required to generate the curve

relating DL's to changes in

ambient illumination.

— —

(Begin on new page; note page numbered sequentially.)

Doe, DL's & Background

Page 5.

References

(References alpha-
betized by first au-
thor; *et al.* not used
for multiple authors;
style varies for jour-
nal article, book, etc.,
always check **APA**
Publication Manual
for correct style.)

Hecht, S. Vision. II. The
nature of the photoreceptor
process. Handbook of general
experimental psychology.
Worcester, Mass.: Clark
University Press, 1934.

Kolrausch, A. Tagessehen.
Dammerschen. Handbook of
normal and pathological
psychology. Berlin: Springer,
1931.

Pirenne, M. H. On the variation
of visual acuity with light
intensity. Proceedings,
cambridge philosophical
society, 1945, 42, 72-82.

(Begin on new page;
note page also num-
bered sequentially.)

Doe, DL's & Background

Page 6.

Figure Caption

(Figure caption should explain figure without reference to text.)

Fig. 1. Mean DL's for 40 $\underline{S}$s tested under two conditions of background illumination. The mean DL for the lower level of ambient illumination is significantly larger than that for the higher level.

- -

(Figure on separate page; note heading omitted; name, short title, and figure number are written lightly in pencil on reverse of figure page; figure in India ink suitable for reproduction; commercial artist recommended.)

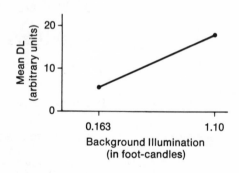

- -

Two copies of the completed article are submitted to the editor of the selected journal. He will assign a reviewing editor who will read the report, criticize it, and decide whether or not the article is appropriate to that journal. He may make acceptance of the article contingent upon completion of suggested changes or modifications.

Just prior to the actual publication, you should receive a set of proofs for the article as it will appear in the journal. You must review these proofs carefully to correct any errors. Charges may be made for any author changes made at this time which are deviations from the original manuscript.

When the report is finally published, the results become a part of the psychological literature and may be referred to by others. Perhaps this report will be responsible for a series of other studies illuminating some previously hazy area. Perhaps it will be a key concept in some theoretical development. You have finished one study and are ready to begin another.

SUMMARY

One requirement for the expansion of any branch of science is the communication of experimental results. Such communication most often takes the form of the scientific report. The reliability of such reports may be greatly reduced by the presence of verbal extraneous variables. Some of these verbal extraneous variables may be at least partially controlled by using objective rather than subjective statements, operational definitions, and factual rather than judgmental statements wherever possible in the research report.

The specific style of research report illustrated was that adopted by the American Psychological Association. The typical report includes: (1) Abstract, (2) Introduction, (3) Method, (4) Results, (5) Discussion, and (6) References. In each of these sections we have stressed the twin requirements of conciseness with sufficient completeness to permit replication. Although the sample report offered an example of each of these sections, an experimenter should always consult the most recent APA *Publication Manual* for detailed instructions.

8. Interactions Between Logic, Design, and Statistics

DETERMINISM, CAUSATION, AND STATISTICS

Let us pause at this point in our study to review some of the general concepts underlying all of psychological research. Many of these were presented in earlier chapters as intuitively developed points of information. Now that you have become acquainted with three inferential statistical techniques (z, t, and F), it is possible to reexamine these concepts within a statistical framework.

Determinism was one of the first concepts to be discussed. Complete determinism was rejected in favor of the more appropriate philosophy of probabilistic determinism. Now you have sufficient knowledge of statistics to show that a definite relationship exists between probabilistic determinism and actual research techniques. For example, any conclusion based on a research study is actually a probabilistic statement, e.g., it is highly probable that the results obtained are not due to chance factors alone. Therefore, analysis of our data should lead to conclusions that are compatible with our underlying philosophy.

Related to this problem of determinism was the entire question of causation. In particular, one of the problems associated with the scientific method was the tendency to infer causation from correlation. We also learned, however, that there are some scientific methods from which one may infer causal relationships. The true experimental technique is one of the methods for developing such inferences. If an experimenter randomly assigns subjects into two groups, he may assume that the preexperiment performances of the groups are approximately equal. The probability that these initial performances are, in fact, different is given by the p values employed in the study. If different treatments are administered to the two groups, and if one group performs significantly better than the other, then this difference in performance may be inferred to have been caused by the difference in treatments.

With correlational or *ex post facto* studies, a somewhat different situation exists. In the true experiment, the p value indicates the probability that such results would have occurred if there were no true differences in the treatments. For the *ex post facto* study, the p value indicates the probability that such results would have been obtained if there were no true differences between the groups initially selected for the study. Thus, the same statistical methods are appropriate for either type of research, and the final p value does not indicate whether or not causation may be inferred in either research technique. This decision must be made by the investigator.

Fortunately, there is one method by which one can approach the goal of inferring causation from multiple *ex post facto* studies. This is the method of converging evidence. A classic example is the statement that smoking cigarettes causes lung cancer. Let us investigate the sequence that has led to an increasing acceptance of this theory. The first several studies of the relationship were obviously *ex post facto* in nature. By investigating the medical histories of individuals who had died from lung cancer and contrasting them with the histories of a group of individuals dying of other causes, it seemed apparent that cigarette smoking and lung cancer were, in some way, related. The *ex post facto* nature of these studies is apparent in that the independent variable (smoking) was not experimentally manipulated. It was not possible to infer a definite causal relationship between lung cancer and smoking from this group of *ex post facto* studies.

A number of alternative explanations for this apparent relationship could be offered at this point. Possibly some aberrant chromosome predisposed an individual to lung cancer and also created in the individual the desire to smoke. If this were the correct explanation, one should expect to find some genetic link or hereditary factor in which selected cases would exhibit a nonchance proportion of either lung cancer or smoking. Another possible explanation of these results could be that both lung cancer and smoking are functions of the stresses and tensions under which the individual must operate. Such an explanation would predict that those individuals in high-stress positions who do not smoke would show a higher incidence of lung cancer than do those in relatively low-stress positions who do not smoke.

The process of gathering converging evidence is one of attempting to formulate all of the possible alternative explanations, make predictions from them, gather the data, and then test the validity of the alternative predictions. When such data for lung cancer were gathered and added to other basic findings, investigators became increasingly confident that a causal relationship did exist between smoking and lung cancer. You should note, however, that since all alternative explanations have not been tested, the possibility still exists that some other factor is responsible. It is evident that the determination of causation from converging evidence is, theoretically at least, an infinitely long process.

From this discussion, we see that the problem of inferring causation from either correlation or *ex post facto* studies is not a limitation inherent within the techniques themselves. Under proper conditions, causation may tentatively be inferred from such studies. If the process of gathering converging evidence has resulted in the rejection of most of the logically derived alternative explanations, one may have considerable confidence that the relationship is indeed a causal one. We are able to see that the problem which exists with respect to causation is predominantly a human factor. Only when such inferences are made in error (from the basis of a single study, without regard to possible alternative explanations, etc.) do they act as a limitation of the scientific method.

From such an example, you may begin to develop a new sense of the role of statistics in psychological research. Simple manipulation of scores—even within the appropriate statistical framework—will never eliminate the necessity for careful judgment and interpretation of results. Statistics can be a valuable aid in assessing the meaning of a set of data and, as a tool for research, can play an intermediate role between the creativity of design and the wisdom and judgment of interpretation.

SYSTEMATIC EXTRANEOUS VARIABLES

The foregoing is not meant to imply that the improper design and conduct of an experiment have no effect upon the subsequent statistical analysis of the data. Consider the effect of the inclusion of systematic extraneous variables upon the conclusions permitted by our statistical analysis. Since these extraneous variables have an effect which extends to all subjects within a group in the experiment, the effect of these variables is indistinguishable from differences caused by manipulation of the independent variable. For example, if an experimenter subconsciously favors any of the groups in an experiment, the effects of such bias are not detectable by standard types of data analysis. This bias, since it is extended to all members of a group, simply adds to the overall treatment effect. We may find a significant difference between our groups and attribute this effect to the experimental variable. If experimenter bias has crept in, this conclusion may be in error.

The effect of such systematic extraneous variables is perhaps made more obvious if we eliminate the mathematical portion of the statistics that we have studied and insert, instead, the sources of the data that are to be analyzed. When viewed in this manner, all of the statistics that we have studied become the ratio:

$$z, t, \text{ or } F = \frac{IV + SEV + E_m}{E_e}$$

where:

$$IV = \text{independent-variable effect}$$
$$\text{(or treatment effect)}$$
$$SEV = \text{systematic extraneous-variable effect}$$
$$E_m = \text{error of measurement}$$
$$E_e = \text{expected error}$$

For the z, t, and F tests, the numerator of this ratio is the effect that we wish to study and, if significant, generalize about. For these statistics, IV is the true difference in the population due to manipulation or selection of the independent variable. In such cases, SEV may be due to experimenter bias, inadequate testing procedures, or any of a number of other systematic extraneous variables. Finally, the last term in the numerator of this ratio (E_m) is due to small random effects expected simply as a function of random sampling. If the study were replicated with a different sample of Ss, it is quite likely that the means for the various groups would not be exactly equal to those found in a prior study. The denominator (E_e) in all three of the techniques that we have studied is based on the variability of the scores within a treatment sample. For both z and t, this is the standard error of the mean and is based on the standard deviation of scores (variability between different Ss). In the technique of analysis of variance, E_e is a direct measure of the variability within the treatment groups.

Note that the existence of systematic extraneous variables in a study may lead either to a Type I or a Type II error. If no IV actually exists due to the independent variable but a large SEV is present due to systematic extraneous variables, the ratio will be large, and significant results may be found. If the experimenter then concludes that these significant results are due to the effect of the independent variable, he will have made a Type I error.

As you recall, a Type I error is the statement that differences exist when in fact no differences are to be found in the population as a whole. We have seen that the probability of a Type I error is given by the p value that we wish to quote in our experiment if no systematic errors have been made. We should, however, realize that the experimental effect analyzed by this F ratio is the total treatment effect for our groups. Perhaps the groups varied in ways other than the stated experimental treatment. The control group may have had a special set of instructions in addition to changes in brightness. As a consequence one may only state that the total treatment differences between his groups have apparently made some differences. If systematic extraneous variables have been included, the experimenter may be further in error in concluding that the p value shown is attributable to his experimentally designed treatment effect.

Similarly, if a large IV is actually present but an opposing SEV exists which cancels the IV, the statistical ratio will be small and the null hypothesis may not be rejected. The inability to find a true effect due to the independent variable's action is a Type II error. Good experimentation, then, should insofar as possible eliminate the effect of systematic extraneous variables so that the statistical answers permit an accurate conclusion to be drawn. Since the accuracy of our conclusions about a study determines the validity of that study, methods for controlling systematic extraneous variables are also methods for increasing the validity of the study.

NONSYSTEMATIC EXTRANEOUS VARIABLES

Nonsystematic extraneous variables also have a severe effect upon the conclusions that may be drawn from a research study. Their action, though, is primarily through the denominator of the statistical ratio computed when analyzing the results of a study. Nonsystematic extraneous variables are those which differentially affect the members within an experimental group. Since the denominator of the statistical ratio (E_e) is directly a measure of within-group variability, any increase in E_e due to nonsystematic extraneous variables tends to decrease the overall value of the ratio and lead to a finding of nonsignificant results.

One of the factors influencing the size of E_e is motivation. The motivational level of subjects participating in an experiment clearly differentially affects various members of each experimental group. This statement should have much more meaning for you after having actually conducted an experiment. The typical beginning experimenter often makes such remarks as "That girl didn't even try to do a good job. She acted in a bored and restless manner—just giving the dial a flip without even looking at it. Can't we eliminate her data?" These annoying aspects of this subject's behavior, however, were not included in the analysis of the data; only the final setting of the dials is indicated. We are, therefore, disregarding behaviors which do influence the factor under study. The inability to analyze total behavior is clearly a limitation to the scientific method.

You may believe it possible to at least partially control an extraneous variable such as motivation. For example, if each subject could have had 10 points added to his final grade in introductory psychology based upon his performance on the above task, the motivational state might have been uniformly high. This represents control of an extraneous variable by the method of keeping conditions constant.

TABLE 8.1. Comparison of basic and experimental measured scores of three subjects

SUBJECT NO.	BASIC PERFORMANCE	MEASURED PERFORMANCE
1	5	1
2	5	5
3	5	9

It is appropriate to investigate whether the control of nonsystematic extraneous variables has an effect upon the outcome of our statistical tests. Let us assume that we have randomly chosen three subjects to participate in an experiment. Further, let us suppose that an extremely fortunate chance factor has permitted us to select subjects who would exhibit identical test scores if the experimental procedures were exactly followed. These true performance scores, which would have been obtained under standard experimental conditions, are listed in the second column of Table 8.1. As noted there, each individual's basic performance score is 5. Since there is no variation within the scores of this group, the *WSS* attributable to this group is zero.

In the experimental test, however, let us say that Subject No. 1 performs under poor lighting conditions with inadequate instructions and a great deal of noise. Although he is capable of a performance score of 5, these detractive effects (extraneous variables) reduce his measured performance to a score of 1. Subject No. 2 performs under the conditions of the experiment as originally stated in our design and consequently achieves his basic possible performance score of 5 units. The third subject is tested by an inept experimenter. He has three more practice trials than should be allowed, is rewarded beyond the conditions originally specified for the experiment and, in addition, detects some cues to his performance from the facial expression of the experimenter. As a consequence Subject No. 3 achieves a measured performance score of 9; had he been tested under standard conditions his basic performance would have been 5. Note that although there is no within-group variation in the basic potential performance of these three individuals, the presence of extraneous variables results in a large within-group variation in the actual measured performance as recorded for our experiment.

We have seen before that the presence of nonsystematic extraneous variables in an experiment reduces the reliability of that experiment. Certainly if the subjects listed in Table 8.1 were tested again on this same task they might well reverse their positions on the measured performance test. We see that a reduction in reliability is shown by an increase in the within-groups variance and, like any increase in the within-groups variance, decreases the likelihood of finding a significant F ratio. Thus, a lack of reliability in an experiment is equivalent to the denial of the goals of the experiment itself.

Several factors can influence the size of the within-groups variance. If every individual within each of our groups were to behave in exactly the same manner as every other member of his group, there would be no within-groups variance. Any differences which did appear between the groups would result in an F ratio so high as to be indeterminant. We might suspect that were we able to control all of the sources of differences between individuals—genetic structure, prenatal environment, experiences, etc.—all individuals would behave identically in any given experimental situation (within the limits of our crude measuring instruments). Due to both practical and philosophical limitations, however, we are unable to control every aspect of an individual's heredity and environment. These differences contribute to within-groups variance in the simple analysis of variance schema. It would appear that the appropriate task of experimental design is not to eliminate within-groups variance, but to minimize it.

In the example previously given in Table 8.1, one of the factors tending to inflate the within-groups mean square was seen to be sloppiness in experimentation. Whenever a standardized procedure is not adhered to by all experimenters (a nonsystematic extraneous variable), the reliability of the study decreases and the within-groups variance increases. It is because of these relationships that the within-groups variance is often termed error variance and was labeled as E_e in the statistical ratio.

Accurate experimental design should include the development of a standardized set of instructions for the subjects, the specification of the values of the experimental variable to be administered, and the planning of each step in the experimental procedure—all contributions towards minimizing error variance. The use of such techniques as constancy of conditions, elimination, balancing, counterbalancing, and randomization for control of extraneous variables also tends to reduce error variance and improve the reliability of the experiment. Since the computed F ratio is an inverse function of the within-groups variance

175

for a given between-groups variance, any design factor which reduces error variance contributes to the finding of significant results.

MAXIMIZING EXPERIMENTAL VARIANCE

The statistical ratio computed on experimental data indicates why differences between experimental treatments are often emphasized in research design. Of primary importance to us as experimenters is the portion of the statistical ratio attributable to the experimental effect (IV). Thus, in the F ratio, we are primarily interested in the ratio of the treatment effect to probable error. Since we must have a large F ratio to support significant results, we should attempt to maximize the treatment effect and minimize the variance due to error.

Very early we stated that one should attempt to obtain a large range of experimental treatments, particularly in exploratory studies. This is equivalent to maximizing the experimental variance. Perhaps it is possible that the particular experimental treatments chosen did have some effect on behavior. However, if we have poorly chosen the range of this effect, the experimental variance will be small with respect to the variation between individuals.

As an example, we might wish to investigate the effect of sleep deprivation on tracking performance in a motor-skills task. We could have one group sleep a full 8 hours, and allow the second group to sleep only 7 hours. It would be unlikely that we would be able to detect such a small difference in our experimental treatments. If we wished to maximize the experimental effect we might test one group following 8 hours sleep and test the second group after 48 hours awake. We would be more likely to find a large treatment effect with this second experimental design than with the first. As a consequence, we would probably find a significant effect of sleep deprivation in the second experiment but not in the first. Thus, particularly for exploratory studies, we may wish to maximize insofar as is feasible the difference between the experimental and control groups.

TYPE II ERRORS

Let us suppose, then, that we have properly minimized the within variance by control of extraneous variables and have also maximized the between variance by providing for a large range of experimental treatments. Does this, then, insure that the conclusions drawn from the results of that experiment are error free? No, even in this situation, we must still consider the possibility of making a Type I or Type II error. However, methods for reducing error variance and increasing treatment variance also tend to decrease the probability of errors in conclusions drawn from the results of a statistical test. Type I errors were previously examined with respect to the necessity for control of systematic extraneous variables. If systematic extraneous variables have been properly controlled, the probability of making a Type I error is given by the p value that we cite for the study.

The Type II error is somewhat more complicated. This is the statement that no differences exist when in fact, for the population as a whole, a true difference does exist. Let us say that we have designed an experiment that has three degrees of freedom associated with the numerator of our F ratio and nine degrees associated with the denominator. Suppose in this experiment that the F ratio experimentally determined is 2.95. When we refer to the F table we find that an F ratio of 3.86 is required for three and nine degrees of freedom; and are unable to conclude that significant differences exist between our groups. However, in the column for three degrees of freedom, we find that at a denominator degrees of freedom of 28 the F ratio of 2.95 would be significant at the .05 level. If the experiment is a reliable and valid experiment within the limitations of sampling error, the same F ratio obtained with a larger group of subjects yields significant results. Thus the number of subjects run may influence a Type II error.

A second factor contributing to a Type II error is, as in the Type I error, a function of random assignment. This error, though, is in the opposite direction of the Type I error. Possibly some differences do exist between our groups, but by random chance alone we may have assigned poor individuals to the experimental group that normally should perform higher and excellent individuals to the group that normally should perform more poorly. As a consequence the two effects tend to cancel out, leaving us with nonsignificant results. Note here that the probability of this type of error is less than the probability of a Type I error. We must find not only nonrandom selection, but nonrandom selection in a specified direction. That is, had the nonrandom assignment of individuals to groups been such that excellent individuals were assigned to the group which should normally perform well, this effect would enhance the significance of the F ratio to be

177

determined. Only when we get nonrandom assignment in the opposite direction will it contribute to a Type II error.

A third and major cause of a Type II error is sloppiness in experimentation. If many nonsystematic extraneous variables are permitted to enter into the experiment, the mean square within groups will be larger than normal. As a consequence the F ratio may be small even though a treatment effect is present. The presence of extraneous variables in an experiment leads to the possibility of an indeterminate conclusion. We should, however, note that this effect is relative. The larger the experimental effect that we expect to obtain, the less the presence of a few extraneous variables will tend to yield a Type II error. If, on the other hand, the expected experimental-treatment effect is relatively small the experiment must be highly controlled to avoid the possibility of a Type II error.

A fourth source of Type II errors is that of using the wrong method of analysis for the data. As we shall discover in later chapters, certain methods of analysis are more powerful for some kinds of data than for others. If we have chosen an inappropriate method it is possible that our experiment will yield nonsignificant results when, in fact, true differences would have been detected with the appropriate technique. It is the correct matching of the experimental design, problem area, and statistical analysis which constitutes good psychological experimentation.

An integration of the factors influencing the Type II error indicates why one does not "prove" the null hypothesis. A finding of no significant differences may actually mean that there are no differences existing in the population. On the other hand, the factors we have just mentioned—(1) lack of sufficient number of subjects, (2) random misplacement of subjects, (3) presence of extraneous variables, and (4) inappropriate analysis—may all lead to a finding of no significant differences. Since we are not able to place a probability value on the presence of these four factors it is impossible for us to "prove" the null hypothesis.

CHOICE OF ANALYSIS AND STATISTICAL ASSUMPTIONS

The last of these factors, inappropriate analysis, requires further discussion. An experiment is not normally designed as was the demonstration experiment presented in the first chapters of this book. In that experiment, the only factors under consideration were the relationship of the study to the background literature and the appropriate design of an experiment to test the hypothesis under question. A third factor usually included when one designs an experiment is the appropriate analysis for that study. Many beginning experimenters have assembled a mass of data, only to find that no suitable technique is available for analyzing it. Often a few changes in the experimental design or method of collecting the data could have yielded data more amenable to analysis.

Simple analysis of variance is not solely a technique for analyzing masses of data. One of the assumptions required prior to such an analysis was that each of the scores be independent of all other scores. The use of this particular technique may reduce the variety of methods available for use in controlling extraneous variables. For example, in an attempt to control for individual differences, we might decide to have the same subjects participate in all of our treatment conditions. This is a legitimate technique for the control of extraneous variables, but it immediately requires a different type of analysis of variance as an appropriate analysis technique. Since a given subject has more than one score, the assumption of independence is violated.

A second assumption required prior to the completion of an analysis of variance is that the scores have been randomly drawn from a normally distributed population of scores. We have previously seen that statistics which require this assumption are termed parametric statistics because they involve the parameters of the normal distribution. Other statistical techniques, to be studied in later chapters, are called nonparametric statistics because they do not involve the assumption that the scores were sampled from a normal distribution of scores. When possible, we should attempt to use parametric statistics in the analysis of experiments.

Given a particular experimental-treatment effect, parametric analyses may yield significant results where some of the nonparametric analyses yield nonsignificant results. For example, one may collect data which indicate the order in which subjects finish a particular task. The first subject to finish would be given a rank of one, the second subject the rank of two, and so forth. With data such as these it is not statistically legitimate to use parametric statistics. Here a relatively simple change in experimental design would have allowed the experimenter to employ parametric techniques. Had he timed each of the subjects and recorded the time it took to finish the particular task under consideration, he possibly could have used parametric analyses.

✗ This power of the parametric tests can, to some extent, overcome the minor deviations from the assumptions required for their use. For example Gayen (12) has shown that limited amounts of nonnormality and heterogeneity of variance may have only small effects on analysis of variance. It has been stated that use of some of the special techniques to determine whether or not an analysis of variance is appropriate is something like "sending a row boat out to sea to find out whether or not the sea is too rough for an ocean liner to make a voyage." In most instances, unless there is a marked deviation from the assumptions underlying a parametric test, parametric techniques should be used.

It is possible to justify a particular analysis in terms of the required assumptions, while it may not be the most appropriate analysis. In such a case, your analysis of the data may be perfectly legitimate (in a statistical sense) but still be rather inefficient. For the study designed as an example in the first portion of this book, the very powerful technique of trials by factorial levels with replications within subjects-analysis of variance could have been completed. In addition to merely deciding that the two groups differed in their differential-brightness thresholds as a function of background illumination, it would have been possible to report whether or not there was a sex difference in this treatment, whether or not ascending trials differed systematically from descending trials, and whether or not subjects differed significantly among themselves. Although none of these answers was required to solve the problem initially posed, they do add a significant amount of new information to the literature at no further cost to the experimenter. Thus, although our use of simple analysis of variance could not be regarded as an inappropriate technique, it was an inefficient one. Proper consideration of the analysis of the experiment at the time of its original design should have pointed to this more efficient analysis.

Viewed in this way, an appropriate sequence of events for the design of a simple experiment in psychology becomes: (1) generation of an initial research idea through either systematic or nonsystematic approaches; (2) a thorough review of the literature to develop the problem area and delineate extraneous variables which might influence the outcome; (3) development of the basic structure of the research design through the use of operational definitions, working hypotheses, independent variables, and the expected relationship between them; (4) development of the method of data collection based upon the working hypothesis and the method of analysis to be used; (5) clarification of the design to increase reliability and validity by reducing possible extraneous variables; and (6) completion of a pilot study.

From the discussion in this chapter, it should be apparent that logic, methodology, and statistics are inextricably interrelated in experimental design. One of your major goals now becomes the acquisition of a working knowledge of the various types of available statistical analyses. In the remainder of this book, we will discuss some of the commonly used statistical measures, the assumptions required for their use, typical experimental designs involving each type of statistic, and the conclusions that one may with justification draw from each such design.

SUMMARY

The purpose of this chapter has been to clarify some of the interrelationships between philosophical concepts, experimental methodology, and statistics. The statistical and design concepts developed in previous chapters were seen to support the conclusions of the earlier discussion of determinism. The problem of causation of behavior was discussed with respect to two types of research: the true experimental design and the *ex post facto* study. Causation could be inferred from a single true experimental study, but the inferrence of causation from *ex post facto* studies was seen to involve the collection of converging evidence from many studies.

From a statistical point of view, experimental design involves minimizing error variance and maximizing treatment variance. The controlling of nonsystematic extraneous variables was effective for minimizing error variance and also increased the reliability of the experiment. Providing a wide range of experimental treatments tended to maximize treatment variance. These same factors were also found to be effective in reducing the possibility of committing a Type I or Type II error when interpreting the results of an experiment. Since the type of data collected would determine the method of analysis used, careful consideration of the selection of statistical techniques was found to be an important factor in experimental design.

9. Confidence Intervals

ESTIMATING POPULATION PARAMETERS

Restrictions on the general applicability of the simple analysis-of-variance technique have been noted in both Chapter 6 and Chapter 8. One such restriction was that the results of an analysis of variance do not indicate differences between individual pairs of sample means unless only two means were tested. A second restriction to the general use of this technique was that the scores to be analyzed must be independent samples. Third, the necessity for assuming that these scores were drawn from a normally distributed population of scores will, in some cases, preclude the use of the simple analysis of variance. In the remaining chapters of this book, additional statistical techniques will be presented which compensate for these restrictions and, consequently, permit a great deal more flexibility in the design of experiments.

The first restriction noted above—an inability to detect differences between individual sample means—is often most vexing to the beginning experimenter. An experiment may have been designed to determine whether or not teaching methods affect learning. Proper experimental design, careful control of extraneous variables, and rigid adherence to structured procedure yield a significant F ratio for the experimental-treatment effect upon three groups. The mean test scores for these three groups are presented in Figure 9.1, where L = lecture only; LD = lecture plus discussion; and LT = lecture plus teaching machine. The lecture-only group has the lowest mean test score, lecture plus

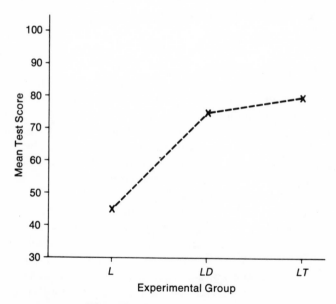

FIGURE 9.1. Hypothetical data resulting from an experiment relating teaching method to mean test scores. (L = Lecture only, LD = Lecture plus discussion, LT = Lecture plus teaching machine.)

discussion has a considerably higher mean test score, while lecture plus teaching machine is slightly higher still.

From simple visual observation, it would appear that the lecture-plus-discussion group and the lecture-plus-teaching-machine group both performed significantly better than did the lecture-only group. However, this visual observation may not be justified on the basis of the significant F ratio determined following the simple analysis of variance. An appropriate technique for testing this observation is known as the Scheffé (31) test for post hoc comparisons.

When an analysis of variance has yielded significant results, we may test for post hoc comparisons to determine the particular sources of such nonchance results. Thus, we are asking specific questions of the data following an overall analysis. Other techniques are available for asking specific questions about data when an overall analysis has not been used.

To understand the logical development of the Scheffé test, let us return to the estimation of population parameters from sample data. We found, in Chapter 5, that our best estimate of the population standard deviation when only sample data are available is:

$$s = \sqrt{\frac{SS}{df}}$$

It was necessary to divide the sum of the squared deviations from the sample mean (SS) by degrees of freedom (df) to compensate for the squared deviations having been computed from the sample mean rather than from the population mean. Following the above formula, the square root of the MS (mean squares) taken from the analysis of variance summary table will yield an estimate of the population σ. This simple correction to the formula permitted us to derive an estimate of the population standard deviation.

But the standard deviation is only one of the parameters of a normal distribution. What will be our best estimate of the second parameter, the mean? A sample mean computed by the formula previously given in Chapter 4 ($\bar{X} = \Sigma X/N$) is, without correction, an unbiased estimate of the true population mean. Recall, from our discussion of the standard error of a mean, that the mean of the distribution of all possible sample means was equal to the population mean. On the average, then, a sample mean will tend to equal the population mean and we are able to state that the best estimate of the true population mean is the computed value of the sample mean.

The phrase *"true* population mean" has been used purposely in the preceding paragraphs. In our earlier discussions of the z test and the t test, it was stated *"If* the true population *IQ* mean is 100, . . ." or *"Assuming* that errors of anticipation and habituation cancel each other for the population, . . ." The z test and the t test are, in effect, tests of a sample mean and assumed population mean. After completing one of these two tests we may find that there is a significant difference between the sample mean and the assumed population mean. We may then state it to be unlikely that the assumed population mean accurately represents the population. That is, rejection of the null hypothesis permits us to reject the assumed value for the population mean.

CONFIDENCE INTERVALS FOLLOWING A z TEST

If the assumed value is rejected, is there a way that one may, with confidence, state a value for the true population mean? We have just determined that the sample mean is the best estimate of the true value of the population mean. However, we know that sample means may vary from one study to the next. Thus, rather than stating that the true mean is the computed mean value of the sample, a more suitable technique is to establish a range of values within which we might reasonably expect to find the true population mean. The formula for this range of values, referred to as a confidence interval, is:

$$CI = C \pm M\sqrt{RV}$$

where:

CI = confidence interval
C = the specific comparison being made (sample data)
M = multiplier
R = reciprocal of the number of subjects involved in the comparison
V = estimate of the population variance

This formula is used for comparisons following a z test, a t test, or an analysis of variance.

Let us see how this formula may be applied to the determination of a confidence interval for the true population mean following a z test. Assume that we have randomly selected 25 individuals from the population of the United States and measured their IQs by means of a standardized test. The theoretical or assumed population mean is 100;

the population standard deviation is 16. Following the administration of this test, we find that the mean of the sample is 108.32. The z test is conducted as follows:

$$z = \frac{\bar{X}_{sample} - \bar{X}_{population}}{\sigma_{\bar{x}}}$$

where:

$$\bar{X}_{sample} = 108.32$$

$$\bar{X}_{population} = 100.00$$

$$\sigma_{\bar{x}} = \frac{\sigma}{\sqrt{N}} = \frac{16}{\sqrt{25}} = \frac{16}{5} = 3.2$$

then:

$$z = \frac{108.32 - 100}{3.2} = \frac{8.32}{3.2} = 2.60$$

Since the observed value of z is greater even than the value of 2.58 required at the .01 level, we are able to reject the null hypothesis and conclude that the differences between the computed sample mean and the assumed population mean are not likely to have occurred as a function of chance alone. If the study has been properly conducted, it would appear that the assumed population mean of 100 is lower than the actual or true mean of the population. What, then, is our best estimate of the true population mean? Since a sample mean is an unbiased estimate of the true population mean, we may state that, to the best of our knowledge, the true population mean is 108.32. However, if the study were repeated with a different sample, we would be unlikely to find the mean of that sample to be exactly 108.32. Thus, instead of citing the sample mean alone, a range of values (confidence interval) is given within which we might expect to find the population mean. This range of values is given by:

$$CI = C \pm \sqrt{RV}$$

where:

C = the specific comparison being made (in this case, $C = \bar{X}_{sample} = 108.32$)

M = multiplier (here, the value 1.96 will yield the 95 percent confidence interval; 2.58 will yield the 99 percent confidence interval)

R = reciprocal of the number of subjects involved in the comparison (25 subjects were tested; thus $R = 1/25$)

V = estimate of the population variance (for this data, the population $\sigma = 16$ and thus $V = \sigma^2 = 256$)

For the 95 percent confidence interval then, we compute:

$$95 \text{ percent CI} = 108.32 \pm 1.96\sqrt{(1/25)(256)}$$
$$= 108.32 \pm 1.96\sqrt{(.04)(256)}$$
$$= 108.32 \pm 1.96\sqrt{10.24}$$
$$= 108.32 \pm 1.96(3.2)$$
$$= 108.32 \pm 6.272$$
$$= 102.048 \text{ to } 114.592$$

There are several points to note carefully about this computation. First, the value of $\sqrt{RV}$ is precisely the same as the value of $\sigma_{\bar{x}}$ computed for the z test. Second, the M value of 1.96 is the same as the critical value of z for the .05 level. Thus, the 95 percent confidence interval is the same as:

$$95 \text{ percent CI} = \bar{X}_{\text{sample}} \pm 1.96\,\sigma_{\bar{x}}$$

The logic underlying this expression was discussed at length in Chapter 5. The probability that a sample mean will deviate, by chance alone, from the population mean more than 1.96 standard error of the mean units is .05. Since we assume that this sample mean is not one of these atypical cases, it should not deviate more than 1.96 $\sigma_{\bar{x}}$ units from the true population mean. The true population mean, then, will probably be found somewhere within the range from 102.048 to 114.592. Finally, note that the original or assumed mean of 100 is not included in this range. Thus, in confirmation of the earlier findings of the z test, we are able to reject 100 as a probable value of the true population mean.

You are probably wondering why we have introduced a new formula instead of using a simple revision of one previously learned. For the z test, such a simple revision would be possible. For comparisons between specific sample means following an analysis of variance, however, this simple formula would be inappropriate.

Confidence Intervals Following a **t** Test

Let us extend this technique for determining a confidence interval to data which follows a t test. Suppose that we wish to determine whether or not, for the population as a whole, an error of anticipation or habituation is present in a discrimination task. We test 10 subjects on this task and obtain the results presented in Table 9.1. For these subjects, the comparison stimulus was set at a value of 200.

TABLE 9.1.   PSE's for a sample of 10 subjects

SUBJECT NO.	PSE
1	207
2	205
3	205
4	200
5	209
6	201
7	203
8	205
9	205
10	210
$\Sigma X =$	2050

$\Sigma X^2 = 420{,}340$

$$\bar{X} = \frac{\Sigma X}{N} = \frac{2{,}050}{10} = 205.00$$

$$\sigma^2 = \frac{\Sigma X^2 - (\Sigma X)^2/N}{N-1} = \frac{420{,}340 - (2{,}050)^2/10}{10-1} = \frac{420{,}340 - 420{,}250}{9} =$$

$$\frac{90}{9} = 10$$

$$\sigma = \sqrt{\sigma^2} = 3.162$$

$$\sigma_{\bar{x}} = \frac{\sigma}{\sqrt{N}} = \frac{3.162}{\sqrt{10}} = \frac{3.162}{3.162} = 1.00$$

As shown in the lower portion of Table 9.1, the mean setting is 205.00, the variance is 10.00, the standard deviation is 3.162, and the standard error of the mean is 1.00. Note that since sample data are used to estimate the population variance and standard deviation, the appropriate correction formula is used. To determine whether this sample mean is significantly different from the assumed population mean of 200, a *t* test is conducted as follows:

$$t = \frac{\bar{X}_{sample} - \bar{X}_{population}}{s_{\bar{x}}}$$

$$= \frac{205.00 - 200}{1.00} = \frac{5.00}{1.00} = 5.00$$

$$df = N - 1 = 10 - 1 = 9$$

Referring to Appendix C, we find (for 9 *df*) that *t* values of 2.262 and 3.250 are required for significance at the .05 and .01 levels, respectively. Since our computed value is larger than either of these values, we may safely reject the null hypothesis. The probability is less than .01 that such a large difference could have occurred as a function of chance alone.

We may also reject the assumed mean of 200 as a likely true mean for the population as a whole. We may then wish to compute an interval within which we might reasonably expect to find the true population mean. Not willing to risk more than 1 percent error in stating this interval, we generate the 99 percent confidence interval by:

$$99 \text{ percent CI} = C \pm M\sqrt{RV}$$

where:

C = the specific comparison (205.00)
M = multiplier for 99 percent level (3.250)
R = reciprocal of number of scores (1/10)
V = variance estimate (10.00)

thus:

99 percent $CI = 205.00 \pm 3.250\sqrt{(1/10)(10.00)} = 205.00 \pm$
$3.250\sqrt{1.00} = 205.00 \pm (3.250)(1.00) = 201.75$ to 208.25

Thus one may, with a relatively high degree of confidence, state that the true population mean for this particular form of discrimination is to be found in the range from 201.75 to 208.25.

There are two points to this example that should be carefully noted. First, the appropriate multiplier for the confidence interval determined following a *t* test must be taken from the table of critical *t* values. This compensates for the fact that sometimes, due to chance alone, we will compute an estimate of the population variance which is much smaller than the true population variance. You should also note that whether the confidence interval is computed following a *t* test or a *z* test, use of the critical value of that statistic for the .05 level is the correct multiplier for determining the 95 percent CI. Use of the critical value of the statistic for the .01 level is the appropriate multiplier for computing the 99 percent CI.

We have seen, in these two examples, that there are specific differences between the computations used to determine a CI following a *z* test and those used following a *t* test: (1) for the *z* test, the population variance is used; for the *t* test, an estimate of this variance is used; and (2) for the *z* test, multiplier values of 1.96 and 2.58 yield the 95 percent and 99 percent CI's, respectively; for the *t* test, critical values of the *t* ratio (at sample *df*) for .05 and .01 yield these confidence intervals.

CONFIDENCE INTERVALS FOLLOWING AN ANALYSIS OF VARIANCE (SCHEFFÉ TEST)

We should expect to develop a similar procedure for the construction of confidence intervals following an analysis of variance; this procedure is referred to as the Scheffé test. The changes in the basic CI formula are, however, more radical since we may have tested three* or more sample means in our original analysis instead of the single sample mean tested in the *t* test or *z* test. Also, the matter of detecting differences between two specific sample means is somewhat more complicated than the method used to establish a range of values for a single mean.

Let us determine what variations to the basic formula ($CI = C \pm M \sqrt{RV}$) are necessary to apply the Scheffé test. First, we have seen that the appropriate value of M for the *t* test confidence interval was simply the tabled value of *t* required for significance at some predetermined level. To deduce what one of the changes should be when using this technique following an analysis of variance, recall from Chapter 6 that: $F = t^2$ (for numerator $df = 1$). If we take the square root of both sides of this equation, we have: $t = \sqrt{F}$. Thus, in the value of M for

---

* Recall that an analysis of variance with two sample means indicates directly the significance of the difference between them. Thus, we shall need to use this CI approach to the detection of differences between specific means only when we have analyzed three or more sample means.

the analysis of variance CI, we must include the square root of the critical value of F for the particular level of significance that we have chosen.

There is a second factor which must be included in the value of M. Consider the distribution of means shown in Figure 9.2. This might possibly represent the results of an analysis of variance which has yielded nonsignificant results. As noted in the figure, the total distribution of these ten means is one which might possibly have occurred as a function of chance alone. This, of course, is what we mean by the statement that no significant differences exist.

Suppose, however, that we examine only $\bar{X}_1$ and $\bar{X}_{10}$. These two specific means are relatively distant from each other and, if no allowance was made for the total distribution of means, one might conclude that they are significantly different. Since the distribution as a whole might have occurred by chance alone, we recognize that no significant

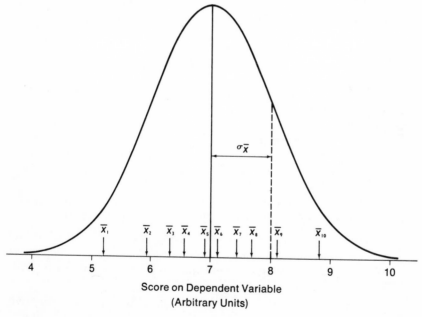

Score on Dependent Variable
(Arbitrary Units)

FIGURE 9.2. A distribution of 10 sample means that might have occurred as a function of random chance alone. The standard deviation of this particular distribution could be computed from the Error MS of the analysis of variance.

differences exist between $\bar{X}_1$ and $\bar{X}_{10}$ when viewed as part of the distribution.

This particular phenomenon has been seen before in a somewhat different context. In determining the appropriate correction for σ when used as an estimator, we found that as the number of scores is increased, the probability that these scores will span the entire distribution is increased. A similar situation exists for sample means. As the number of sample means is increased, there is also an increased likelihood that one or more of these means will come from one or both of the tails of the distribution.

To offset the possibility of such differences being detected as significant by the Scheffé test, the M value of the CI includes the factor: $\sqrt{(J-1)}$ where J is the number of sample means tested by the analysis of variance. Combining this factor with the $\sqrt{F}$ value discussed above yields the following formula for M:

$$M = \sqrt{(J-1)} \cdot \sqrt{F} \qquad \text{or} \qquad M = \sqrt{(J-1)F}$$

where:

J = number of means in the overall test
F = critical value of F for the overall test at a predetermined level of significance

Of the remaining terms in the general expression for the confidence interval ($CI = C \pm M\sqrt{RV}$), the estimate of population variance (V) requires no revision. Since we know that the within-groups MS is our best estimate of the population variance, this error MS may be taken directly from the summary table constructed following the original analysis of variance.

The last term, R, does require some revision. Once again, consider the distribution of sample means illustrated in Figure 9.1. If we were considering any one of these means—say, $\bar{X}_1$—we should expect to find deviations from the overall mean greater than $1.96 \, \sigma_{\bar{x}}$ only 5 percent of the time by chance alone. Note that only this one sample mean is free to vary since the overall mean is a fixed value.

When we consider the range of possible differences between two sample means, we find a much larger value. For example, $\bar{X}_1$ and $\bar{X}_{10}$ are both sample means and, consequently, both are free to vary from the overall mean. Some of the time, by chance alone, $\bar{X}_1$ might be 1.00 $\sigma_{\bar{x}}$ below the overall mean when $\bar{X}_{10}$ is 1.00 $\sigma_{\bar{x}}$ above the overall mean.

In such an instance, the difference between these two sample means would be 2.00 $\sigma_{\bar{x}}$ even though the placement of either sample mean is one that might reasonably be expected as a function of chance.

A simple correction may be made to compensate for the fact that both sample means are free to vary. Instead of taking the reciprocal of the total number of scores included in these two sample means, find the sum of the R values for both means. For example, say that $\bar{X}_1$ and $\bar{X}_{10}$ each contain the scores of five subjects. Rather than computing R on the total number of subjects involved ($1/10 = .1$), we compute the sum of the R values for each mean ($R = 1/5 + 1/5 = 2/5 = .4$). Thus, the appropriate formula for R is:

$$R = 1/N_1 + 1/N_2$$

where:

N_1 and N_2 are the number of scores included in the two specific means under test.

Combining all of these revisions, we find that:

$$CI = C \pm M\sqrt{RV}$$

where:

C = difference between means for which CI is to be obtained
$M = \sqrt{(J-1)F}$
J = number of means in the overall test
F = critical F ratio for the overall test
$R = 1/N_1 + 1/N_2$
N_1, N_2 = number of scores included in each of the specific means tested
V = Error MS (from the summary table)

Let us apply this Scheffé test to the data presented in Table 9.2. These are final examination scores for three groups of students who attended class taught either by lecture only, by lecture plus discussion, or by lecture plus teaching machine. The analysis of variance yields a significant value of F and, consequently, the null hypothesis of no differences between the three groups is rejected.

Although the mean for the lecture-only group ($\bar{X}_L = 59.00$) appears to be lower than either the mean for lecture plus discussion ($\bar{X}_{LD} = 85.33$) or the mean for lecture plus teaching machine ($\bar{X}_{LT} = 89.20$), this judgment cannot be validated from the results of the analysis of

TABLE 9.2. Analysis of variance: teaching methods experiment

	LECTURE ONLY	LECTURE + DISCUSSION	LECTURE + TEACHING MACHINE
	45	78	95
	73	85	87
	56	93	92
	62		81
			91
	$\Sigma_L = \overline{236}$	$\Sigma_{LD} = \overline{256}$	$\Sigma_{LT} = \overline{446}$
	$N_L = 4$	$N_{LD} = 3$	$N_{LT} = 5$
	$\bar{X}_L = 59.00$	$\bar{X}_{LD} = 85.33$	$\bar{X}_{LT} = 89.20$

$TSS = 45^2 + 73^2 + \ldots + 91^2 - 938^2/12 = 76,192 - 73,320.33 = 2,871.67$

$BSS = 236^2/4 + 256^2/3 + 446^2/5 - 938^2/12 = 75,552.53 - 73,320.33 = 2,232.20$

$WSS = 2,871.67 - 2,232.20 = 639.47$

SOURCE	SS	df	MS	F	p
Between	2,232.20	2	1,116.10	15.71	$< .01$
Within	639.47	9	71.05		
Total	2,871.67	11			

variance alone. Since a significant *F* ratio was obtained, we may use the Scheffé test for comparing the specific means.

Let us first determine the 99 percent CI for the differences between the means for lecture only and lecture plus teaching machines. The actual comparison (*C*) based on sample data is the difference between these two means:

$$C = \bar{X}_{LT} - \bar{X}_L = 89.20 - 59.00 = 30.20$$

The value for *M* is given by:

$$M = \sqrt{(J - 1)F}$$

Since three means were tested by the analysis of variance, $J = 3$. For significance at the .01 level with 2, 9 *df*, an *F* ratio of 8.02 is required.

Thus:

$$M = \sqrt{(3-1)(8.02)} = \sqrt{2(8.02)} = \sqrt{16.04} = 4.005$$

Since four students participated in the lecture-only group and five participated in the lecture plus teaching machine, the value of R is:

$$R = 1/4 + 1/5 = 9/20 = .45$$

The value of V, taken from the summary table for the within MS, is 71.05.

The Scheffé CI is then computed as:

99 percent $CI = C \pm M\sqrt{RV}$

$$= 30.20 \pm 4.005 \sqrt{(.45)(71.05)} = 30.20 \pm 4.005 \sqrt{31.97}$$
$$= 30.20 \pm 4.005 \,(5.654) = 30.20 \pm 22.64$$
$$= 7.56 \text{ to } 52.84$$

We are relatively confident that the mean for students attending lecture only will be from 7.56 to 52.84 points lower than for students attending lecture plus teaching machine. Note that the null hypothesis (that the difference between the two groups is zero) is *not* included in this interval. As a consequence, we may reject the null hypothesis and conclude that a true difference does exist: The two means are significantly different.

We have, in this analysis, compared two of the means and found significant differences. May we now proceed to analyze other combinations? Yes, the Scheffé test for post hoc comparisons may be used for all possible comparisons that one may desire to make, provided that an overall significant F ratio was found preceding such analyses.

Let us next determine whether or not the mean for the lecture-plus-discussion group is significantly different from that of the lecture-only group. Note that the value of M remains the same since we are still working from the same overall analysis of variance. Similarly, the value for V will be the same. The only changes will be the value of C (the actual difference) and R (since the lecture-plus-discussion group contains only three subjects). For this analysis:

$$C = \bar{X}_{LD} - \bar{X}_{L} = 85.33 - 59.00 = 26.33$$

and:

$$R = \frac{1}{N_{LD}} + \frac{1}{N_{L}} = \frac{1}{3} + \frac{1}{4} = \frac{7}{12} = .583$$

thus:

99 percent CI $= C \pm M\sqrt{RV}$

$$= 26.33 \pm 4.005\sqrt{(.583)(71.05)} = 26.33 \pm 4.005\sqrt{41.446}$$

$$= 26.33 \pm (4.005)(6.438) = 26.33 \pm 26.78$$

$$= -.45 \text{ to } +53.11$$

Note that the null hypothesis may not be rejected at this confidence level. That is, the null hypothesis states that the difference between these two groups is zero. Since this is one of the possible values specified by this 99 percent confidence interval, we may not reject it.

This does not necessarily mean that there are no significant differences between these two means, for we have used a rather strict value in computing the 99 percent CI. Perhaps we should also compute the 95 percent CI. The only value to change from the 99 percent CI computation will be M. Since an F ratio of 4.26 is required at 2, 9 *df* for significance at the .05 level, M becomes:

$$M = \sqrt{(J-1)F} = \sqrt{(2)(4.26)} = \sqrt{8.52} = 2.919$$

Substitution of this value in the preceding analysis yields:

95 percent CI $= C \pm M\sqrt{RV} = 26.33 \pm (2.919)(6.44) = 26.33 \pm 18.80$

$$= 7.53 \text{ to } 45.13$$

The null hypothesis value of 0 is not included in this interval and may be rejected. We may reject the null hypothesis at the 95 percent CI, but may not reject it when using the 99 percent CI. Therefore, this difference between sample means is significant at the $p = .05$ level but not at the $p = .01$ level.

As a final step in this analysis, we may determine whether or not significant differences exist between the means for lecture plus discussion and for lecture plus teaching machine. When these values are computed, you will find that the null hypothesis can be rejected neither in the 99 percent CI nor in the 95 percent CI. As a consequence, you must conclude that no significant differences exist between these two means. We are able to state that both lecture plus discussion and lecture plus teaching machine yield significantly higher final examination scores than does lecture alone. However, there appears to be no significant difference between the final examination scores of those students participating in lecture plus discussion and those receiving lecture plus teaching machine.

It is apparent that the Scheffé technique removes one of the sources of discontent with the analysis-of-variance technique—that the final p value reflects only the probability that the total distribution of means might have occurred by chance alone. Specific differences may be detected by application of the Scheffé technique following such analyses.

DESIGN CONSIDERATIONS

The technique used for determination of confidence intervals considerably increases the flexibility of experimental design. When designing an experiment to be analyzed by either the t test or the z test, one may determine whether the sample mean differs significantly from the assumed population mean and, if such a difference does exist, determine the probable true population parameter. This is particularly appropriate for both psychometric work and for quantification of some of the significant parameters influencing behavior.

The addition of the Scheffé test to your store of statistical techniques will probably influence your subsequent experimental design. It is now possible for you to select a wide variety of possible experimental treatments, determine the overall significance levels, and compare the individual treatments with one another. Prior to learning this technique, it would have been necessary to design a separate two-group experiment for each specific comparison to be tested.

This Scheffé test is a conservative test and is designed for post hoc comparisons. There may be instances in which the overall test by simple analysis of variance yields results significant at the .05 level, yet none of the specific comparisons are significant at that level. In general, this is due to the fact that any two samples have a smaller N than does the overall distribution. In such cases, further testing with increased N is indicated.

Although sample size is a consideration in all experimental designs, it should be given special consideration when making post hoc comparisons by the Scheffé test. For example, if the experiment is designed so that all of the samples drawn are of equal size, one need only compute a single value of $M\sqrt{RV}$ in order to test all possible comparisons between pairs of means.

Finally, both the confidence-interval approach and the Scheffé test are parametric techniques. Thus, one must first fulfill the assumptions required by the specific test (z test, t test, or analysis of variance) before computing a CI. In designing an experiment for such post hoc analyses, then, one should also consider carefully the design criteria for the underlying test.

SUMMARY

In this chapter, a method for the generation of a confidence interval (CI) for the true population comparison was developed. For all such comparisons, the appropriate computational formula was given as:

$$CI = C \pm M\sqrt{RV}$$

where:

$$CI = \text{confidence interval}$$
$$C = \text{the specific comparison}$$

The remaining parts of this computational formula (M, R, and V) were seen to be a function of the particular prior test of significance. For generation of a confidence interval for the true population mean following a z test, these values became:

$M = 1.96$ for the 95 percent CI or 2.58 for the 99 percent CI
$R = $ reciprocal of the number of scores in the sample $(1/N)$
$V = $ the population variance (σ^2)

For generation of a confidence interval for the true population mean following a t test, these values were:

$M = $ value of t required for significance at $N - 1$ df
$R = $ reciprocal of the number of scores in the sample $(1/N)$
$V = $ estimate of the population variance based on sample data (s^2)

When this technique (referred to as the Scheffé test) was used to test for the significance of a difference between specific means following an overall test by analysis of variance, these values became:

$$M = \sqrt{(J - 1)F}$$

where:

$J = $ the number of means in the overall test
$F = $ value of F required for significance in the overall test

R = sum of the reciprocals of the number of scores in each sample under test $(1/N_1 + 1/N_2)$

V = error MS from the overall test

Use of the CI approach for post hoc comparisons was seen as extending the range of possible experimental designs, in that all possible comparisons between treatments may be made on the basis of a single overall test.

10. Correlation

CORRELATION AS THE RATIO OF TWO VARIANCES

We have indicated that the Scheffé technique may be used to compensate for one restriction to the use of the simple analysis-of-variance technique—the fact that differences between specific pairs of means are not indicated. The second restriction to the use of the simple analysis-of-variance technique is the fact that the scores to be analyzed must be independent samples from the population. The data from psychological experiments, however, are often drawn from correlated, or noninde-pendent samples. In this chapter, a method for determining the strength of the relationship between such correlated scores will be presented. The following chapter will present the technique used for correlated-scores analysis of variance.

Let us, then, turn to correlation and its measurement. We previously encountered the term correlation in relation to the prediction of be-havior when, in Chapter 1, we noted the error of inferring causation from a predictive relationship. The meaning of the term correlation possibly becomes clearer if we divide it: co-relation. That is, a correla-tion indicates a joint relationship between two variables. The word "joint" is important in this definition because it implies that we must have some method of pairing the observations on the variables under consideration. We may pair scores on two variables for a given subject, year, or any of a number of possible items. Of these, you are probably most familiar with the technique of pairing two scores for each subject in an experiment. For example, one might test a person's basic mathe-matical ability and pair the resulting score with his score on a final examination in a math class. Other subjects would be tested to obtain a distribution of these paired scores. In this case, the pairing is across subjects since each subject has both a test score and an examination score. From these data, a correlation between tested mathematical ability and class performance could be obtained.

Other items may also be used as the basis for this pairing. In the facetious example given in the first chapter, the amount of diaper rash was correlated with the number of miles of highway built in Ireland. In this case, month of the year was used for pairing. In each month a number of babies had diaper rash and, for the same month, a number of miles of highway were built in Ireland.

From this particular example, it is easily seen that a correlation, as a way of examining data, is quite different from the methods used to determine the significance of a difference. It is, of course, ridiculous to ask whether there were significantly more babies having diaper rash than there were miles of highway being built in Ireland.

This distinction may become blurred in some studies. For example, if we were to test a person's reaction time following his drinking of a coffee substitute and then retest him following his drinking of coffee, both types of analysis are possible. To ask whether or not drinking coffee increases reaction time is to ask whether or not a significant difference between the two conditions (coffee and no coffee) exists.

To ask whether a correlation exists between the two values, on the other hand, is to ask whether or not the two scores tend to co-vary. That is, do subjects who have a slower than average reaction time after drinking the coffee substitute also tend to have a slower than average reaction time after drinking coffee? This correlational question may legitimately be asked regardless of whether the coffee increases, decreases, or has no effect upon the mean reaction time for the group.

The basic point of a correlation, then, is a question about the variability within two distributions; the differences between means are not involved. Consequently, one might expect the computational formula for determining a correlation to be similar to the formula previously used to compute variance. Although we shall later simplify this equation slightly, the basic formula for a correlation is:

$$r = \frac{\dfrac{\Sigma XY - \dfrac{(\Sigma X)(\Sigma Y)}{N}}{N}}{\sqrt{\left[\dfrac{\Sigma X^2 - \dfrac{(\Sigma X)^2}{N}}{N}\right]\left[\dfrac{\Sigma Y^2 - \dfrac{(\Sigma Y)^2}{N}}{N}\right]}}$$

where:

X, Y = paired scores on two variables, X and Y
N = number of pairs

The denominator of this formula is simply the square root of the product of σ_x^2 and σ_y^2. Thus, this denominator is a type of variance estimate itself. It may be seen that if the two distributions were exactly equal ($X = Y$), this denominator would be:

$$\sqrt{(\sigma_X^2)(\sigma_Y^2)}$$

But if $X = Y$, then:

$$\sqrt{(\sigma_X^2)(\sigma_Y^2)} = \sqrt{(\sigma_X^2)(\sigma_X^2)} = \sqrt{(\sigma_X^2)^2} = \sigma_X^2$$

Only rarely will $X = Y$ and, as a consequence, this denominator expresses the variance of the joint distribution of Xs and Ys. Recall that the computation of variance is independent of the order in which the scores are placed. Thus, this denominator yields the variance of the joint distribution of Xs and Ys without regard to any pairing.

Let us now turn to the numerator of the basic formula. Again, consider what this numerator would be if $X = Y$. The numerator is:

$$\frac{\Sigma XY - \frac{(\Sigma X)(\Sigma Y)}{N}}{N}$$

But if $X = Y$, then:

$$\frac{\Sigma XY - \frac{(\Sigma X)(\Sigma Y)}{N}}{N} = \frac{\Sigma(X \cdot X) - \frac{(\Sigma X)(\Sigma X)}{N}}{N} = \frac{\Sigma X^2 - \frac{(\Sigma X)^2}{N}}{N} = \sigma_x^2$$

The numerator is also an expression of variance, but with one basic difference. The first term, XY, indicates that we are to sum the products of the *paired* scores. This numerator, called the covariance term, reflects the variance of the joint distributions of X and Y when pairing is taken into account. The denominator, as presented above, disregards pairing. A correlation, then, is a ratio between covariance (numerator) and joint, unpaired variance (denominator).

Let us simplify the basic formula and demonstrate both the computational method to be followed and the interrelationship of this covariance to joint variance. The basic formula was:

$$r = \frac{N \dfrac{\Sigma XY - \frac{(\Sigma X)(\Sigma Y)}{N}}{N}}{N\sqrt{\left[\dfrac{\Sigma X^2 - \frac{(\Sigma X)^2}{N}}{N}\right]\left[\dfrac{\Sigma Y^2 - \frac{(\Sigma Y)^2}{N}}{N}\right]}}$$

Multiplying both the numerator and the denominator of this equation by N will not change its value (e.g., multiplying both numerator and denominator of the fraction 1/2 by 4 does not change its value; $1/2 = (1 \cdot 4)/(2 \cdot 4) = 4/8$). This multiplication by N permits us to cancel Ns and yields:

$$r = \frac{\Sigma XY - \frac{(\Sigma X)(\Sigma Y)}{N}}{\sqrt{\left[\Sigma X^2 - \frac{(\Sigma X)^2}{N}\right]\left[\Sigma Y^2 - \frac{(\Sigma Y)^2}{N}\right]}}$$

Repeating this multiplication of both numerator and denominator by N finally yields the computational formula to be used for the remainder of the chapter:

$$r = \frac{N\Sigma XY - (\Sigma X)(\Sigma Y)}{\sqrt{[N\Sigma X^2 - (\Sigma X)^2][N\Sigma Y^2 - (\Sigma Y)^2]}}$$

COMPUTATIONAL EXAMPLE

As an example of the use of this formula, consider the two fictitious distributions of scores given in Table 10.1. The X scores are IQ scores and the Y scores are college GPA's. The pair of scores, P_1, would be an IQ score and college GPA for a single individual. The second pair, P_2, would be IQ and GPA scores for a second individual, etc. The scores illustrated in Table 10.1 are obviously not typical scores that one might expect to obtain by random sampling but are scores which were spe-

TABLE 10.1.   IQ and college GPA for four college students

PAIR	X (IQ)	Y (GPA)
P_1	90	1.00
P_2	100	2.00
P_3	110	3.00
P_4	120	4.00

$$\Sigma X = 420 \qquad \Sigma Y = 10.00$$
$$\Sigma X^2 = 44,600 \qquad \Sigma Y^2 = 30.00$$
$$\Sigma XY = 1,100$$
$$N = 4$$

$$r = \frac{N\Sigma XY - (\Sigma X)(\Sigma Y)}{\sqrt{[N\Sigma X^2 - (\Sigma X)^2][N\Sigma Y^2 - (\Sigma Y)^2]}}$$

$$= \frac{4(1,100) - (420)(10)}{\sqrt{[4(44,600) - (420)^2][4(30) - (10)^2]}}$$

$$= \frac{4,400 - 4,200}{\sqrt{[178,400 - 176,400][120 - 100]}}$$

$$= \frac{+200}{\sqrt{(2,000)(20)}} = \frac{+200}{\sqrt{40,000}} = \frac{+200}{200} = +1.00$$

cifically drawn to illustrate the maximum value of the correlation coefficient, $r = +1.00$.

All of the computations follow the procedures previously given for variance derivations with the exception of ΣXY. This term indicates that we are to sum the cross products of the pairs of scores, where a *cross product* is an X score multiplied by its corresponding Y score. In this example, $\Sigma XY = (90)(1.00) + (100)(2.00) + (110)(3.00) + (120)(4.00) = 1100$. Here N is the number of *pairs*, not the total number of different scores. The final computation of r follows logically once ΣX, ΣX^2, ΣY, ΣY^2, ΣXY, and N are found. In the example in Table 10.1, the final value of r is found to be $+1.00$.

What does this value of r indicate? It indicates the existence of a perfect (or invariant), direct, linear relationship between the two variables of IQ and college GPA. To illustrate the meaning of each of these terms, consider what the original data would look like if graphed. This graph is shown in Figure 10.1. As noted there, each pair of points lies exactly on a straight line (called a regression line). The $r = +1.00$ is termed a perfect, or invariant, relationship because all of the points fall exactly on this regression line. If the points were merely close to the regression line, but not exactly on it, the value of r would be less than 1.00.

The term "direct relationship" indicates that as IQ values increase, values of college GPA also increase. The directionality of the relation-

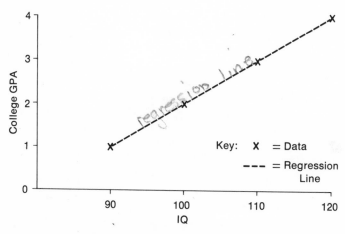

FIGURE 10.1. Graph illustrating the $r = +1.00$ relationship for the data presented in Table 10.1.

ship is expressed by the sign of the correlation. A positive correlation (such as the +1.00 in this example) is a direct relationship whereas a negative correlation indicates an inverse relationship.

Finally, by the term linear we mean that the correlation coefficient measures only the tendency for the paired data points to fall on a straight line. Suppose, in this respect, that paired data for five subjects on two variables resembled that presented in Table 10.2.

The computed value of r for these five paired scores is zero. One of the common mistakes made in the interpretation of a correlation coefficient is to assume that an $r = 0$ indicates no relationship between the pairs. The fallacy of such an interpretation is easily seen when the data of this example are graphed as in Figure 10.2. As illustrated there, an inverted U function fits the data quite nicely. This relationship, however, is curvilinear rather than linear and consequently the $r = 0$. The correlation coefficient, then, is a measure only of the linear relationship between two variables.

TABLE 10.2.   Hypothetical measurements of five subjects on two variables

PAIR NO.	X	Y
P_1	1	1
P_2	2	2
P_3	3	3
P_4	4	2
P_5	5	1
	$\Sigma X = 15$	$\Sigma Y = 9$
	$\Sigma X^2 = 55$	$\Sigma Y^2 = 19$
	$\Sigma XY = 27$	
	$N = 5$	

$$r = \frac{N\Sigma XY - (\Sigma X)(Y)}{\sqrt{[N\Sigma X^2 - (\Sigma X^2)][N\Sigma Y^2 - (\Sigma Y)^2]}}$$

$$= \frac{5(27 - (15)(9)}{\sqrt{[5(55) - (15)^2][5(19) - (9)^2]}} = \frac{135 - 135}{\sqrt{[275 - 225][95 - 81]}}$$

$$= \frac{0}{\sqrt{(50)(14)}} = \frac{0}{\sqrt{700}} = 0$$

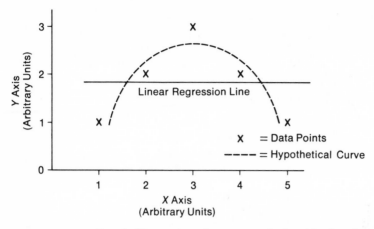

FIGURE 10.2. Graph illustrating the $r = 0$ relationship for the data presented in Table 10.2. Note that this relationship is curvilinear and so is not detected by the correlation coefficient, which measures only linear relationships.

Let us examine some of the other characteristics of the correlation coefficient which differentiate it from other statistics that we have discussed. Perhaps you have discovered through trial and error that a negative sum of squares in an analysis of variance design indicates the presence of an arithmetic mistake, since less than no variance is impossible to attain. In computation of a correlation coefficient, though, a negative covariance term is possible. Perhaps a computational example will serve to illustrate this point. Consider the hypothetical data in Table 10.3, listing errors in a verbal learning task as a function of the IQ of the subject.

The computation of the correlation coefficient from the data given in this table yields a value of $r = -1.00$; and we can see that a correlation coefficient may have either positive or negative values. The data illustrated in Table 10.1 presents the maximum positive value of r ($+1.00$); the data from Table 10.3 illustrates the maximum negative value of r (-1.00). All correlation coefficients must fall between these two values. If a value of r greater than $+1.00$ or less than -1.00 is obtained, one may assume that an arithmetic mistake in computation has been made.

The relationship between the errors in a verbal learning task and Ss

207

TABLE 10.3. IQ and errors in a verbal learning task

PAIR	X (IQ)	Y (ERRORS)
P_1	90	4
P_2	100	3
P_3	110	2
P_4	120	1

$$\Sigma X = 420 \qquad \Sigma Y = 10$$
$$\Sigma X^2 = 44{,}600 \qquad \Sigma Y^2 = 30$$
$$\Sigma XY = 1{,}000$$
$$N = 4$$

$$r = \frac{N\Sigma XY - (\Sigma X)(\Sigma Y)}{\sqrt{[N\Sigma X^2 - (\Sigma X)^2][N\Sigma Y^2 - (\Sigma Y)^2]}}$$

$$= \frac{4(1{,}000) - (420)(10)}{\sqrt{[4(44{,}600) - (420)^2][4(30) - (10)^2]}}$$

$$= \frac{4{,}000 - 4{,}200}{\sqrt{[178{,}400 - 176{,}400][120 - 100]}}$$

$$= \frac{-200}{\sqrt{(2{,}000)(20)}} = \frac{-200}{\sqrt{40{,}000}} = \frac{-200}{200} = -1.00$$

IQ is visually presented in Figure 10.3. The relation illustrated here is a perfect (invariant), inverse, linear relationship. That is, as the subject's IQ increases, the number of errors made in the verbal learning task decreases. A negative correlation coefficient, then, indicates that values of one variable are increasing simultaneously with decreases in the second variable. You should note that a negative correlation coefficient is not a "bad" correlation coefficient to obtain. The negative sign merely indicates the direction of the slope of the line when the data are plotted graphically. In this particular case, you will notice that, had the number of correct responses in the verbal task been plotted, the resulting correlation coefficient would have been +1.00. One often finds that the sign of the correlation coefficient is a function of the measure used as one of the variables.

Other examples might include the possible use of either speed of a rat's running or the latency of his running response. A correlation coefficient between speed of a rat's running and deprivation time is

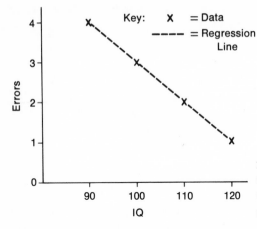

FIGURE 10.3. Graph illus-
trating the $r = -1.00$ relationship for the data presented in Table 10.3.

likely to be positive. If, on the other hand, one were to compute the
coefficient between the latency of the rat's running response and deprivation time, the correlation coefficient would probably be negative;
i.e., the hungrier the rat is, the shorter time it will take him to reach a
food reward.

Let us examine in greater detail the factor which causes correlation
coefficients to vary between $+1.00$ and -1.00. The formula that we
have previously given for r is in every respect algebraically equivalent
to the following:

$$r = \frac{\Sigma xy}{N\sigma_x \sigma_y}$$

where x and y are deviation values (see Chapter 4). Use of this formula
would, however, be very difficult computationally. For each value of
X, we would be required to determine a deviation value and multiply
it by the corresponding deviation value for the Y score. If each of the
deviation values for the X variable corresponded to similar deviation
values for the Y variable, the upper portion of this formula would be
the sum of squared deviations from the mean. In such an instance the
numerator and denominator would be equal, resulting in a correlation
coefficient of 1.00. This would be the typical method of finding the
variance of a single distribution, i.e., to square the deviations from the
mean. Consider now the negative correlation that we have previously
illustrated. In each pair of scores, a positive deviation from the mean
on one variable was accompanied by a negative deviation from the

TABLE 10.4. Relationships of deviation cross products (data derived from Tables 10.1 and 10.3)

FROM TABLE 10.1			FROM TABLE 10.3		
x (IQ)	y (GPA)	xy	x (IQ)	y (ERRORS)	xy
−15	−1.5	22.5	−15	1.5	−22.5
− 5	− .5	2.5	− 5	.5	− 2.5
5	.5	2.5	5	− .5	− 2.5
15	1.5	22.5	15	−1.5	−22.5
Σx = 0	Σy = 0	Σxy = 50.0	Σx = 0	Σy = 0	Σxy = −50.0

mean on the other variable. The cross product of these would be a negative value. This point is illustrated more clearly in Table 10.4 which combines the data previously presented in Tables 10.1 and 10.3. Note that we have replaced each of the original observations by its appropriate deviation score. In the data originally presented in Table 10.1, all of the products of the X scores are positive. Each positive x deviation value is accompanied by a positive y deviation value. Each negative x deviation value is accompanied by a negative y deviation value. In contrast, the data from Table 10.3 indicate that each positive X deviation value is paired with a negative Y deviation value and vice versa. Each of the products, then, is a negative value, resulting in a total sum negative value.

Of course, correlations may have values other than +1.00, −1.00 or 0, although all of the examples so far used to illustrate some of the characteristics of the correlation coefficient have yielded only these values. Actually, it would be very unusual for data gathered from an actual experiment to yield a perfect correlation. For example, consider the data presented in Table 10.5. These data are horizontal and vertical errors made in a two-dimensional performance task (17). The scores are for 20 subjects for the tenth trial of this task. Note that in this case the pairing variable is subjects. The computation of the value of the correlation coefficient for these data is presented in the lower portion of Table 10.5 and follows the form of the computational formula rather than that of the deviation formula.

The Regression Equation

What meaning may we attach to this computed value of r? One use that we may make of the correlation coefficient is predicting what

TABLE 10.5. X-axis and Y-axis errors in a two-dimensional performance

SUBJECT NO.	X-AXIS ERROR	Y-AXIS ERROR	PREDICTED Y (Y')
1	15.6	21.3	20.68
2	11.4	12.1	15.77
3	6.7	9.4	10.27
4	7.4	12.0	11.09
5	12.0	15.3	16.47
6	9.9	11.3	14.01
7	4.3	1.2	7.46
8	14.3	25.8	19.16
9	7.5	12.6	11.21
10	11.7	22.5	16.12
11	9.2	12.1	13.19
12	17.2	27.9	22.55
13	14.7	15.0	19.63
14	4.1	10.7	7.23
15	11.5	14.4	15.89
16	20.0	24.6	25.83
17	7.7	15.3	11.44
18	15.6	13.5	20.68
19	10.2	15.6	14.36
20	4.6	8.1	7.81

$$\Sigma X = 215.6 \qquad \Sigma Y = 300.7$$
$$\Sigma X^2 = 2{,}704.58 \qquad \Sigma Y^2 = 5{,}328.47$$
$$\Sigma XY = 3{,}687.29$$
$$N = 20$$

$$r = \frac{N\Sigma XY - (\Sigma X)(\Sigma Y)}{\sqrt{[N\Sigma X^2 - (\Sigma X)^2][N\Sigma Y^2 - (\Sigma Y)^2]}}$$

$$= \frac{(20)(3{,}687.29) - (215.6)(300.7)}{\sqrt{[(20)(2{,}704.58) - (215.6)^2][(20)(5{,}328.47) - (300.7)^2]}}$$

$$= \frac{8{,}914.88}{\sqrt{122{,}864{,}783}} = +.804$$

value on one variable would be obtained when a particular value on the
other is known. For example, from the data listed in Table 10.5 it is
apparent that high X-axis errors correspond rather closely to high
Y-axis errors. If, then, we knew an individual's X score, would it be

possible to predict his error in the Y axis? It seems apparent from the graphic illustration of the data in Table 10.5 that although an exact relationship does not exist between these two types of errors, a systematic relationship does exist. The line drawn in Figure 10.4 is known as a regression line. This line is drawn to minimize the sum of the squared deviations of the plotted points from that line. Note that this regression line comes close to many data points but actually touches very few of them. The regression line that is shown here gives our best prediction of a Y score from a known X score. The equation for finding this line is very simple. The regression equation for determining a predicted Y score (Y') from a given X score is:

$$Y' = r \frac{\sigma_y}{\sigma_x} (X - \bar{X}) + \bar{Y}$$

The predicted value of Y is given the symbol Y' to indicate that it is not an actual score but rather is a predicted score. Given this equation, we can determine the best prediction of the value of Y from any X value, when the values of $r, \sigma_x, \sigma_y, \bar{X},$ and $\bar{Y}$ are known.

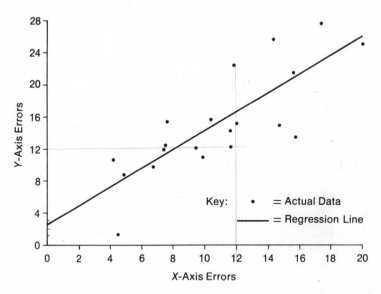

FIGURE 10.4. Graphic illustration of the data previously presented in Table 10.5 relating X-axis and Y-axis errors in a two-dimensional performance. The equation of the regression line is: $Y' = 1.17X + 2.43$.

For the data listed in Table 10.5, the regression equation for estimating Y from X is:

$$Y' = (.804)\frac{(6.35)}{4.36}(X - 10.78) + 15.04 = 1.17\,(X - 10.78) + 15.04 =$$

$$1.17X - 12.61 + 15.04 = 1.17X + 2.43$$

where:

$$\sigma_x = 4.36$$
$$\sigma_y = 6.35$$
$$\bar{X} = 10.78$$
$$\bar{Y} = 15.04$$

Predicted values of Y for each of the X values are given in the right-hand side of Table 10.5. Although the predicted values of Y do not agree exactly with the actual value of Y, the difference between predicted and actual scores is very small with respect to the total range of Y-axis errors.

The predicted value of Y is a measure of the stability of a person's performance on both X- and Y-axis performance. If those who perform well on the X-axis portion also perform well on the Y-axis portion, a high correlation will be obtained. In turn, then, the predictions of Y from known values of X will be relatively accurate (i.e., the errors in prediction, $Y' - Y$, will be small). If systematic differences between individuals on this task are minimal (an individual who is high on X-axis tracking errors may have high, medium, or low Y-axis errors), the resulting correlation coefficient will be low. The $Y' - Y$ errors of prediction from the regression equation would, in this case, tend to be nearly as large as the original range of Y scores. Thus, the degree to which errors in prediction are minimized is an indication of the extent of systematic individual differences.

The extremes of this effect are given by r values of ± 1.00 and 0. For r values of ± 1.00, there are no errors in prediction; each Y value may be predicted exactly. With an r of 0, the variance of errors of prediction is equal to the variance of the original Y values.

In an experiment one might employ a regression equation to determine whether or not a particular treatment had an effect. Let us say that we have used a different instructional set for our task and believe that it should reduce the Y-axis errors. If we have been able to predict these Y-axis errors through a regression equation similar to that given above then we may determine how much the new instructions *improve* each person's performance. In this instance, we would not be concerned with the total range of performances (differences between individuals), but with the amount of improvement irrespective of the actual level of performance. To some extent, this would eliminate individual differences between the subjects as a source of error variance. This will be discussed in more detail in the next chapter.

One might also use a regression equation in predicting performance on one test from known scores on another test. For example, admission to college may be based on aptitude tests. In the selection of those individuals who are to be admitted to school, an implicit regression equation is assumed between college grades (Y scores) and performance on an intellectual aptitude test (X scores). Such a regression equation permits the college officials to determine which applicants for admission would be most likely to succeed in college and which would be most likely to fail.

Note, in the regression equation formulated above, that this prediction will not be exactly correct in most cases. It is possible that some students for whom success is predicted will, in fact, fail college. It is also possible that some of the students for whom failure is predicted would have succeeded in college, had they been given the chance. The regression equation, when used in such cases, predicts for the average rather than for any individual. An individual prediction from a regression equation is always subject to error, although the resulting prediction is more accurate than a prediction made without such an equation.

If the correlation coefficient used to determine the equation of the regression line is not zero, and provided that the underlying relationship between the two variables is linear, the use of this regression equation is a better method of prediction than any alternative. Further, we have seen that as the correlation coefficient approaches either +1.00 or −1.00, i.e., as the size of the correlation coefficient increases (irrespective of the sign of that correlation) the predictions become increasingly accurate. One of the primary uses of the correlation coefficient is in the prediction of the value of one variable from another variable.

Sampling Distribution of r

In addition to the value of correlation in prediction, a second use of the correlation coefficient is as a descriptive measure. For example, although we find that there is a correlation of +.673 between the measured IQ's of identical twins, we may have no interest in predicting one twin's IQ from the other twin's. In such a case, we may wish to use the correlation coefficient simply as a descriptive coefficient to describe the strength of the existing relationship. In such an instance, it is necessary to realize that, as with an analysis of variance or a *t* test, the correlation coefficient exhibits a distribution of values which would be expected to occur by chance alone. This distribution enables us to determine whether or not a given correlation coefficient is significantly different from zero.

Consider the possibility that we have only two pairs of data from which to work. As illustrated in Figure 10.5, the *X* score of one of these scores may either be paired with the low *Y* score or with the high *Y* score. Similarly, the low *X* score may either be paired with the high *Y* score or the low *Y* score. In such an instance, the correlation coefficient would always be either +1.00 or −1.00, and we see that a perfect correlation is to be expected when only two pairs are included in the data. This may also be demonstrated by the regression lines drawn in each portion of Figure 10.5. Given any two paired data points, a straight line can always be drawn through them. Even a perfect correlation of 1.00 may not be significant if the number of pairs is too small.

This, then, indicates that the important variable to consider when determining the significance of a correlation is the number of pairs involved in that correlation. In fact, the *only* significant parameter influencing the variability of a correlation is the number of pairs, and the standard error of a correlation may be expressed only in terms of *N*.

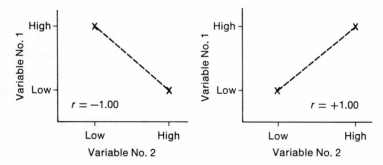

FIGURE 10.5. When only two pairs of data points are available for analysis, only two unique relationships are possible.

SIGNIFICANCE OF *r*

Since no other values are required, tabled values of significant correlations at various levels of N have been determined. These are presented in Appendix E, listing the significant levels of r for the 5 percent and 1 percent levels of confidence. If the computed value of the correlation is greater than or equal to the tabled value, irrespective of whether the value is positive or negative, we may conclude that we have a significant correlation. Entry to this table requires the use of degrees of freedom, similar to that previously used for both the t test and analysis of variance. In this case, however, $df = N - 2$, where N is the *number of pairs* involved in the correlation.

Let us determine the significance of the correlation coefficient for the data in Table 10.5. The computed value was +.804 with 20 pairs. For these data, the degrees of freedom is $N - 2$ or 18. Appendix E shows that for 18 degrees of freedom the smallest significant r at the 1 percent level is .561. Therefore, the obtained r of +.804 is clearly significant at the .01 level.

Since the null hypothesis states that our sample r is not different from a population coefficient of zero, we may reject it. If the study were replicated under the same conditions, a positive value of r would probably be obtained again. There is less than one chance in 100 of obtaining a sample r of +.804 if the population coefficient were 0.

As seen in Appendix E, relatively small values of r may be significant when computed from a sufficiently large number of pairs. For example, at 125 degrees of freedom, the 1 percent r is .228. In addition to knowing the probability that such a coefficient might have occurred by chance alone, we might also like to know the predictive power of this correlation. In general, we would find that the predictive power of a correlation is equal to the square of the correlation itself. A correlation of .50 is not just half the value of a correlation of 1.00, but rather is only about one quarter as valuable in the elimination of errors of prediction.

At 125 degrees of freedom, then, a correlation coefficient that is significant at the .01 level ($r = .228$) has only approximately 1/20 the value in eliminating errors of prediction as a correlation of 1.00 from the same number of pairs. It is for this reason that many of our standardized tests of intelligence, reading, achievement abilities, and so forth insist that the reliability correlation not only be significant but also be high (usually .90 or higher). As the correlation drops, predictability (reliability) also suffers. There might appear to be very little difference between a reported correlation coefficient of .95 and one of .90. However, we find that the lower of these two correlations is approximately 90 percent as accurate as is the higher of the two (.95² = .9025; .90² = .8100).

This approximation of the value of a correlation coefficient stems from the relationship between errors of prediction from a regression line and the original scores of that distribution. If we have computed a correlation coefficient between two variables, X and Y, we may form a regression equation for the prediction of Y values from known values of X. The variance of the original distribution of Y scores would be σ_y^2. If we now subtract predicted value of Y from each actual value of Y, we tend to eliminate that portion of the variance due to individual differences, leaving only a distribution of the errors of prediction. If such a procedure were followed, we would find that the variance of this distribution of errors of prediction would be $(1 - r^2)\sigma_y^2$. Thus, we may speak of the reduction of the variance of a distribution through use of a correlation. It is this reduction in variance that we shall use in the following chapter when we discuss correlated-scores analysis of variance.

DESIGN CONSIDERATIONS

One of the first factors to consider when designing a correlational study is that causation may not be inferred from the results. As noted in Chapter 8, the process of gathering converging evidence to determine causation from such studies is, theoretically, an infinite one. If the detection of causal relationships is to be the research goal, then one should use an experimental method, not the correlational approach.

However, the correlational method is nonetheless of considerable value to the progress of psychology as a science. There are many problems which cannot be investigated experimentally, yet are of both theoretical and practical importance. Such studies have provided psychology with much of its systematic knowledge regarding the interrelationships of the various parameters of behavior occurring naturally.

In the design of correlational studies, it is important to know the range of scores likely to occur in both variables. Since the correlation coefficient involves the cross products of values of the two variables, it is necessary to have an adequate sample of the total range of values which might be expected to occur. Any restriction in this range reduces the value of the correlation coefficient. If this reduced value of *r* is then employed in a regression equation for purposes of prediction, the resulting predictions are likely to be seriously in error.

A second factor to be considered is the reliability of the measures of the two variables being correlated. Since reliability is the correlation of the variable with itself (in a test–retest situation), any reduction in reliability will necessarily reduce the value of a subsequent correlation of that variable with another. Thus, where there is a choice of measures of the variables studied, preference should be given to the most reliable.

The reliabilty of measurement also has definite implications for the actual conduct of the study. The fact that causation cannot be inferred from correlation does not excuse a poorly controlled study. As noted earlier, the lack of adequate control reduces reliability. This, in turn, would decrease the value of any correlation coefficient computed from the study.

Finally, correlational studies usually involve a larger *N* than may typically be found in an experimental test. This helps to insure that the total range of values of the two variables has been tested and also increases the probability of detecting a systematic relationship.

SUMMARY

We have developed a method for determining the strength of the relationship between correlated scores. The computational formula was presented as:

$$r = \frac{N\Sigma XY - (\Sigma X)(\Sigma Y)}{\sqrt{[N\Sigma X^2 - (\Sigma X)^2][N\Sigma Y^2 - (\Sigma Y)^2]}}$$

where:

r = Pearson product-moment correlation coefficient
N = number of pairs of scores
X = an individual's score on variable X
Y = an individual's score on variable Y

The significance of the resulting coefficient is determined by entry to Appendix E, using:

$$df = N - 2$$

Values of r range from $+1.00$ to -1.00. Complete linear association is indicated by an r coefficient of ± 1.00. The absence of a linear relationship between the variables is indicated by an r value of 0.

Predictions of any Y value can be made from known X values if a regression equation has been formulated. This equation is:

$$Y' = r \frac{\sigma_y}{\sigma_x} (X - \bar{X}) + \bar{Y}$$

where:

Y' = predicted value of Y

σ_y, σ_x = standard deviations of the distributions of Y and X variables, respectively

The degree to which a given value of r is effective in reducing errors of prediction was found to be equal to the square of that correlation coefficient. The division of the variance of a distribution of scores into parts attributable to individual differences and to errors of prediction was shown to be important in the development of a technique for the analysis of variance of correlated scores.

11. Correlated=Scores Analysis of Variance

CORRELATIONAL VS. ANALYTIC ANALYSES

We have studied one method for analyzing nonindependent scores—
the correlation coefficient. This method, however, is limited to answer-
ing questions about the degree of relationship existing between two
distributions. We have also seen that the value of the correlation coef-
ficent is independent of the means of the two distributions. Thus, with
a test of reaction time under normal conditions followed by a similar

test under experimental conditions, the value of r may be positive irrespective of whether the experimental condition increased, decreased, or had no effect upon reaction time.

As a result of this characteristic of r, the correlational approach to data analysis is unsuited for many experimental questions that one might like to ask. For such questions, though, the material in the previous chapter leads to a method which can be used for the analysis of variance of correlated scores.

If we have measured the performance of a group of subjects under standard conditions and also under experimental conditions, the scores obtained might resemble those presented in Table 11.1. Note that both a correlational approach and an analytic approach are possible with these data. The correlation coefficient would be computed to determine whether or not individuals tend to retain their relative positions under the two conditions. The analytic question is concerned with whether or not there is a significant difference between the mean performances for the two conditions.

Had the scores in Table 11.1 been independent samples, a simple analysis of variance could have been computed to answer the analytic question. The results of such an analysis would have indicated no significant difference between the two means, since the observed difference (the between MS) is small with respect to the large range of scores within each group (within MS). This would indicate a high probability that the experimental treatment had no effect on the performance of this task.

When we inspect these data as correlated rather than independent scores, we arrive at a somewhat different conclusion. Visual inspection

TABLE 11.1. Correlated scores obtained under standard and experimental conditions

SUBJECT NO.	NORMAL SCORE	EXPERIMENTAL SCORE
1	1	3
2	5	6
3	6	9
4	25	30
5	100	105
	$\bar{X}_C = 27.4$	$\bar{X}_E = 30.6$

of the data in Table 11.1 shows that every subject's score increased under the experimental condition. This improvement ranged between one and five points. Now we must ask a somewhat different question of the data. What is the probability that, due to chance alone, all of the subjects would have shown this increase in performance? Restated, we are interested in whether or not the treatment effect is large with respect to the within-groups variance when differences between individuals are eliminated.

Let us examine this question in more detail. The correlational approach to data analysis presented in the last chapter was specifically designed to detect systematic relationships between paired scores. Since the basic explanation of r was in terms of variance, it seems apparent that some communality should exist. This relationship becomes more apparent if one examines the concept of the variance of errors in prediction as based on a regression equation.

We saw in Chapter 6 that the total variance from the combined distribution of two or more samples could be divided into its component parts: that portion of the total variance due to differences between groups and that portion attributable to within groups variability. In the last chapter, a similar situation was shown to exist for correlated scores. The total variance in a distribution of correlated scores could be divided into a portion due to systematic individual differences and a portion attributable to errors in prediction.

LOGICAL DEVELOPMENT

The technique used for the analysis of variance of samples of correlated scores simply combines two techniques. That is, if two or more samples of correlated scores are available for analysis, the total variance of the combined distribution may be apportioned between (1) differences between samples (the treatment effect), (2) systematic differences between individuals (the correlated portion), and (3) error.

The only problem associated with such an analysis is the determination of where these three aspects of the distribution of scores are represented and a demonstration of independence of these portions of the scores. Consider, in this respect, the hypothetical data represented in Table 11.2. The scores here represent data from three individuals, where each has participated under three different experimental conditions. In part A of this table, the scores (X) for each sub-

TABLE 11.2.   Analysis of treatment, subjects, and error effects

A. BASIC DATA

SUBJECT	TREATMENT 1	TREATMENT 2	TREATMENT 3	ΣX_I
1	2	1	3	6
2	3	5	4	12
3	4	6	8	18
ΣX_J	9	12	15	
$\bar{X}_J$	3	4	5	
— (Deviation)	1	0	−1	

B. CORRECTED FOR TREATMENT EFFECT

SUBJECT	TREATMENT 1	TREATMENT 2	TREATMENT 3	$\Sigma \dot{X}_I$	$\bar{X}_I$
1	3	1	2	6	2
2	4	5	3	12	4
3	5	6	7	18	6
ΣX_J	12	12	12		

C. CORRECTED FOR INDIVIDUAL DIFFERENCES

SUBJECT	TREATMENT 1	TREATMENT 2	TREATMENT 3	ΣX_I
1	5	3	4	12
2	4	5	3	12
3	3	4	5	12
ΣX_J	12	12	12	

ject (I) under each condition (J) are listed, together with the sums of the scores for each treatment (ΣX_J) and for each subject (ΣX_I). If each of the treatment means was expressed as a deviation from the over-all mean of four, then one could eliminate all treatment effects by add-ing this deviation with sign changed to each score. This has been accomplished in part B of Table 11.2. Since the Treatment-1 mean of 3 is a deviation of −1 from the overall mean of 4, we add −(−1) or +1 to each of the three scores in that treatment. A similar process has been followed for the other two treatments.

You should note that the effect of the various treatments has been completely eliminated in part B of the table. Since differences between the three subjects still remain, changes in treatment effects may be considered to be independent of individual differences. This is shown in the ΣX_I column of the A and B portions of the table. Further, if one had first corrected for the differences in ΣX_I, he would find that these changes would not affect differences due to treatment effects.

The third source of variation in the basic data may be illustrated by correcting part B for individual differences. Again, since S_1's mean of 2 is a deviation of -2 from the overall mean, we add $-(-2)$ or $+2$ to each of S_1's treatment-corrected scores, e.g., $3 + 2 = 5, 1 + 2 = 3$, etc. These scores, shown in part C of the table, have been doubly corrected. We find no differences due either to ΣX_J or to ΣX_I.

The remaining differences between the scores in part C of the table may be called error, and are similar to the errors of prediction based on a regression equation. We may compute an estimate of population variance based on these errors and use it as the denominator in an F ratio for determining the significance of our treatment effects. This is the basis for correlated-scores analysis of variance.

Fortunately, the actual computaton procedures usually employed are not as complicated as the previous analysis might indicate. In view of the possible rounding errors in the correction process, such a direct computation of the error variance is usually avoided.

Computational Methods

In the indirect method both the Total Sum of Squares and the Treatment Sum of Squares are found in a manner identical to that previously used for simple analysis of variance. In addition, however, a Subjects Sum of Squares is computed by using the ΣX_I column as if it also reflected a treatment effect. Finally, the Error Sum of Squares is found by:

$$\text{Error } SS = \text{Total } SS - \text{Treatment } SS - \text{Subjects } SS$$

As an example, let us assume that an experiment has been conducted to determine the effect of sleep deprivation on the accuracy of dart throwing. Each subject is tested under conditions of 0, 24, and 48 hours sleep deprivation and the order of participation of subjects in these conditions is counterbalanced to eliminate both the effects of practice and of cumulative fatigue. A recording of the data for six subjects might resemble that shown in Table 11.3. For these data, a higher score indicates greater accuracy of performance.

There may be some confusion in the interpretation of such a table

TABLE 11.3.   Dart-throwing scores as a function of sleep deprivation

| | HOURS SLEEP DEPRIVATION | | | |
SUBJECT NO.	0	24	48	ΣX_I
1	10	8	5	23
2	12	10	8	30
3	9	6	4	19
4	14	12	9'	35
5	18	15	13	46
6	15	14	10	39
	$\Sigma X_J = 78$	65	49	$\Sigma\Sigma_{i,j} = 192$

$$\text{Total } SS = 10^2 + 8^2 + \ldots + 10^2 - \frac{(192)^2}{18} = 242.00$$

$$\text{Treatment } SS = \frac{(78)^2}{6} + \frac{(65)^2}{6} + \frac{(49)^2}{6} - \frac{(192)^2}{18} = 70.33$$

$$\text{Subjects } SS = \frac{(23)^2}{3} + \frac{(30)^2}{3} + \ldots + \frac{(39)^2}{3} - \frac{(192)^2}{18} = 169.33$$

$$\text{Error } SS = 242.00 - 70.33 - 169.33 = 2.34$$

unless there is some systematic method for designating any particular score or sum derived from the table. It is convenient to use subscripts for this purpose. Since we have previously used J to indicate the number of treatment means in the Scheffé test, we have used the same notation here. The subjects are designated as I, so that the score of any one of the subjects (I) on any one of the treatments (J) is $X_{i,j}$. As an example, if we refer to $X_{2,3}$ we mean the score of Subject No. 2 on Treatment 3. In Table 11.3, the value of $X_{2,3}$ is 8. A sum for a particular subject—say, Subject No. 4—would then become $\overset{J}{\underset{j=1}{\Sigma}} X_{4,j}$ where the additonal indicators above and below the summation sign indicate that values of j are to be successively taken from one to J. For this particular example then, we would take the values $X_{4,1}, X_{4,2}, X_{4,3}$; and sum them. The sum for Subject No. 4 is $14 + 12 + 9 = 35$. Similarly,

225

$\sum\limits_{i=1}^{I} X_{i,2}$ will be the sum for Treatment 2 and is determined by letting i successively take the values 1, 2, 3, 4, 5, and 6. Finally, the sum for the overall table $(X_{i,j})$ may be designated as $\sum\limits_{i=1}^{I} \sum\limits_{j=1}^{J} X_{i,j}$.

The computations for all sums of squares are shown in the lower portion of Table 11.3. The Total SS is given by:

$$\text{Total } SS = \Sigma X_{i,j}^{2} - \frac{\left[\sum\limits_{i=1}^{I} \sum\limits_{j=1}^{J} X_{i,j} \right]^{2}}{N}$$

or:

$$= 10^{2} + 8^{2} + \cdots + 10^{2} - \frac{(192)^{2}}{18} = 242.00$$

The Treatment SS is given by:

$$\text{Treatment } SS = \sum\limits_{j=1}^{J} \frac{\left[\sum\limits_{i=1}^{I} X_{i,j} \right]^{2}}{I} - \frac{\left[\sum\limits_{i=1}^{I} \sum\limits_{j=1}^{J} X_{i,j} \right]^{2}}{N}$$

or:

$$= \frac{(78)^{2}}{6} + \frac{(65)^{2}}{6} + \frac{(49)^{2}}{6} - \frac{(192)^{2}}{18} = 70.33$$

The Subjects SS is given by:

$$\text{Subjects } SS = \sum\limits_{i=1}^{I} \frac{\left[\sum\limits_{j=1}^{J} X_{i,j} \right]^{2}}{J} - \frac{\left[\sum\limits_{i=1}^{I} \sum\limits_{j=1}^{J} X_{i,j} \right]^{2}}{N}$$

or:

$$= \frac{(23)^{2}}{3} + \frac{(30)^{2}}{3} + \cdots + \frac{(39)^{2}}{3} - \frac{(192)^{2}}{18} = 169.33$$

Finally, the Error SS is:

$$\text{Error } SS = \text{Total } SS - \text{Treatment } SS - \text{Subjects } SS$$

or:

$$= 242.00 - 70.33 - 169.33 = 2.34$$

Key
I = number of subjects
i = individual subject
J = number of treatments
j = individual treatment
$X_{i,j}$ = single score of subject i with treatment j
ΣX_I = sum of subject scores
ΣX_J = sum of treatment scores

As you recall, these SS are not variance estimates but must be divided by their respective df in order to yield estimates of the population variance. Again the Total df will be equal to $N - 1$. For the data of Table 11.3, total df is $18 - 1 = 17$. Similarly, the Treatment df will be $J - 1$ or $3 - 1 = 2$. May we then say that the remaining df are associated with the Error SS? No, for we have the additional restriction that each subject's scores must total to his particular sum. Thus, of the remaining df, $I - 1$ or $6 - 1 = 5$ are associated with the Subjects SS. Of the original 17 df, then, two are associated with treatments and five are associated with subjects, leaving $(I - 1)(J - 1)$ or $(2)(5) = 10$ df to be associated with the error. These df, and the subsequent computations of MS, are shown in Table 11.4. As before, the MS column is derived by dividing each SS by its corresponding df.

Finally, F ratios are computed for both systematic effects (Treatments and Subjects) by dividing their MS by the Error MS. The determination of the p values for each of these F ratios follows the same procedure previously used for simple analysis of variance. That is, the required value of F for Treatment is found by using 2, 10 df as an entry into the F table, and the required F value for Subjects is found with 5, 10 df.

TABLE 11.4. Summary table: analysis of variance (correlated) for data in Table 11.3

SOURCE	SS	df	MS	F	p
Treatment	70.33	2	35.17	150.30	<.001
Subjects	169.33	5	33.87	144.74	
Error	2.34	10	.234		
Total	242.00	17			

In some cases, the entire row for Subjects as a source of variance may be excluded from the final summary table, since a significant F ratio there indicates that different subjects do, in fact, perform differently on the basic task. This value has been included in the present summary table (Table 11.4) because of its further implications to experimental design and the understanding of the basic concept of correlated-scores analysis of variance.

Correlated vs. Simple Analysis of Variance

Let us examine this Subjects SS more closely. Consider what the analysis of the data would have been had each of the scores listed in Table 11.3 been derived from different subjects. The Treatment SS would not change, because there would be no change in the sums for each group. We would not be able to derive a ΣX, or a Subjects SS, however, since the scores would be independent. As a consequence, all of the difference between Total SS and Treatment SS would have been attributed to Error (or within SS as we used that term in Chapter 6). This would yield an Error SS of 171.67 rather than 2.34. In the computation of MS, this increase would have been partially offset, since the within df would have been 15 rather than the 10 listed in Table 11.4. Still, the Error MS for this simple analysis of variance would have been 11.44 as compared to the correct value of .234. By use of a correlated scores analysis, we have achieved nearly a 50 : 1 reduction in the denominator of our F ratio. You should especially note that the treatment effect, when correctly analyzed, is highly significant (F obtained $= 150.30$, $F_{.01}$ required $= 7.56$) whereas the incorrect simple analysis of variance yields nonsignificant results (F obtained $= 3.07$, $F_{.05}$ required $= 3.68$).

One of the advantages, then, to the use of correlated scores rather than independent scores is that we may extract a portion of the total variance and attribute it to differences between subjects. However, there are times when a correlated-scores analysis of variance will yield lower treatment-significance levels than would a simple analysis of variance. This may result from two sources—a Subjects F ratio of less than 1.00 and the higher required F ratio for significance at the reduced df. Suppose that the experimental treatment requires subjects to change their basic method of problem solving as compared to their control performance. In such a case, performances on the two tasks may have a population correlation coefficient of zero. This, in turn, would imply that the Subjects *MS* and the Error *MS* should both be estimates of the same population variance. At times, though, due to chance alone the Subjects *MS* might be smaller than the Error *MS*. In such a case the within *MS* of a simple analysis of variance would be larger and, consequently, yield a smaller treatment *F* ratio than would the Error *MS* of a correlated design.

Even in cases in which the Subjects *MS* is larger than the Error *MS*, it is possible to achieve a less significant *p* value with a correlated design than would have been determined with independent scores. Note in Table 11.4 that the treatment *F* ratio was evaluated at 2, 10 *df*. The *F* ratio required for significance at the .05 level for these degrees of freedom is 4.10. Had this been an independent scores design, the obtained *F* ratio would have been evaluated against the 3.68 required for 2, 15 *df*. An obtained *F* ratio of 4.00 would be regarded as significant for the independent scores design but nonsignificant for the correlated scores design.

Methodological Considerations

Other methodological considerations should be reviewed before one accepts a research design involving correlated scores. For example, what assumptions or control measures must be used in order to limit possible interactions between the treatment conditions? One might wish to have a group of subjects learn a list of nonsense syllables under one condition, later returning to learn the same list under a different condition. It takes very little experimental sophistication to detect the possibility that learning might influence this comparison. To correct for this, subjects usually are presented with a different, but equated, list of words on the second trial. Any differences between the two lists contribute to a reduction in test–retest reliability. This lack of test–retest reliability will, in turn, increase the Error *MS* and reduce the likelihood of finding a significant *F* ratio. Once again we find the concept of experimental reliability entering into the analysis of variance.

There is a second and more subtle effect in the design above. Consider the possibility that some "learning to learn" nonsense syllables results from the presentation of the first list. Some of the difference in performance on the second list may therefore be due to this "learning to learn" rather than to the second treatment. The technique of counterbalancing can be used in such situations to reduce the influence of practice, fatigue, or similar variables. For the particular case outlined above, one approach might be to use the following assignment of subjects to lists and conditions:

Group I List A, Treatment 1; then List B, Treatment 2
Group II List B, Treatment 1; then List A, Treatment 2
Group III List A, Treatment 2; then List B, Treatment 1
Group IV List B, Treatment 2; then List A, Treatment 1

Notice that half of the groups have List A first and half have List B first. A similar situation exists for Treatment 1 and Treatment 2. This arrangement should, if we are fortunate, counterbalance most of the effects which might influence our results. However, differential effects (e.g., learning List A first has a greater effect on List B than learning List B first has upon List A) will not be eliminated by this particular scheme.

The counterbalancing method of reducing extraneous variables is relatively easy to accomplish with only two groups, but becomes more demanding as the number of treatments is increased. With three groups, for example, one must consider whether a given treatment (say Treatment 3) comes at the first, in the middle, or last. In addition, it is necessary to consider the possibility that the administration of Treatment 1 followed by Treatment 2 will have a different effect on Treatment 3 than would reversing the first two treatments. To take this order effect into account, one might have the following six groups:

1. T_1, T_2, T_3 4. T_2, T_3, T_1
2. T_1, T_3, T_2 5. T_3, T_1, T_2
3. T_2, T_1, T_3 6. T_3, T_2, T_1

The use of all possible orders helps to eliminate not only position effects but also some of the interaction effects as possible variables affecting the outcome of the study.

When the number of treatments expands much beyond four, this method becomes very cumbersome. For example, there would be 40,320 possible arrangements of 8 treatments, and it is highly unlikely that many of us will conduct laboratory experiments with this many subjects. As a result, many investigators either use random assignment of subjects to treatment orders or else assure that each treatment occurs an equal number of times in each position.

It is seen, even from this brief discussion, that the use of a correlated scores design implies some restrictions which may not be associated with a design utilizing independent scores. Like all analyses, a correlated-scores design should be used only when it is appropriate to the particular study. This does not mean, however, that we may never use a correlated design if we can anticipate the existence of some complex interactions between our various treatments. In such circumstances, it may be possible to use matched subjects for the various experimental treatments rather than using the same subjects in all conditions. The basic requirement for successful matching is that the matching variable should correlate highly with the dependent variable under study.

For example, one might use IQ scores as a matching variable for a study having correct responses to a verbal learning task as the dependent variable. Use of subjects' heights as a matching variable in this example would probably be useless as we might expect no correlation between height and verbal learning. Here one would pair two subjects with 110 IQ and assign one of them to each experimental condition. The analysis would then proceed exactly as was outlined in the first portion of this chapter. The ΣX_I, in this case, does not represent the sum for a given individual, but rather reflects the sum of a matched pair. Thus, the Subjects SS would be an indication of the amount of variance due to differences in IQ in the performance of this test. Since these IQ differences are only one part of the total individual differences between subjects, one normally would expect to find both a smaller Subjects MS and a larger Error MS when using matched subjects than when using the same individuals in all groups.

The decision to use matched subjects, then, is a decision to sacrifice some of the accuracy of the same-subjects design in order to eliminate possible interactions between treatments. This kind of balance is also evident when one decides to use the correlated-scores analysis. The correlated-scores design is usually more accurate than an independent-scores design, but a conclusion based on independent scores is more general than one based on an equivalent p value stemming from correlated scores. The conclusion based on independent scores indicates that the effect is sufficiently powerful to be detected over and above individual differences between subjects.

It is this kind of decision making that comes closest to art in experimentation. A given study can usually be designed in a number of different ways, and part of the real challenge in psychological research is the determination of the particular experimental design and method of analysis which will most likely provide an answer to the specific question being asked.

231

DESIGN CONSIDERATIONS

A correlated-scores analysis of variance shares some of the design problems of both correlation and simple analysis of variance. In common with correlation, the dependent variable should be carefully selected so its test–retest reliability will be high. High reliability insures that the Subjects *MS* will be high; i.e., that a significant portion of the variability of scores will be extracted as due to individual differences. In common with simple analysis of variance, the treatment effects should be both linear and additive; i.e., the various treatments should not have differential effects upon the measures of performance.

In addition to these special requirements, the correlated-scores analysis of variance technique requires that the usual parametric assumptions be fulfilled. Whenever possible, the scores within each treatment (when corrected for individual differences), should have been drawn from a normally distributed population of scores.

Some of the methodological problems specifically associated with the correlated-scores analysis of variance design were briefly outlined in this chapter. These included the necessity for balancing the order of treatments, the consideration of equated forms of the test used as the dependent variable, and the possibility of using matched subjects rather than having the same subject participate in all treatment conditions.

Other, more practical, factors should also be considered by the experimenter when he decides to use the correlated-scores design. For example, when a subject does not show up to participate in an experiment designed for *t*-test analysis, it is usually a simple matter to schedule a replacement subject. The experimenter loses only the few minutes that he waits for the "no-show." When one decides to use a correlated-scores design, however, he risks the possibility that a subject may cooperate for several of the treatments and then refuse to participate in further treatments. In such a case, all of the previously collected data must be discarded.

Another practical factor to be considered is that of the time required to set up the experimental treatment. In a simple analysis-of-variance design, a particular experimental environment can be constructed and a group of subjects tested; then another experimental environment constructed for the second treatment, etc. If the correlated-scores design requires counterbalancing, this highly efficient procedure becomes impossible since the order of treatments must be varied from individual to individual.

If the experimenter has the patience and the ingenuity to adequately balance all of these considerations, he will find that the correlated-scores design is the most sensitive to experimental treatment effects of all of the designs that we shall study.

SUMMARY

The technique for correlated-scores analysis of variance was shown to stem from the fact that the total variance of two or more samples of scores may be divided into parts attributable to: (1) differences between treatments, (2) differences between subjects, and (3) error. The computational formulae for the sums of squares in such analyses were given as:

$$\text{Total } SS = \Sigma X_{i,j}^2 - \frac{\left[\displaystyle\sum_{i=1}^{I}\sum_{j=1}^{J} X_{i,j}\right]^2}{N}$$

$$\text{Treatment } SS = \sum_{j=1}^{J} \frac{\left[\displaystyle\sum_{i=1}^{I} X_{i,j}\right]^2}{I} - \frac{\left[\displaystyle\sum_{i=1}^{I}\sum_{j=1}^{J} X_{i,j}\right]^2}{N}$$

$$\text{Subjects } SS = \sum_{i=1}^{I} \frac{\left[\displaystyle\sum_{j=1}^{J} X_{i,j}\right]^2}{J} - \frac{\left[\displaystyle\sum_{i=1}^{I}\sum_{j=1}^{J} X_{i,j}\right]^2}{N}$$

$$\text{Error } SS = \text{Total } SS - \text{Treatment } SS - \text{Subjects } SS$$

where:

I = number of subjects
i = the ith subject
J = number of treatments
j = the jth treatment
$X_{i,j}$ = the score of the ith subject under the jth treatment
N = total number of scores in the entire distribution

The procedure for computing the various SS is thus identical to that used for simple analysis of variance except that an additional SS is extracted by using the ΣX_I as a second type of treatment effect.

The remaining computations required to complete a correlated-scores analysis of variance are given in the summary table below:

SS	df	MS	F	p
Treatment	$J-1$	Divide each SS by its respective df	$\dfrac{\text{Treatment } MS}{\text{Error } MS}$	Evaluate at $J-1$, $(J-1)(I-1)$ df
Subjects	$I-1$		$\dfrac{\text{Subjects } MS}{\text{Error } MS}$	Evaluate at $I-1$, $(J-1)(I-1)$ df
Error	$(J-1)(I-1)$			
Total	$N-1$			

In most cases, this type of analysis is more sensitive to the experimental effects than is simple analysis of variance. In some cases, however, the converse may be found. This may be caused by a Subjects F ratio less than 1.00 or by the higher value of F required for significance at the reduced df.

The methodological aspects to be considered in the selection of this design were (1) balancing order effects, (2) equated measurements, and (3) the use of matched subjects. The decision to use this technique was shown to require the weighing of several such factors against the benefits of using such a sensitive method.

12. Rank-Order Techniques

SCALES OF MEASUREMENT

The study of nonparametric methods of analysis necessitates some knowledge of the theory of measurement. Most of the measurements used to derive scores for analysis in our experiments stem from either ratio, interval, ordinal, or nominal scales. The most rigorous and exacting of these is the ratio scale, exemplified by a ruler measuring in inches. The ratio scale has a true zero point (0″ on the ruler), the units are both additive ($1'' + 2'' = 3''$) and multiplicative ($2 \times 1'' = 2''$), and meaningful ratios may be formed ($1'':2'' :: 3'':6''$). Although this type of scale is aspired to as the model, very few (if any) of our common psychological tests can be considered to have the attributes of the ratio scale.

A somewhat less restrictive type of measurement is implied with the interval scale. Two such common scales are the Centigrade and Fahrenheit scales for temperature measurement. For such a scale, the zero point is arbitrary ($0°F$ is not equal to $0°C$), but differences between numerically equally distant points are, in fact, equal within either scale ($20°F - 10°F = 70°F - 60°F$). As these are both interval scales, a translation of the type $AX + B$ can be meaningfully made ($9/5°C + 32° = °F$). If we can assume that intelligence is actually normally distributed in the population as a whole, then the range of IQ scores may be regarded as an equal interval scale. A score of zero on one of these tests would not necessarily indicate zero intelligence. Neither may we state with any degree of certainty that an individual with an IQ of 100 is twice as smart as an individual with an IQ of 50. As a consequence, it seems apparent that IQ cannot be regarded as a ratio scale. If, however, we can state that the difference between 80 and 90 IQ is the same as the difference between 115 and 125 IQ, then perhaps we are justified in using IQ as an interval scale.

Most of our current tests should properly be classified as ordinal scales—typified in the physical world by the hardness scale for testing minerals. Here 10 basic minerals differing in hardness have been set as the standards. A mineral of hardness 8 will scratch the surface of a mineral of hardness 7, etc. Only rank order may be determined by such a scale, for no true zero point exists. Nor may one assume that the difference in hardness from 1 to 2 is equivalent to the difference in hardness from 5 to 6. Many of our rating scales make no pretense at yielding even the interval scale and report their findings directly in terms of ranks (e.g., your rank in class is 16 out of 34 individuals). Other psychological tests, however, are often reported in numbers which seem to imply a higher order of measurement than can be justified. As a consequence, even though a particular test may report a "score" of 126 for an individual, that score may be no more meaningful than to indicate that the individual is higher than all people with scores of 125 or lower.

The last, or nominal scale, can hardly be termed a true scale as the assignment of numbers is completely arbitrary. An example of such a scale would be the numbers assigned to men on a football team. With the nominal scale, not even the concept of ordinality is assumed (the player with the number 50 on his back is not necessarily a better or worse player than the one with the number 36 on his back). Of what use is the nominal scale then? Many of the phenomena we might like to investigate are primarily of a nominal classification such as "right-handedness" vs. "left-handedness." Such a classification could also be assigned the numbers 0 and 1 or 13 and 15, etc., in a completely arbitrary fashion. The only requirement for such a scale is that all "zero" individuals must be identifiably different in some specific respect from the "one" individuals. You should note that some of our nominal classifications may actually be a reduction from the higher-order scales. For example, cans in a food-processing plant may be labeled "satisfactory" or "unsatisfactory" with respect to their weight, even though that weight is capable of specification on the ratio scale of grams. In general, a higher-order scale may be reduced to a lower one, but the converse is not true. Each reduction in scale, however, results in a loss of some of the information available in the higher scale.

You are perhaps wondering how the type of scale from which the data are derived may influence its subsequent statistical analysis. The parametric statistics that we have studied are appropriate only when the measurement is derived from either a ratio or an interval scale. Thus, in addition to the requirements that we must have randomly and independently sampled our scores from a normally distributed population of scores, we must also assume either ratio or interval scales of measurement. Unless all of these requirements are met, one cannot in theory justify using a parametric technique in the analysis of the data. We have previously seen that the requirement for assuming an underlying normal distribution of scores can be relaxed somewhat without completely destroying the validity of our conclusions. The matter of scale of measurement, though, is a somewhat more restrictive requirement. If the data are either ranks (ordinal scale) or classification (nominal scale), then any parametric analysis of variance is very nearly meaningless.

One may decide to use one of the nonparametric techniques for data analysis either when he cannot legitimately fulfill the distribution assumptions of the parametric techniques or when his data are not derived from a ratio or an interval scale. In general, these are the only times that nonparametric statistical analyses should be used, since the more powerful parametric techniques are to be preferred whenever appropriate.

(handwritten: ① Normal distributional (is you can not assume that it comes from a norm distribution))

KRUSKAL-WALLIS ONE-WAY ANALYSIS OF VARIANCE BY RANKS

With this in mind, let us proceed directly to a discussion of a non-parametric method for determining the significance of a difference when the data are drawn from at least an ordinal scale. The particular technique we will investigate for determining the significance of a difference is called the Kruskal-Wallis (20) one-way analysis of variance by ranks. This method parallels the simple analysis of variance technique discussed in Chapter 6 and has some similar requirements. That is, the scores to be analyzed must be independent samples from the population under consideration though the samples may be of different sizes. It is not necessary, however, to make assumptions concerning the shape of the distribution of scores in the population.

(handwritten margin note: Imp)

The Kruskal-Wallis test, like simple analysis of variance, is an overall test of differences between the treatments; a significant finding indicates only that the distribution of the various treatment sums of ranks is unlikely to have occurred by chance alone. One of the major differences between the two techniques is that all of the observations must be expressed as ranks for the Kruskal-Wallis test. This means that one must determine the lowest score in the entire distribution, give it a rank of 1, find the next lowest score and give it a rank of 2, etc., until all of the scores have been assigned a rank. In the event of ties, the tied scores are given the mean of the ranks that they would have occupied had slight differences enabled the experimenter to differentiate between them. The ranking then proceeds from that point.

As an illustration of the method of resolving ties, consider the fictitious data reported in Table 12.1. The assignment of the first two ranks presents no difficulties: 10 is the lowest score and receives the rank of 1; 12 is the next lowest score and receives the rank of 2. Next are two tied scores of 13. Since these two scores would normally receive the ranks of 3 and 4 if there were some method of discriminating between them, we assign each of them the mean of these two ranks, or 3.5. As the first four ranks have been used, the next score in order (the 14) receives the rank of 5. The three tied scores of 15, which would occupy the ranks 6, 7, and 8, are assigned the mean rank of 7.

TABLE 12.1.   Example of assigning tied ranks

ORIGINAL DATA (SCORES)	ASSIGNED RANK
10	1
12	2
13	3.5
13	3.5
14	5
15	7
15	7
15	7
17	9
20	10

For scores of 13: Occupy ranks 3 and 4; $(3 + 4)/2 = 7/2 = 3.5$
For scores of 15: Occupy ranks 6, 7, and 8; $(6 + 7 + 8)/3 = 21/3 = 7$

Finally, the score of 17 is assigned the rank of 9 and the score of 20 is given the last rank of 10.

Once this ranking procedure has been completed, the formula for the computation of the Kruskal-Wallis statistic (called H) is quite simple:

$$H = \frac{12}{N(N + 1)} \left[\sum_{j=1}^{J} \frac{(\Sigma R_j)^2}{n_j} \right] - 3(N + 1)$$

where:

J = number of treatments
n_j = number of cases in the jth treatment
N = total number of observations
ΣR_j = sum of the ranks in the jth treatment

As an example of the computational procedures to be followed, consider the data presented in Table 12.2. At the beginning of a class in introductory psychology, a questionnaire was administered to the 24 students. This questionnaire included, among other items, a place for the student to check whether his political tendency was Democratic, Independent, or Republican. At a later date, an experimenter was interested in determining whether or not these three groups differed

239

TABLE 12.2. Rigidity scores as a function of preferred political affiliation

TYPE OF SCORE	DEMOCRAT	INDEPENDENT	REPUBLICAN
	21	5	16
	13	14	24
	24	12	11
	33	10	31
Original	11	31	43
	26	2	26
	3	16	
	42	8	
		24	
		7	
	14	3	12.5
	10	11	16
	16	9	7.5
Expressed as Ranks	22	6	20.5
	7.5	20.5	24
	18.5	1	18.5
	23	12.5	$\Sigma R = 99.0$
	$\Sigma R = 113.0$	5	$n = 6$
	$n = 8$	16	
		4	
		$\Sigma R = 88.0$	
		$n = 10$	
	$N = 24,$	$\Sigma\Sigma R = 300.0$	

significantly in performance on a test of conceptual rigidity. Scores on this test could range from 0 (very flexible) to 50 (very rigid). The test scores for the three groups are shown in Table 12.2.

These data seem to indicate positive skewness, and it was unlikely that the rigidity-test scores could be considered drawn from an interval scale. Consequently, analysis of these data was by means of the Kruskal-Wallis one-way analysis of variance by ranks. The original data is shown in the upper portion of the table with the conversion to ranks in the lower portion. Note that the four sets of two tied scores and the single set of three tied scores were assigned ranks according to the preceding discussion.

The analysis of this data proceeded directly from the computational formula previously given, as applied to the scores listed in the lower portion of Table 12.2. The computation of H was:

$$H = \frac{12}{N(N+1)} \left[\sum_{j=1}^{J} \frac{(\Sigma R_j)^2}{n_j} \right] - 3(N+1)$$

$$= \frac{12}{(24)(25)} \left[\frac{113^2}{8} + \frac{88^2}{10} + \frac{99^2}{6} \right] - 3(25)$$

$$= .02(1596.125 + 774.400 + 1633.500) - 75$$

$$= .02(4{,}004.025) - 75 = 80.081 - 75 = 5.081$$

This value of H is apparently due to the lower mean rank of the Independent group. Simple division indicates that the treatment mean ranks are: Democrat, 14.125; Independent, 8.800; and Republican, 16.500. As is true of all of our statistical tests, however, the simple indication of a difference does not indicate whether or not these differences may have been the result of chance factors. The value of H is judged for significance in Appendix F where degrees of freedom is found by: $df = J - 1$ (the number of treatments minus 1).

Since this experiment used three treatment groups, the appropriate *df* for evaluating this computed value of H is $J - 1 = 3 - 1 = 2$. In Appendix F we find that the required value of χ^2 for 2 *df* is 5.991. Thus we cannot claim that the results of the experiment are significantly different from those which might have occurred as a function of chance alone. Since computed value of 5.081 is relatively close to the $p = .05$ level of 5.991, perhaps our best decision is to reserve judgment pending further evidence. With results this close to the required level for significance, the study may be worth repeating with a larger sample chosen randomly from the population.

The computation and interpretation of the Kruskal-Wallis one-way analysis of variance by ranks is a relatively straightforward procedure once the original data have been converted to ranks. Before leaving this technique and turning to the question of correlation based on ranks, however, several points regarding this method of analysis should be raised. First, you should be aware of the fact that this method of analysis is applicable only in situations where the scores have been independently drawn from the population. The Kruskal-Wallis test is not appropriate for analyzing correlated data.

Second, the Kruskal-Wallis test, when evaluated in the manner described above, is not appropriate when any of the treatment groups contains less than five observations. Special techniques derived for handling such small samples may be found in texts of nonparametric statistics.

Third, the obtained value of H is not exactly accurate if the data exhibit ties. The correction factor accounting for the presence of ties usually has only a very minor effect, however, and in most cases may be disregarded. For the data given above, where 11 of the 24 observations were involved in ties, the corrected value of H is 5.098 compared to the uncorrected value of 5.081. Notice that the effect of ignoring ties in the data is to decrease the value of H. Use of the uncorrected value is conservative, and does not increase the likelihood of a Type I error.

Finally, this nonparametric test is slightly less powerful than simple analysis of variance. If the assumptions of a parametric, simple, analysis of variance can be met, the Kruskal-Wallis test requires 200 subjects to match the same level of significance reached by the F test on 191 observations of the same data.

SPEARMAN RANK CORRELATION

Let us now turn to a second nonparametric technique appropriate for the analysis of data which may be assumed to stem from at least an ordinal scale of measurement. This is the Spearman rank correlation coefficient, r_s (17). As you recall from the discussion of the parametric correlation coefficient in Chapter 10, a correlation differs from an analysis of variance in that r is a measure of relative placement of two variables, rather than a test of the mean difference between two treatments. A similar situation exists with respect to the relationship between the Spearman rank correlation coefficient and the Kruskal-Wallis one-way analysis of variance by ranks. The former tests for relative placement; the latter tests for significance of a difference.

This relationship is perhaps more easily seen in the procedures for computing r_s than in those for computing r. The scores that we wish to analyze by r_s are ranked *independently* for the two sets of observations. Thus the sums of the ranks for the two variables are equal, regardless of the mean differences which may have existed in the raw data prior to ranking. This aspect of the computational procedure is demonstrated in the data presented in Table 12.3. These data represent X- and Y-axis tracking errors in a two-dimensional performance task and were previously presented as Table 10.5 in the chapter on parametric correlation. In the left-hand portion of Table 12.3 are the original data; in the right-hand portion the conversion to ranks. When the original data are considered we find the X-axis mean to be 10.78 and the Y-axis mean to be 15.04. Note that this difference disappears when these data are converted to ranks; the sum of both X- and Y-axis ranks is 210. This is a method for checking the assignment of ranks, since the sum of any given set of ranks will always be $N(N + 1)/2$. For the 20 ranks of Table 12.3 this sum is $N(N + 1)/2 = 20(21)/2 = 420/2 = 210$. This same check may also be used with other techniques which involve ranking, e.g., the sum of the 24 ranks of Table 12.2 illustrating the Kruskal-Wallis test was 300:

$$\frac{N(N + 1)}{2} = \frac{24(25)}{2} = \frac{600}{2} = 300.$$

TABLE 12.3.   X-axis and Y-axis errors in a two-dimensional performance

X-AXIS ERRORS	Y-AXIS ERRORS	RANK X	RANK Y
15.6	21.3	17.5	16
11.4	12.1	11	7.5
6.7	9.4	4	3
7.4	12.0	5	6
12.0	15.3	14	13.5
9.9	11.3	9	5
4.3	1.2	2	1
14.3	25.8	15	19
7.5	12.6	6	9
11.7	22.5	13	17
9.2	12.1	8	7.5
17.2	27.9	19	20
14.7	15.0	16	12
4.1	10.7	1	4
11.5	14.4	12	11
20.0	24.6	20	18
7.7	15.3	7	13.5
15.6	13.5	17.5	10
10.2	15.6	10	15
4.6	8.1	3	2
$\overline{X} = 10.78$	$\overline{Y} = 15.04$	$\Sigma R_X = 210$	$\Sigma R_Y = 210$

The computational formula for the determination of r_s once the data have been converted to ranks is:

$$r_s = 1 - \frac{6 \Sigma D^2}{(N - 1)(N)(N + 1)}$$

where:

$D =$ difference $R_X - R_Y$ for each pair of ranks

$N =$ number of pairs of observations

The denominator of the subtractive portion of the formula is expressed in this form because the sequence of three successive numbers will always permit the easy reduction of the six in the numerator. For the 20-rank case presented in Table 12.3, the formula reduces to:

$$r_s = 1 - \frac{6 \Sigma D^2}{(N - 1)(N)(N + 1)}$$

$$= 1 - \frac{\overset{1}{\cancel{6}} \Sigma D^2}{\underset{(10)(7)}{(19)(\cancel{20})(\cancel{21})}}$$

$$= 1 - \frac{\Sigma D^2}{1330}$$

The ΣD^2 required for the completion of this computation is shown in Table 12.4, where the first two columns reproduce the X- and Y-axis ranks presented in the preceding table. The third column of Table 12.4 is labeled D and is found by direct subtraction of an individual's Y-axis error rank (R_Y) from his X-axis error rank (R_X). The last column is labeled D^2 and is the square of each of the D values listed in the third column. The ΣD^2 value at the bottom of this column (230.50) is the value required for the completion of the computation of r_s by the formula given above. The actual computation is:

$$r_s = 1 - \frac{6 \Sigma D^2}{(N - 1)(N)(N + 1)}$$

$$= 1 - \frac{\Sigma D^2}{1330} = 1 - \frac{230.50}{1330} = 1 - .173$$

$$= +.827$$

This value of r_s is very close to the value of r previously computed $(r = +.804)$, but one should not regard the two types of correlation co-

TABLE 12.4.   Example of the computational procedure for r_s

RANK X	RANK Y	D	D^2
17.5	16	1.5	2.25
11	7.5	3.5	12.25
4	3	1.0	1.00
5	6	−1.0	1.00
14	13.5	.5	.25
9	5	4.0	16.00
2	1	1.0	1.00
15	19	−4.0	16.00
6	9	−3.0	9.00
13	17	−4.0	16.00
8	7.5	.5	.25
19	20	−1.0	1.00
16	12	4.0	16.00
1	4	−3.0	9.00
12	11	1.0	1.00
20	18	2.0	4.00
7	13.5	−6.5	42.25
17.5	10	7.5	56.25
10	15	−5.0	25.00
3	2	1.0	1.00
			$\Sigma D^2 = \overline{230.50}$

$$r_s = 1 - \frac{6\Sigma D^2}{(N-1)(N)(N+1)} = 1 - \frac{\Sigma D^2}{1330} = 1 - \frac{230.50}{1330} = 1 - .173 = + .827$$

efficients as identical. The parametric r is based on the variance of two normally distributed populations of scores, whereas the nonparametric r_s is based on the cross product of rank deviations when the population distributions are unknown. The primary value of r_s is in the description of the relationship between two distributions of scores in situations where the assumptions of the parametric method cannot be justified.

The nonparametric r_s does present one problem common to all of the statistical methods so far discussed, that of determining the level of significance. The distribution of possible Spearman rank correlations that might occur as a function of chance alone is easily demonstrated. Consider that we have only two pairs of scores to rank. Since each pair may be ranked only as 1–2 or as 2–1, the only possible combinations are below.

	Combination 1		Combination 2		Combination 3		Combination 4	
	X	Y	X	Y	X	Y	X	Y
S_1	1	1	1	2	2	1	2	2
S_2	2	2	2	1	1	2	1	1

Of these, only combinations 1 and 2 are unique, since combinations 3 and 4 only reverse these ranks by assigning them to the other subject. For all four of the combinations shown above, the computed r_s value will be either $+1.00$ or -1.00. As a consequence, when one has only two ranks to compare, even a coefficient of ± 1.00 will not be significant, since we would expect either value to occur 50 percent of the time by chance alone. Fortunately, it is not necessary for us to go through each of the possible rank correlations for every combination in order to determine the significance of a given r_s. Appendix G lists those values of r_s which would be expected to occur .05 or .01 proportion of the time by chance alone when the true population $r_s = 0$. Entry to this table is obtained by a knowledge of the number of pairs of ranks, N. Inspection of Appendix G for $N = 20$ pairs indicates that our obtained value of $+.827$ is much greater than that value required at the .01 level. This result is consistent with the finding of a highly significant value of r as determined in Chapter 10.

Let us end this discussion of the rank-order correlation technique with some precautions concerning the use of r_s. First, like the Kruskal-Wallis test, r_s may not be evaluated when less than five pairs of observations are available for analysis. Even values of ± 1.00 are not significant if computed for four or less pairs of ranks.

Second, the obtained value of r_s, like the obtained value of H in the Kruskal-Wallis test, is not exact if the data exhibit ties. Once again, however, the effect of ties is relatively minor and for most practical cases may be disregarded. Finally, if the assumptions of the parametric r can be met, the Spearman rank correlation requires 100 pairs of observations to reach the same level of significance obtained by r on 91 observations from the same data. Thus, the power of r_s is less than that of r, and the technique should be used only when the assumptions of distribution or measurement are untenable.

DESIGN CONSIDERATIONS

When planning studies to be analyzed by either the Kruskal-Wallis one-way analysis of variance by ranks or the Spearman rank-correlation coefficient, a prime consideration is the relationship between these techniques and their parametric counterparts. If a particular set of data could have been analyzed by simple analysis of variance had those scores fulfilled the parametric assumptions, then the Kruskal-Wallis technique is appropriate. Similarly, if the correlation r could have been used except for violation of the parametric assumptions, then the Spearman r_s may be computed. Even though a study has been designed for analysis by a parametric technique, the data may fail to meet all of the assumptions required by that technique. The experimenter may then turn to the nonparametric method appropriate for the analysis of the data.

Too often, an inexperienced investigator will omit some of the desirable controls in a study because he regards them as unnecessary when using a nonparametric technique. This is completely incorrect; only underlying assumptions may be relaxed—not control. If this experimenter were to consider the loss of power due to the use of the nonparametric techniques, he should be unwilling to commit any error which would further reduce the possibility of finding significant results.

The reduction in power when nonparametric methods are used for data analysis can be compensated for by an increase in the number of subjects tested in the experiment. If, when the experiment is originally designed it appears that the parametric assumptions may not be fulfilled, one may decide in advance to use either the Kruskal-Wallis test or the Spearman r_s to analyze the data. In such instances, an increase of 10 percent in the number of subjects tested over that desired in a parametric study will more than compensate for the loss of power.

A final consideration in the decision to use nonparametric techniques for data analysis is their general lack of subsequent expansion. If several groups' scores yield a significant F ratio, one may then test for differences between specific groups by use of the Scheffé technique. Such post hoc comparisons may not be made when the data are analyzed by the Kruskal-Wallis technique. Similarly, a regression equation based on a significant r may be interpreted by variance explanations. This is not possible when the data has been analyzed by r_s. Thus the decision to use a nonparametric technique should be based upon the requirements of the situation, not upon ease of computation or other irrelevant considerations.

SUMMARY

A brief overview of the theory of measurement served as an introduction to the study of nonparametric techniques. Four of the typical scales from which most of our experimental data are derived were discussed. The ratio scale has a true zero point, the units are both additive and multiplicative, and meaningful ratios may be formed. The interval scale has an arbitrary zero point and the differences between numerically equidistant points are equal. The ordinal scale also has an arbitrary zero point, but numerically equidistant points only imply order of magnitude rather than true distances. The last, or nominal scale, is scaling by classification only and neither order nor magnitude may be assumed.

It was seen that the scale of measurement places another restriction on the application of parametric techniques, in that either ratio or interval scale measurement must be assumed. The remainder of the chapter was devoted to development of two nonparametric techniques which may be used when only ordinal scale measurement may be assumed.

The first of these techniques—the Kruskal-Wallis one-way analysis of variance by ranks—was shown to be an analog of simple analysis of variance. Once the entire distribution of scores has been ranked, the appropriate computational formula is:

$$H = \frac{12}{N(N+1)} \left[\sum_{j=1}^{J} \frac{(\Sigma R_j)^2}{n_j} \right] - 3(N+1)$$

where:

J = number of treatments
n_j = number of cases in the jth treatment
N = total number of observations
ΣR_j = sum of the ranks for the jth treatment

The resulting value of H is evaluated for significance by entry to Appendix F using as df:

$$df = J - 1$$

The interpretation of the results of this test are similar to those for simple analysis of variance.

The second nonparametric method of data analysis discussed in this chapter was the Spearman rank correlation coefficient r_s. This technique was shown to be an analog of the parametric correlation coefficient, r. In contrast to the Kruskal-Wallis test, the data to be analyzed by r_s must first be ranked separately for each variable. The computational formula, once this ranking is complete is:

$$r_s = 1 - \frac{6\Sigma D^2}{(N-1)(N)(N+1)}$$

where:

$D =$ difference $(R_x - R_y)$ for each pair of ranks
$N =$ number of pairs of observations

The significance of the resulting coefficient is determined by entry to Appendix G using $df = N$.

These two nonparametric techniques were shown to be less powerful than their parametric counterparts. Consequently, use of these methods should be directed by the requirements of the data rather than by irrelevant considerations.

13. Classification Techniques

CHI-SQUARE

We have explored two methods for analyzing ordinal-scale data: (1) a method for the determination of the significance of a difference, and (2) a method for determining the correlation. For both methods, it was necessary to assume that the data were derived from at least ordinal-scale measurement. In the present chapter we shall consider two techniques for the analysis of data when no more than nominal scale measurement may be assumed. Again, one of these methods (chi-square) may be used to test for the significance of a difference and the other (phi) to test for the correlation between two variables.

We have previously seen that nominal-scale measurement is simply a function of classification. For example, one nominal scale that might be used in an experiment is that of male vs. female. A second nominal scale might be right-handed vs. left-handed. In this study, the independent variable would be the position of a particular individual on the male–female scale. A subsequent test would determine whether each individual previously scaled on the male–female classification was right-handed or left-handed. In the definition of these nominal scales, each individual tested may fit into only one of four possible categories: male right-handed, male left-handed, female right-handed, or female left-handed. It would not be possible, using this scale of measurement, for an individual to be both masculine and feminine or to be both right-handed and left-handed.

What would the data from such a study look like? It would seem fairly obvious that not even ordinality is assumed in this measurement. One would not say, without exposing oneself to considerable heated discussion, that males were "better" than females, or vice versa. Similarly, one would be unable to state whether right-handed was "better" than left-handed. As a consequence, the only data available would be whether or not the person was male right-handed, male left-handed, female right-handed or female left-handed. The only method of measurement available (given these categories) is that of counting the number of individuals that fit into each of the four categories.

Suppose that we test 50 males and 50 females for their classification on the right-handed vs. left-handed variable and find that 20 are left-handed and 80 are right-handed. If there are no significant differences between the right-handed vs. left-handed scores of males and females, we should expect about half of each of these right-handed vs. left-handed scores to be male and about half female. Thus, on the basis of chance alone, we should expect to find 40 right-handed males, 10 left-handed males, 40 right-handed females and 10 left-handed females. These expected values are shown in the left-hand portion of Table 13.1. It was relatively easy to compute these expected values because an equal number of males and females were tested. In general, though, the expected value for a given cell may be computed by the formula:

$$E_{r,c} = \frac{\Sigma_r \Sigma_c}{N}$$

TABLE 13.1.   Joint classification on male–female and right-handed vs. left-handed scales

| | EXPECTED VALUES | | | | OBSERVED VALUES | | |
	MALE	FEMALE	Σ		MALE	FEMALE	Σ
Right-handed	40	40	80		37	43	80
Left-handed	10	10	20		13	7	20
	50	50	100		50	50	100

where:

r = any row
c = any column
$E_{r,c}$ = expected cell frequency at the junction of row r and column c
N = total number
Σ_r = observed frequency for row r
Σ_c = observed frequency for column c

For the sample data collected, we may apply this formula for right-handed males as follows:

$$E_{r,c} = \frac{\Sigma_r \Sigma_c}{N} = \frac{(80)(50)}{100} = \frac{4000}{100} = 40$$

In this particular table, where we have two rows and two columns, this is the only expected value that we actually need to compute. If we have found that we have 40 right-handed males and we know that 80 of our Ss are right-handed, then we must have 40 female right-handed Ss. Similarly, if 40 of our males are right-handed, then the other 10 must be left-handed to bring us to our total of 50 males. Finally, having previously computed that we have 40 right-handed females, we know that we must have 10 left-handed females in order to equal our total of 50. Thus (given that the row and column totals must be accurate), we have only one degree of freedom to place a number in a 2 × 2 table such as this. For more complicated tables, the general formula for degrees of freedom is:

$$df = (R - 1)(C - 1)$$

where:

$$R = \text{number of rows}$$
$$C = \text{number of columns}$$

For the tables shown in Table 13.1, then:

$$df = (R - 1)(C - 1) = (2 - 1)(2 - 1) = (1)(1) = 1$$

For these data we may specify both the expected value and the degrees of freedom. Our knowledge of sampling, however, might lead us to expect that we would not obtain exactly these values from a sample of data. Suppose that our actual observations were those shown in the right-hand portion of Table 13.1. The question now confronting us is, "Are these data significantly different from what we might expect to obtain by chance alone?" Upon casual inspection, it would appear that almost twice as many of the males are left-handed as are females (13 to 7). The difference between the values observed and those expected, however, is relatively small—only three more male left-handed subjects than would be expected by chance alone.

A test of the significance of the difference is given by the chi-square (χ^2) formula:

$$\chi^2 = \sum \frac{(O - E)^2}{E}$$

where:

O = observed frequency for any cell (the junction of row r and column c)
E = expected frequency for any cell
Σ = sum for all $R \times C$ cells

For the observed data and expected values shown in Table 13.1, we may compute a chi-square value as follows:

$$\chi^2 = \sum \frac{(O - E)^2}{E} = \frac{(37 - 40)^2}{40} + \frac{(13 - 10)^2}{10} + \frac{(43 - 40)^2}{40} +$$

$$\frac{(7 - 10)^2}{10}$$

$$= \frac{(-3)^2}{40} + \frac{(+3)^2}{10} + \frac{(+3)^2}{40} + \frac{(-3)^2}{10} = \frac{9}{40} + \frac{9}{10} + \frac{9}{40} + \frac{9}{10}$$

$$= 2.25$$

The probability of finding, by chance alone, a chi-square value this large or larger may be determined by an inspection of Appendix E. This table lists those values of χ^2 which might be expected to occur either .05 or .01 proportion of the time by chance alone. Entry to this table requires that we use the degrees of freedom previously computed ($df = 1$). In Appendix F we find that a χ^2 value of 3.841 is required for significance at the .05 level. Since our obtained value of chi-square is much lower than this required value, we may state that males and females do not vary significantly on the variable of handedness. For our sample, though we counted nearly twice as many left-handed males as left-handed females, no significant differences were found. When we inspect the actual differences (only three more left-handed males out of 50 than might be expected by chance alone), this conclusion seems more tenable.

Let us consider a slightly more complex example. An investigator was interested in determining whether average yearly income was a function of the level of education of the individual. Level of education for 300 subjects was classified as: (1) nongraduate, (2) high-school graduate, or (3) at least some college. Level of income was similarly classified into three groups: (1) less than $4000, (2) $4000 to $7500, and (3) more than $7500. These data are summarized in Table 13.2. Note that each individual surveyed may fit into one and only one of these nine categories. The expected values for each of the nine cells in Table 13.2 were computed according to the formula previously given. For

TABLE 13.2. Yearly income as a function of amount of formal education (number of individuals)

	NON-GRADUATE	HIGH-SCHOOL GRADUATE	AT LEAST SOME COLLEGE	TOTALS
Less than $4,000	$E = 20.40$ $O = 32$	$E = 35.04$ $O = 35$	$E = 16.56$ $O = 5$	72
$4,000 to $7,500	$E = 32.87$ $O = 36$	$E = 56.45$ $O = 58$	$E = 26.68$ $O = 22$	116
More than $7,500	$E = 31.73$ $O = 17$	$E = 54.51$ $O = 53$	$E = 25.76$ $O = 42$	112
Totals	85	146	69	300

254

example, the expected value (E) for nongraduates earning less than $4000 a year is:

$$E_{r,c} = \frac{\Sigma_r \Sigma_c}{N} = \frac{(72)(85)}{300} = 20.40$$

Our expression for degrees of freedom for this table—$df = (R - 1)$ $(C - 1) = (3 - 1)(3 - 1) = (2)(2) = 4$—indicates that at least four of these computations must be made in order to complete the expected frequencies for this table. Computation of the value of chi-square for this table again follows the formula:

$$\chi^2 = \sum \frac{(O - E)^2}{E}$$

$$= \frac{(32 - 20.40)^2}{20.40} + \frac{(35 - 35.04)^2}{35.04} + \cdots + \frac{(42 - 25.76)^2}{25.76}$$

$$= \frac{(11.60)^2}{20.40} + \frac{(-.04)^2}{35.04} + \cdots + \frac{(16.24)^2}{25.76}$$

$$= \frac{134.5600}{20.40} + \frac{.0016}{35.04} + \cdots + \frac{263.7376}{25.76}$$

$$= 6.5961 + .0000 + \cdots + 10.2382 = 32.9455$$

This value is evaluated at four degrees of freedom in Appendix E. The required value of χ^2 for significance at the .01 level with four degrees of freedom is 13.277. Since our computed value of chi-square is much larger than the value required for significance, we may state that a classification on the income scale is a function of the classification on the education scale.

You should note that this is the only legitimate conclusion that can be derived from a chi-square analysis. A significant value of chi-square indicates only that the distribution of observed frequencies is non-random; we may not say that the nongraduates earn significantly less than do the high-school graduates or those with at least some college education. For example, suppose that all of those individuals with at least some college education fell into either the less-than-$4000 category or the more-than-$7500 category. With such a distribution, the median income for the group might be approximately the same as that for the nongraduates. But a significant value of chi-square would have been found, indicating that the distribution of frequencies is a non-chance event.

In addition to its lack of sensitivity to differences between the medians of two different groups, the chi-square test is also quite inefficient in the detection of order. Thus in the current example a significant value of χ^2 could have been obtained had high-school graduates earned the least median income, those with at least some college education earned the next highest income, and nongraduates earned the highest median income. This particular result might have been contrary to a previous hypothesis which indicated the order of median incomes shown in Table 13.2.

The data in Table 13.1 may be used to illustrate another restriction to the use and interpretation of chi-square. In this table, each of the O values was three observations greater or smaller than the E value expected on the basis of chance alone. In the computation of the χ^2 value, however, the two cells with an expected frequency of 10 contribute four times as much to the final chi-square as do the two cells with expected frequencies of 40. Thus we see that small expected frequencies contribute disproportionately to the final computed value of chi-square. Consequently, when using χ^2, no expected value for any cell should have a frequency of less than 5, and preferably not less than 10. It is important to note that this restriction applies to expected values rather than to observed values. A much higher (and legitimate) value of chi-square will be obtained for any table where the observed value is zero.

Chi-square Correction for Continuity

The data in Table 13.1 also serve to illustrate the correction for continuity used in all 2×2 tables. Consider the three distributions shown in the upper portion of Figure 13.1. The first of these distributions is clearly bimodal, the second approximates a normal distribution, and the third is a rectangular distribution. The middle portion of Figure 13.1 illustrates the relative frequencies that might be obtained if each of these distributions was divided into two classifications: (1) above the median, and (2) below the median. Note that this particular classification does not permit us to discriminate between the three distributions shown in the upper portion. In the lower third of this figure is shown a classification which divides the score line into three equal intervals. The bimodality of the first distribution, the normality of the

(A) Basic Distributions of Scores

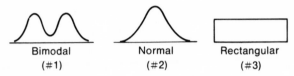

Bimodal	Normal	Rectangular
(#1)	(#2)	(#3)

(B) Two Category Classification of Basic Distributions

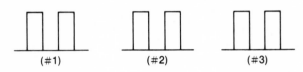

(#1) (#2) (#3)

(C) Three Category Classification of Basic Distributions

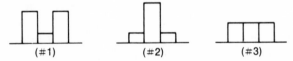

(#1) (#2) (#3)

FIGURE 13.1. (B) and (C) illustrate dichoto-
mized and three-category divisions of the continuous distribution shown in the upper portion.

second distribution, and the rectangularity of the third distribution
are clearly seen with this division. As may be seen in this figure, use of
only two classifications in an ordinal-scale measurement yields very
little information about the shape of the underlying distribution of
scores.

To correct for this factor we subtract the value .5 from the $O - E$
value when signs are disregarded. The correct computation of the value
of χ^2 for the data originally given in Table 13.1, then, is the following.

$$\chi^2 = \frac{(/37 - 40/ - .5)^2}{40} + \frac{(/13 - 10/ - .5)^2}{10} + \frac{(/43 - 40/ - .5)^2}{40} +$$

$$\frac{(/7 - 10/ - .5)^2}{10}$$

$$= \frac{(3 - .5)^2}{40} + \frac{(3 - .5)^2}{10} + \frac{(3 - .5)^2}{40} + \frac{(3 - .5)^2}{10}$$

$$= \frac{(2.5)^2}{40} + \frac{(2.5)^2}{10} + \frac{(2.5)^2}{40} + \frac{(2.5)^2}{10}$$

$$= \frac{6.25}{40} + \frac{6.25}{10} + \frac{6.25}{40} + \frac{6.25}{10} = 1.56$$

This value of chi-square is considerably lower than was the value previously computed (2.25) because the correction for continuity tends to lower the computed value of χ^2. This, in turn, reduces the probability that a significant finding will be obtained.

As a final point, let us reconsider the concept of degrees of freedom in a chi-square table. The degrees of freedom associated with a χ^2 test indicates the number of cell totals that are free to vary and is not a function of the number of individuals tested. Consequently, for this test, we must revise to some extent the concept of degrees of freedom developed over the preceding twelve chapters. Since the degrees of freedom for a given chi-square table are independent of the number of observations, does this imply that the number of people tested has no effect on chi-square? No, quite to the contrary, it may be demonstrated that an increase in the number of observations decreases the likelihood of finding a chance result and increases the probability of detecting a true effect. This is because the factor of N is included directly in the computational formula for χ^2.

THE PHI COEFFICIENT

Let us now turn to a second method for analyzing data when the results of an experiment or study are derived from nominal-scale classification— the correlation coefficient, phi (ϕ). A correlation coefficient based on nominal-scale data occurs frequently in psychometrics where a common problem is that of determining the correlation between two items on a test. For each of these items, only a nominal-scale measurement may be assumed, i.e., a given individual may either pass or fail the item. An illustration of such data is presented in Table 13.3. Listed here are the pass–fail scores for two items of the test administered to 50 students. Rather than listing each of the individuals as passed or failed, we have listed them as either 1 (passed) or 0 (failed). If we computed the parametric correlation coefficient (r) on these data, the cross product (ΣXY) would simply be the number of people who passed both questions. A pass score of 1 on question X times a pass score of 1 on question Y equals 1, and all other cross products would involve zeros. Similarly, the value of ΣX is the number of students who pass question X, and the value of ΣY is the number who pass question Y. Further,

TABLE 13.3.　Responses of 50 individuals to two items of a test

INDIVIDUAL NO.	QUESTION X	QUESTION Y	INDIVIDUAL NO.	QUESTION X	QUESTION Y
1	1	1	26	0	0
2	1	1	27	0	0
3	1	1	28	0	0
4	1	1	29	0	0
5	1	1	30	0	0
6	1	1	31	0	0
7	1	1	32	0	0
8	1	1	33	0	0
9	1	1	34	0	0
10	1	1	35	0	0
11	1	1	36	0	0
12	1	1	37	0	0
13	1	1	38	0	0
14	1	1	39	0	0
15	1	1	40	0	0
16	1	1	41	0	0
17	1	1	42	0	0
18	1	1	43	0	0
19	1	1	44	0	0
20	1	1	45	0	0
21	1	0	46	0	0
22	1	0	47	0	0
23	0	1	48	0	0
24	0	1	49	0	0
25	0	1	50	0	0

TABLE 13.4.   Data from table 13.3 recast into a 2 × 2 table

		QUESTION X		
		PASS	FAIL	TOTALS
Question Y	Pass	$A = 20$	$B = 3$	$(A + B) = 23$
	Fail	$C = 2$	$D = 25$	$(C + D) = 27$
	Totals	$(A + C) = 22$	$(B + D) = 28$	$N = 50$

it may be seen that the values for ΣX^2 and ΣY^2 are also the number of people passing each of the questions. It would thus appear that we could simplify the data presented in Table 13.3 by constructing a table listing the number of people who jointly pass and fail each of the two questions. We see in Table 13.4 that 20 students passed both questions, 25 failed both questions, and the remaining five individuals each failed only one of the two questions. In Table 13.4, the individual cells have been identified by a letter. The number of individuals who passed both question X and question Y is A; the number of people who failed question X but passed question Y is B; the number of people passing question X but failing question Y is C; and the number of people failing both questions is D. The row and column totals may be expressed as $A + C$ for those who passed question X, $B + D$ who failed question X, $A + B$ who passed question Y, $C + D$ who failed question Y, and N for the total number.

Labeling the table in this manner permits us to provide a simplified version of the formula for the parametric correlation, r, computed on these data. In the following formula we refer to the resulting correlation coefficient as ϕ rather than r to indicate that we have not satisfied the assumptions of normality of distribution. Thus the formula expressed below is only an analog of the parametric correlation, and restrictions upon its interpretation must be made. The appropriate formula for determining this correlation is:

$$\phi = \frac{AD - BC}{\sqrt{(A + B)(C + D)(A + C)(B + D)}}$$

To determine this nonparametric correlation coefficient based on nominal-scale data, then, we determine the product of those passing and failing both items and subtract from it the product of those who pass one item and fail the other. This is then divided by the square root of the product of the four marginal totals. The determination of the correlation coefficient for the data presented in Table 13.4 is:

$$\phi = \frac{AD - BC}{\sqrt{(A+B)(C+D)(A+C)(B+D)}}$$

$$= \frac{(20)(25) - (3)(2)}{\sqrt{(23)(27)(22)(28)}} = \frac{500 - 6}{\sqrt{382{,}586}}$$

$$= \frac{+494}{616} = +.80$$

A relatively strong relationship is thus shown between questions X and Y. It appears that any individual who passes or fails one item is very likely to repeat his performances on the other item. In psychometric terms, this is evidence for the homogeneity of the two items, i.e., it is likely that the two items tend to test the same types of material.

The method of category sorting shown in Table 13.4 resembles the chi-square tables presented earlier in this chapter. A definite relationship does, in fact, exist between these two types of analysis. We have found that:

$$\phi = \sqrt{\frac{\chi^2}{N}}$$

Such a formulation for the 2 × 2 table is only accurate when the correction for continuity is not used. It appears from this relationship that one may then test for the significance of a ϕ coefficient by first computing: $\chi^2 = N\phi^2$. The significance of this value of chi-square may be determined by reference to the table of χ^2 under one degree of freedom. For the data presented in Table 13.4 this value is:

$$\chi^2 = N\phi^2 = (50)(+.80)^2 = (50)(.64) = 32$$

Reference to the table of chi-square presented in Appendix *E* indicates that this value of χ^2 is highly unlikely to have been obtained by chance alone. As a consequence, we may say that we have a highly significant value of ϕ for the original data.

You may note, from the computations above, that a ϕ value could be computed from any 2 × 2 table by use of the relationship between χ^2 and ϕ. In the data presented in Table 13.1, showing the joint classification on male–female and right-handed vs. left-handed scales, the χ^2 value was 3.841. A ϕ value for this table would be as follows.

$$\phi = \sqrt{\frac{\chi^2}{N}} = \sqrt{\frac{3.841}{100}} = \sqrt{.03841} = .196$$

The relatively small value of ϕ computed for these data substantiates our earlier conclusion that no significant differences between the right-handed vs. left-handed classifications are apparent as a function of classification on the male–female scale. We have not assigned a plus or minus sign to the ϕ value computed on that data. If we had classified males as 1s and females as 0s and right-handed as 1s and left-handed as 0s, then the value of phi would have been negative. Such assignment of signs to a phi coefficient is apparently meaningless, and the value of phi for such data is primarily that of determining the magnitude of a relationship rather than its direction. From this standpoint one may use phi as an indication of the overall strength of a relationship and thus compare two tables where the N's are unequal.

PHI PRIME

Let us now extend this method of determining a correlation coefficient with nominally scaled data to tables larger than 2×2. It becomes immediately apparent that we may no longer think of the resulting correlation coefficient as analogous to a Pearson product-moment correlation (r). In the two previous examples utilizing 2×2 tables as entries, the resulting sign of the value of phi is determined by which variable is designated as 0 or 1. If classification were possible on three categories of a variable, one could assign the numbers 0, 1, and 2 to these categories. If the parametric correlation coefficient were computed using one arrangement of the numbers 0, 1, or 2, the magnitude of the correlation would differ from one computed using a different system of assigning numbers.

One may, however, use the previous expression for phi as a function of chi-square when it is modified by the number of classifications of the variables involved. The proper formula for computation of a correlation coefficient where more than two categories of classification are used substitutes ϕ' for ϕ as follows:

$$\phi' = \sqrt{\frac{\chi^2}{N(L-1)}}$$

where:
$$L = \text{smaller of } R \text{ or } C$$
$$R = \text{number of rows}$$
$$C = \text{number of columns}$$

Notice that the earlier expression for phi is identical to the expression for ϕ' since $L = 2$ in a 2×2 table.

Let us return to the data originally presented in Table 13.2 relating degree of education to income. The classification of acquired level of formal education was: (1) nongraduate; (2) high-school graduate; (3) at least some college. The classification of income was: (1) less than \$4000; (2) \$4000 to \$7500; (3) more than \$7500. For this particular table then, $R = 3$ and $C = 3$. Thus, in the expression for ϕ', L also will be 3 since it is the lower of either the number of rows or the number of columns. The computed value of χ^2 for Table 13.2 was 32.9455 with 4 degrees of freedom. Inspection of the table of chi-square indicated that this value was an unlikely event to have happened by chance alone ($p < .01$).

Computation of a ϕ' value for the data of this table proceeds as follows:

$$\phi' = \sqrt{\frac{\chi^2}{N(L-1)}} = \sqrt{\frac{32.9455}{300(2)}} = \sqrt{.0549} = .2343$$

This value of ϕ' gives us a somewhat different interpretation of the original data than does the chi-square value. The values of ϕ' may range from a low of .00 (indicating no association between the classifications of the two variables) to a high of 1.00 (indicating a complete dependence of classification of one variable upon the other). The obtained value of ϕ' for Table 13.2 indicates that, although a relationship exists, there are other determiners, i.e., the relationship between level of education and level of income is not perfect. It is interesting to note that the data of Table 13.3 relating pass–fail on two questions of an examination ($N = 50$) also yielded a chi-square value of 32. The phi coefficient for that data, however, was $+.80$. For the larger N included in education–income data a similar level of chi-square yielded a phi prime value of only .23. Thus the degree of relationship exhibited between pass–fail criteria on the two items of the test is much stronger than the relationship exhibited between income and formal educational level.

One final item concerning ϕ' should be mentioned. We noted earlier that a significant value of χ^2 indicates a relationship between distributions rather than overall differences between central tendency. Extending this concept, we see that ϕ' is not necessarily an indication of a linear relationship between two variables, but rather indicates the total strength of the relationship existing between the variables. Consequently, the interpretation of a ϕ' value must necessarily be different from the parametric correlation coefficient r. In addition one must meet all of the other assumptions of χ^2—independent observations, unique categories that admit any observation to only one category, and expected values of five or more observations per cell. Provided that these criteria are met, ϕ' is a valuable addition to the statistician's fund of knowledge.

DESIGN CONSIDERATIONS

One of the mistakes made by students of statistics and experimental design is to allow the scale of measurement of the independent variable to determine the choice of the analysis technique. For example, if one is attempting to determine whether or not males have a higher IQ than females, the classification of male–female is clearly that of a nominal scale. This does not necessarily indicate that subsequent analysis of the data should be accomplished by the χ^2 technique. The important determiner of the appropriate statistical test is the scale of measurement assumed by the dependent variable. In this example, since IQ scores may be assumed to fulfill the requirements of interval scale measurement, the correct method of data reduction is probably that of simple analysis of variance.

The methods of χ^2 and ϕ are, however, exceedingly useful techniques for the analysis of data. This is particularly true for the analysis of observations that may be made outside of a laboratory situation. As noted in Chapter 8, many of the phenomena that one might wish to study are exceedingly difficult to reproduce in an experimental laboratory. For example, the cause and prediction of riot behavior is of extreme practical importance. It would, however, be difficult to reproduce, in the laboratory, the conditions which lead to riots. An experimenter studying this question would be required to conduct a field study and, since accurate measurement is often difficult in such circumstances, would probably analyze most of his data by the techniques of χ^2 and ϕ.

Of primary consideration in the design of studies to be analyzed by either of these two techniques is the factor of sample size. Often, through literature review, one may estimate the likely proportions of individuals falling into the various classifications. From this it should be possible to estimate the sample size necessary to fulfill the requirement that no cell has an expected frequency of less than five. In situations where this requirement cannot be met, it is sometimes possible to collapse categories. In the example cited in this chapter relating income to level of education, it would have been possible to reclassify educational level as either (1) did not graduate from high school or (2) graduated from high school. This would eliminate small expected value cells if very few at-least-some-college subjects had been surveyed.

Finally, the size of the N is doubly important in the design of studies to be analyzed by these two nonparametric techniques. We find that the power of both χ^2 and ϕ is a direct function of sample size. As N increases, the power of these techniques also increases relative to the parametric techniques. If the sample size is infinitely large, both χ^2 and ϕ are just as powerful in the detection of true differences as are their parametric counterparts.

SUMMARY

Paralleling the development of two techniques for the analysis of ordinal-scale data in the previous chapter, two techniques for the analysis of nominal-scale data were presented. The first of these, chi-square (χ^2), is a method for determining the significance of a difference between two or more classifications. The computational formula was given as:

$$\chi^2 = \sum \frac{(O - E)^2}{E}$$

where:

O = observed frequency for any cell
E = expected frequency for that cell

The expected frequency for any cell could be computed by:

$$E_{r,c} = \frac{(\Sigma_r)(\Sigma_c)}{N}$$

where:

$E_{r,c}$ = expected frequency for the cell formed by the junction of row
r and column c
Σ_r = number of observations in row r
Σ_c = number of observations in column c
N = total number of observations

The significance of this value of χ^2 is determined by entry to Appendix E using:

$$df = (R - 1)(C - 1)$$

where: R = number of rows
C = number of columns

The value of χ^2 for tables having only one df must be corrected for continuity by use of the computational formula:

$$\chi^2 = \sum \frac{(/O - E/ - .5)^2}{E}$$

The second technique discussed in this chapter was a method for determining the correlation when only nominal-scale measurement may be assumed. When dichotomous classifications on both variables tested are made, this correlation is termed phi (ϕ), and may be determined by the formula:

$$\phi = \frac{AD - BC}{\sqrt{(A + B)(C + D)(A + C)(B + D)}}$$

where the letters are indicated by the following diagram:

Variable 1

	+	−	
Variable 2 +	A	B	A + B
−	C	D	C + D
	A + C	B + D	N

The significance of a given ϕ value is determined by first computing:

$$\chi^2 = N\phi^2$$

This value of χ^2 (and of ϕ) is tested for significance in Appendix E under $df = 1$.

When classification on either of the variables is into three or more categories, a χ^2 value for that table is first computed. The correlation coefficient for this data is then determined by use of the formula:

$$\phi' = \sqrt{\frac{\chi^2}{N(L-1)}}$$

where:

$$L = \text{the lesser of } R \text{ or } C$$

If the value of χ^2 is significant at $(R-1)(C-1)$ df, then the resulting ϕ' is also significant at that level.

It was noted that neither ϕ nor ϕ' may be interpreted as a parametric r. In particular, ϕ' indicates the total strength of the relationship between the two variables, rather than a linear relationship. Finally, it was seen that the factor of sample size is extremely important since it determines both the expected frequency for any cell and also the power of these two techniques relative to their parametric counterparts.

References

1. Bacon, F. *Novum organum.* From the excerpts given in F. H. Sanford, & E. J. Capaldi, *Advancing Psychological Science.* Vol. 1. Belmont, Calif.: Wadsworth, 1964.
2. Bingham, H. C. Size and form perception in *gallus domesticus. J. Anim. Behav.,* 1913, **3,** 65–113.
3. Blackwell, H. R. Contrast thresholds of the human eye. *J. opt. Soc. Amer.,* 1946, **36,** 624–643.
4. Brackbill, Yvonne, & Kappy, M. S. Delay of reinforcement and retention. *J. comp. physiol. Psychol.,* 1962, **55,** 14–18.
5. Bridgman, P. W. *The logic of modern physics.* New York: Macmillan, 1927.

6. Carlsmith, J. M., & Aronson, E. Some hedonic consequences of the confirmation and disconfirmation of expectancies. *J. abnorm. Soc. Psychol.,* 1963, **66**, 151–156.
7. Conrad, H. S., & Jones, H. E. A second study of familial resemblance in intelligence. *39th Yearb. nat. Soc. Stud. Educ.* Chicago: University of Chicago Press, 1940 (II), 97–141.
8. Cronbach, L. *Essentials of psychological testing.* New York: Harper & Row, 1960.
9. Cronbach, L., & Meehl, P. Construct validity of psychological tests. *Psychol. Bull.,* 1955, **52**, 281–302.
10. Du Bois, P. H. *An introduction to psychological statistics.* New York: Harper & Row, 1965.
11. Festinger, L. *A theory of cognitive dissonance.* New York: Harper & Row, 1957.
12. Gayen, A. K. Significance of a difference between the means of two non-normal samples. *Biometrika,* 1950, **37**, 399–408.
13. Hayakawa, S. I. *Language in thought and action.* New York: Harcourt, Brace & World, 1949.
14. Hecht, S. Vision. II. The nature of the photoreceptor process. *Handbook of general experimental psychology.* Worcester, Mass.: Clark University Press, 1934, pp. 704–828.
15. Heisenburg, W. *The physicist's conception of nature.* Translated by A. J. Pomerans. New York: Harcourt, Brace & World, 1958.
16. Hilgard, E. R. *Introduction to psychology.* (3rd ed.) New York: Harcourt, Brace & World, 1953.
17. Hotelling, H., & Pabst, M. R. Rank correlation and tests of significance involving no assumption of normality. *Ann. Math. Statist.,* 1936, **7**, 29–43.
18. Hull, C. L. *Principles of behavior.* New York: Appleton-Century-Crofts, 1943.
19. Kerlinger, F. N. *Foundations of behavioral research.* New York: Holt, Rinehart & Winston, 1964.
20. Kruskal, W. H. A nonparametric test for the several sample problem. *Ann. Math. Statist.,* 1952, **23**, 525–540.
21. Kuenne, M. R. Experimental investigation of the relation of language to transposition behavior in young children. *J. exp. Psychol.,* 1946, **36**, 471–490.
22. Kuhn, T. S. *The structure of scientific revolutions.* Chicago: University of Chicago Press, 1962.
23. Lathrop, R. G. Error correlations in a two-dimensional compensatory tracking task. *Percept. mot. Skills,* 1965, **21**, 653–654.
24. Lathrop, R. G. First order response dependencies at a differential brightness threshold. *J. exp. Psychol.,* 1966, **72**, 120–124.
25. Lott, D. F. Threat and submission signals in mature male American bison. *Proc. 75th Amer. Psychol. Assoc.,* 1967, **2**, 121–122.

26. Marx, M. H. (Ed.) *Theories in contemporary psychology.* New York: Macmillan, 1963.
27. McLelland, D. C. *The achievement motive.* New York: Appleton-Century-Crofts, 1953.
28. Nagel, E., & Newman, E. R. *Gödel's proof.* New York: New York University Press, 1958.
29. Platt, J. R. Strong inference. *Science,* 1964, **146,** 347–353.
30. Rosenthal, R., & Lawson, R. A longitudinal study of the effects of experimenter bias on the operant learning of laboratory rats. *J. Psychiatric Res.,* 1964, **2,** 61–72.
31. Scheffé, H. *The analysis of variance.* New York: Wiley, 1959.
32. Sears, P. R. Some child-rearing antecedents of aggression and dependency in young children. *Genet. Psychol. Monogr.,* 1953, **47,** 135–234.
33. Spence, K. W. The differential response in animals to stimuli varying within a single dimension. *Psychol. Rev.,* 1937, **44,** 430–444.
34. Steinhardt, J. Intensity discrimination in the human eye: I. The relation of $\Delta I/I$ to intensity. *J. gen. Psychol.,* 1936, **20,** 185–209.
35. Sturges, Persis T. Verbal retention as a function of the informativeness and delay of feedback. Presented at the Western Psychological Association Convention, 1966.
36. Walker, H. M., & Lev, J. *Statistical inference.* New York: Holt, Rinehart & Winston, 1953.
37. Whitehead, A. N. *Science and the modern world.* New York: Macmillan, 1925.
38. Woodworth, R. S., & Schlosberg, H. *Experimental psychology.* (Rev. ed.) New York: Holt, Rinehart & Winston, 1954.

Appendixes

KEY TO ABBREVIATIONS AND SYMBOLS

BSS   Between-groups sum of squares
c   Any one column (χ^2)
C   Specific comparison being made (CI); number of columns (χ^2)
CI   Confidence interval
D   Difference for paired ranks (r_s)
df   Degrees of freedom

DL	Differential threshold
E	Expected frequency (χ^2)
E_e	Expected error
E_m	Error of measurement
f	Frequency
F	Ratio of two variances (analysis of variance)
H	Kruskal-Wallis statistic
i	Individual subject
I	Number of subjects
IV	Independent-variable effect
j	Individual treatment
J	Number of sample means
L	The smaller of R or C (χ^2)
M	Multiplier (CI)
MS	Mean squared deviation (from sample mean)
n	Number in subsample
N	Total number; number of pairs of observations
NS	Not significant
O	Observed frequency (χ^2)
P	Probability
PSE	Point of subjective equality
r	Parametric correlation; any one row (χ^2)
r_s	Spearman rank correlation coefficient
R	Rank (Kruskal-Wallis); reciprocal of N (CI); number of rows (χ^2)
s	Standard deviation of sample
$s_{\bar{x}}$	Standard error of sample mean
s^2	Variance of sample
S	Subject
SEV	Systematic extraneous variable effect
σ	Standard deviation of population
σ^2	Variance of population (mean squared deviation)
$\sigma_{\bar{x}}$	Standard error of the mean
Σ	Sum
SS	Sum of squared deviations from the mean
t	Inferential t test
TSS	Total sum of squared deviations from the mean
ϕ	Phi (nonparametric correlation coefficient)
ϕ'	Phi prime (nonparametric correlation coefficient for three or more variables)

V	Estimate of population variance (CI)
WSS	Within-group sum of squares
x	deviation from $\bar{X}$
$\bar{X}$	Mean of X scores
X	Any individual score
χ^2	Chi-squared
y	Deviation from $\bar{Y}$
$\bar{Y}$	Mean of Y scores
z	Inferential z test

Appendix A

Squares, square roots

Roots of numbers other than those given directly may be found by the following relations:

$$\sqrt{100n} = 10\sqrt{n}; \ \sqrt{1000n} = 10\sqrt{10n}; \ \sqrt{\frac{1}{10}n} = \frac{1}{10}\sqrt{10n}; \ \sqrt{\frac{1}{100}n} = \frac{1}{10}\sqrt{n};$$

$$\frac{1}{1000}n = \frac{1}{100}\sqrt{10n}.$$

n	n^2	$\sqrt{n}$	$\sqrt{10n}$
1	1	1.000 000	3.16228
2	4	1.414 214	4.47214
3	9	1.732 051	5.47723
4	16	2.000 000	6.32456
5	25	2.236 068	7.07107
6	36	2.449 490	7.74597
7	49	2.645 751	8.36660
8	64	2.828 427	8.94427
9	81	3.000 000	9.48683
10	100	3.162 278	10.00000
11	121	3.316 625	10.48809
12	144	3.464 102	10.95445
13	169	3.605 551	11.40175
14	196	3.741 657	11.83216
15	225	3.872 983	12.24745
16	256	4.000 000	12.64911
17	289	4.123 106	13.03840
18	324	4.242 641	13.41641
19	361	4.358 899	13.78405
20	400	4.472 136	14.14214
21	441	4.582 576	14.49138
22	484	4.690 416	14.83240

n	n^2	$\sqrt{n}$	$\sqrt{10n}$
23	529	4.795 832	15.16575
24	576	4.898 979	15.49193
25	625	5.000 000	15.81139
26	676	5.099 020	16.12452
27	729	5.196 152	16.43168
28	784	5.291 503	16.73320
29	841	5.385 165	17.02939
30	900	5.477 226	17.32051
31	961	5.567 764	17.60682
32	1 024	5.656 854	17.88854
33	1 089	5.744 563	18.16590
34	1 156	5.830 952	18.43909
35	1 225	5.916 080	18.70829
36	1 296	6.000 000	18.97367
37	1 369	6.082 763	19.23538
38	1 444	6.164 414	19.49359
39	1 521	6.244 998	19.74842
40	1 600	6.324 555	20.00000
41	1 681	6.403 124	20.24846
42	1 764	6.480 741	20.49390
43	1 849	6.557 439	20.73644
44	1 936	6.633 250	20.97618
45	2 025	6.708 204	21.21320
46	2 116	6.782 330	21.44761
47	2 209	6.855 655	21.67948
48	2 304	6.928 203	21.90890
49	2 401	7.000 000	22.13594
50	2 500	7.071 068	22.36068
51	2 601	7.141 428	22.58318
52	2 704	7.211 103	22.80351
53	2 809	7.280 110	23.02173
54	2 916	7.348 469	23.23790
55	3 025	7.416 198	23.45208
56	3 136	7.483 315	23.66432
57	3 249	7.549 834	23.87467
58	3 364	7.615 773	24.08319
59	3 481	6.681 146	24.28992
60	3 600	7.745 967	24.49490
61	3 721	7.810 250	24.69818

Squares, square roots (*Continued*)

n	n^2	$\sqrt{n}$	$\sqrt{10n}$
62	3 844	7.874 008	24.89980
63	3 969	7.937 254	25.09980
64	4 096	8.000 000	25.29822
65	4 225	8.062 258	25.49510
66	4 356	8.124 038	25.69047
67	4 489	8.185 353	25.88436
68	4 624	8.246 211	26.07681
69	4 761	8.306 624	26.26785
70	4 900	8.366 600	26.45751
71	5 041	8.426 150	26.64583
72	5 184	8.485 281	26.83282
73	5 329	8.544 004	27.01851
74	5 476	8.602 325	27.20294
75	5 625	8.660 254	27.38613
76	5 776	8.717 798	27.56810
77	5 929	8.774 964	27.74887
78	6 084	8.831 761	27.92848
79	6 241	8.888 194	28.10694
80	6 400	8.944 272	28.28427
81	6 561	9.000 000	28.46050
82	6 724	9.055 385	28.63564
83	6 889	9.110 434	28.80972
84	7 056	9.165 151	28.98275
85	7 225	9.219 544	29.15476
86	7 396	9.273 618	29.32576
87	7 569	9.327 379	29.49576
88	7 744	9.380 832	29.66479
89	7 921	9.433 981	29.83287
90	8 100	9.486 833	30.00000
91	8 281	9.539 392	30.16621
92	8 464	9.591 663	30.33150
93	8 649	9.643 651	30.49590
94	8 836	9.695 360	30.65942
95	9 025	9.746 794	30.82207
96	9 216	9.797 959	30.98387
97	9 409	9.848 858	31.14482
98	9 604	9.899 495	31.30495
99	9 801	9.949 874	31.46427
100	10 000	10.00000	31.62278

Appendix B

Percent of total area under the normal curve between mean ordinate
and ordinate at any given sigma distance from the mean

$\frac{x}{\sigma}$	.00	.01	.02	.03	.04	.05	.06	.07	.08	.09
0.0	00.00	00.40	00.80	01.20	01.60	01.99	02.39	02.79	03.19	03.59
0.1	03.98	04.38	04.78	05.17	05.57	05.96	06.36	06.75	07.14	07.53
0.2	07.93	08.32	08.71	09.10	09.48	09.87	10.26	10.64	11.03	11.41
0.3	11.79	12.17	12.55	12.93	13.31	13.68	14.06	14.43	14.80	15.17
0.4	15.54	15.91	16.28	16.64	17.00	17.36	17.72	18.08	18.44	18.79
0.5	19.15	19.50	19.85	20.19	20.54	20.88	21.23	21.57	21.90	22.24
0.6	22.57	22.91	23.24	23.57	23.89	24.22	24.54	24.86	25.17	25.49
0.7	25.80	26.11	26.42	26.73	(27.04)	27.34	27.64	27.94	28.23	28.52
0.8	28.81	29.10	29.39	29.67	29.95	30.23	30.51	30.78	31.06	31.33
0.9	31.59	31.86	32.12	32.38	32.64	32.90	33.15	33.40	33.65	33.89
1.0	34.13	34.38	34.61	34.85	35.08	35.31	35.54	35.77	35.99	36.21
1.1	36.43	36.65	36.86	37.08	37.29	37.49	37.70	37.90	38.10	38.30
1.2	38.49	38.69	38.88	39.07	39.25	39.44	39.62	39.80	39.97	40.15
1.3	40.32	40.49	40.66	40.82	40.99	41.15	41.31	41.47	41.62	41.77
1.4	41.92	42.07	42.22	42.36	42.51	42.65	42.79	42.92	43.06	43.19
1.5	43.32	43.45	43.57	43.70	43.83	43.94	44.06	44.18	44.29	44.41
1.6	44.52	44.63	44.74	44.84	44.95	45.05	45.15	45.25	45.35	45.45
1.7	45.54	45.64	45.73	45.82	45.91	45.99	46.08	46.16	46.25	46.33
1.8	46.41	46.49	46.56	46.64	46.71	46.78	46.86	46.93	46.99	47.06
1.9	47.13	47.19	47.26	47.32	47.38	47.44	(47.50)	47.56	47.61	47.67
2.0	47.72	47.78	47.83	47.88	47.93	47.98	48.03	48.08	48.12	48.17
2.1	48.21	48.26	48.30	48.34	48.38	48.42	48.46	48.50	48.54	48.57
2.2	48.61	48.64	48.68	48.71	48.75	48.78	48.81	48.84	48.87	48.90
2.3	48.93	48.96	48.98	49.01	49.02	49.06	49.09	49.11	49.13	49.16
2.4	49.18	49.20	49.22	49.25	49.27	49.29	49.31	49.32	49.34	49.36
2.5	49.38	49.40	49.41	49.43	49.45	49.46	49.48	49.49	49.51	49.52
2.6	49.53	49.55	49.56	49.57	49.59	49.60	49.61	49.62	49.63	49.64
2.7	49.65	49.66	49.67	49.68	49.69	49.70	49.71	49.72	49.73	49.74
2.8	49.74	49.75	49.76	49.77	49.77	49.78	49.79	49.79	49.80	49.81
2.9	49.81	49.82	49.82	49.83	49.84	49.84	49.85	49.85	49.86	49.86
3.0	49.87									
3.5	49.98									
4.0	49.997									
5.0	49.99997									

Appendix C

Values of t significant at .05 and .01 levels

DEGREES OF FREEDOM (df)	PROBABILITY .05	.01
1	12.706	63.657
2	4.303	9.925
3	3.182	5.841
4	2.776	4.604
5	2.571	4.032
6	2.447	3.707
7	2.365	3.499
8	2.306	3.355
9	2.262	3.250
10	2.228	3.169
11	2.201	3.106
12	2.179	3.055
13	2.160	3.012
14	2.145	2.977
15	2.131	2.947
16	2.120	2.921
17	2.110	2.898
18	2.101	2.878
19	2.093	2.861
20	2.086	2.845
21	2.080	2.831
22	2.074	2.819
23	2.069	2.807
24	2.064	2.797
25	2.060	2.787
26	2.056	2.779
27	2.052	2.771
28	2.048	2.763
29	2.045	2.756
30	2.042	2.750

Appendix D

Values of F significant at .05 and .01 levels

df ASSOCIATED WITH THE DENOMINATOR		df ASSOCIATED WITH THE NUMERATOR																		
		1	2	3	4	5	6	7	8	9	10	12	14	16	20	30	40	50	100
1	5%	161	200	216	225	230	234	237	239	241	242	244	245	246	248	250	251	252	253
	1%	4052	5000	5403	5625	5764	5859	5928	5982	6022	6056	6106	6142	6169	6208	6258	6286	6302	6334
2	5%	18.5	19.0	19.2	19.2	19.3	19.3	19.4	19.4	19.4	19.4	19.4	19.4	19.4	19.4	19.5	19.5	19.5	19.5
	1%	98.5	99.0	99.2	99.2	99.3	99.3	99.4	99.4	99.4	99.4	99.4	99.4	99.4	99.5	99.5	99.5	99.5	99.5
3	5%	10.1	9.55	9.28	9.12	9.01	8.94	8.89	8.85	8.81	8.78	8.74	8.71	8.69	8.66	8.62	8.60	8.58	8.56
	1%	34.1	30.3	29.5	28.7	28.2	27.9	27.7	27.5	27.3	27.2	27.1	26.9	26.8	26.7	26.5	26.4	26.3	26.2
4	5%	7.71	6.94	6.59	6.39	6.26	6.16	6.09	6.04	6.00	5.96	5.91	5.87	5.84	5.80	5.74	5.71	5.70	5.66
	1%	21.2	18.0	16.7	16.0	15.5	15.2	15.0	14.8	14.7	14.5	14.4	14.2	14.2	14.0	13.8	13.7	13.7	13.6
5	5%	6.61	5.79	5.41	5.19	5.05	4.95	4.88	4.82	4.77	4.74	4.68	4.64	4.60	4.56	4.50	4.46	4.44	4.40
	1%	16.3	13.3	12.1	11.4	11.0	10.7	10.5	10.3	10.2	10.1	9.89	9.77	9.68	9.55	9.38	9.29	9.24	9.13
6	5%	5.99	5.14	4.76	4.53	4.39	4.28	4.21	4.15	4.10	4.06	4.00	3.96	3.92	3.87	3.81	3.77	3.75	3.71
	1%	13.7	10.9	9.78	9.15	8.75	8.47	8.26	8.10	7.98	7.87	7.72	7.60	7.52	7.39	7.23	7.14	7.09	6.99
7	5%	5.59	4.74	4.35	4.12	3.97	3.87	3.79	3.73	3.68	3.63	3.57	3.52	3.49	3.44	3.38	3.34	3.32	3.28
	1%	12.2	9.55	8.45	7.85	7.46	7.19	6.99	6.84	6.72	6.62	6.47	6.35	6.27	6.15	5.98	5.90	5.85	5.75
8	5%	5.32	4.46	4.07	3.84	3.69	3.58	3.50	3.44	3.39	3.34	3.28	3.23	3.20	3.15	3.08	3.05	3.03	2.98
	1%	11.3	8.65	7.59	7.01	6.63	6.37	6.18	6.03	5.91	5.82	5.67	5.56	5.48	5.36	5.20	5.11	5.06	4.96
9	5%	5.12	4.26	3.86	3.63	3.48	3.37	3.29	3.23	3.18	3.13	3.07	3.02	2.98	2.93	2.86	2.82	2.80	2.76
	1%	10.6	8.02	6.99	6.42	6.06	5.80	5.61	5.47	5.35	5.26	5.11	5.00	4.92	4.80	4.64	4.56	4.51	4.41

10	5%	4.96	4.10	3.71	3.48	3.33	3.22	3.14	3.07	3.02	2.97	2.91	2.86	2.82	2.77	2.70	2.67	2.64	2.59
	1%	10.0	7.56	6.55	5.99	5.64	5.39	5.20	5.06	4.94	4.85	4.71	4.60	4.52	4.41	4.25	4.17	4.12	4.01
11	5%	4.84	3.98	3.59	3.36	3.20	3.09	3.01	2.95	2.90	2.86	2.79	2.74	2.70	2.65	2.57	2.53	2.50	2.45
	1%	9.65	7.21	6.22	5.67	5.32	5.07	4.89	4.74	4.63	4.54	4.40	4.29	4.21	4.10	3.94	3.86	3.80	3.70
12	5%	4.75	3.89	3.49	3.26	3.11	3.00	2.91	2.85	2.80	2.76	2.69	2.64	2.60	2.54	2.46	2.42	2.40	2.35
	1%	9.33	6.93	5.95	5.41	5.06	4.82	4.64	4.50	4.39	4.30	4.16	4.05	3.98	3.86	3.70	3.61	3.56	3.46
13	5%	4.67	3.81	3.41	3.18	3.03	2.92	2.83	2.77	2.71	2.67	2.60	2.55	2.51	2.46	2.38	2.34	2.32	2.26
	1%	9.07	6.70	5.74	5.21	4.86	4.62	4.44	4.30	4.19	4.10	3.96	3.85	3.78	3.67	3.51	3.42	3.37	3.27
14	5%	4.60	3.74	3.34	3.11	2.96	2.85	2.76	2.70	2.65	2.60	2.53	2.48	2.44	2.39	2.31	2.27	2.24	2.19
	1%	8.86	6.51	5.56	5.04	4.70	4.46	4.28	4.14	4.03	3.94	3.80	3.70	3.62	3.51	3.34	3.26	3.21	3.11
15	5%	4.54	3.68	3.29	3.06	2.90	2.79	2.71	2.64	2.59	2.55	2.48	2.43	2.39	2.33	2.25	2.21	2.18	2.12
	1%	8.68	6.36	5.42	4.89	4.56	4.32	4.14	4.00	3.89	3.80	3.67	3.56	3.48	3.36	3.20	3.12	3.07	2.97
16	5%	4.49	3.63	3.24	3.01	2.85	2.74	2.66	2.59	2.54	2.49	2.42	2.37	2.33	2.28	2.20	2.16	2.13	2.07
	1%	8.53	6.23	5.29	4.77	4.44	4.20	4.03	3.89	3.78	3.69	3.55	3.45	3.37	3.25	3.10	3.01	2.96	2.86
17	5%	4.45	3.59	3.20	2.96	2.81	2.70	2.61	2.55	2.49	2.45	2.38	2.33	2.29	2.23	2.15	2.11	2.08	2.02
	1%	8.40	6.11	5.18	4.67	4.34	4.10	3.93	3.79	3.68	3.59	3.45	3.35	3.27	3.16	3.00	2.92	2.86	2.76
18	5%	4.41	3.55	3.16	2.93	2.77	2.66	2.58	2.51	2.46	2.41	2.34	2.29	2.25	2.19	2.11	2.07	2.04	1.98
	1%	8.29	6.01	5.09	4.58	4.25	4.01	3.84	3.71	3.60	3.51	3.37	3.27	3.19	3.07	2.91	2.83	2.78	2.68
19	5%	4.38	3.52	3.13	2.90	2.74	2.63	2.54	2.48	2.42	2.38	2.31	2.26	2.21	2.15	2.07	2.02	2.00	1.94
	1%	8.18	5.93	5.01	4.50	4.17	3.94	3.77	3.63	3.52	3.43	3.30	3.19	3.12	3.00	2.84	2.76	2.70	2.60
20	5%	4.35	3.49	3.10	2.87	2.71	2.60	2.51	2.45	2.39	2.35	2.28	2.23	2.18	2.12	2.04	1.99	1.96	1.90
	1%	8.10	5.85	4.94	4.43	4.10	3.87	3.70	3.56	3.46	3.37	3.23	3.13	3.05	2.94	2.77	2.69	2.63	2.53
21	5%	4.32	3.47	3.07	2.84	2.68	2.57	2.49	2.42	2.37	2.32	2.25	2.20	2.15	2.09	2.00	1.96	1.93	1.87
	1%	8.02	5.78	4.87	4.37	4.04	3.81	3.64	3.51	3.40	3.31	3.17	3.07	2.99	2.88	2.72	2.63	2.58	2.47
22	5%	4.30	3.44	3.05	2.82	2.66	2.55	2.46	2.40	2.34	2.30	2.23	2.18	2.13	2.07	1.98	1.93	1.91	1.84
	1%	7.95	5.72	4.82	4.31	3.99	3.76	3.59	3.45	3.35	3.26	3.12	3.02	2.94	2.83	2.67	2.58	2.53	2.42

Values of F significant at .05 and .01 levels (Continued)

df ASSOCIATED WITH THE NUMERATOR

df ASSOCIATED WITH THE DENOMINATOR		1	2	3	4	5	6	7	8	9	10	12	14	16	20	30	40	50	100
23	5%	4.28	3.42	3.03	2.80	2.64	2.53	2.44	2.37	2.32	2.28	2.20	2.14	2.10	2.04	1.96	1.91	1.88	1.82
	1%	7.88	5.66	4.76	4.26	3.94	3.71	3.54	3.41	3.30	3.21	3.07	2.97	2.89	2.78	2.62	2.53	2.48	2.37
24	5%	4.26	3.40	3.01	2.78	2.62	2.51	2.42	2.36	2.30	2.26	2.18	2.13	2.09	2.02	1.94	1.89	1.86	1.80
	1%	7.82	5.61	4.72	4.22	3.90	3.67	3.50	3.36	3.26	3.17	3.03	2.93	2.85	2.74	2.58	2.49	2.44	2.33
25	5%	4.24	3.39	2.99	2.76	2.60	2.49	2.40	2.34	2.28	2.24	2.16	2.11	2.06	2.00	1.92	1.87	1.84	1.77
	1%	7.77	5.57	4.68	4.18	3.86	3.63	3.46	3.32	3.22	3.13	2.99	2.89	2.81	2.70	2.54	2.45	2.40	2.29
26	5%	4.23	3.37	2.98	2.74	2.59	2.47	2.39	2.32	2.27	2.22	2.15	2.10	2.05	1.99	1.90	1.85	1.82	1.76
	1%	7.72	5.53	4.64	4.14	3.82	3.59	3.42	3.29	3.18	3.09	2.96	2.86	2.77	2.66	2.50	2.41	2.36	2.25
27	5%	4.21	3.35	2.96	2.73	2.57	2.46	2.37	2.31	2.25	2.20	2.13	2.08	2.03	1.97	1.88	1.84	1.80	1.74
	1%	7.68	5.49	4.60	4.11	3.78	3.56	3.39	3.26	3.15	3.06	2.93	2.83	2.74	2.63	2.47	2.38	2.33	2.21
28	5%	4.20	3.34	2.95	2.71	2.56	2.45	2.36	2.29	2.24	2.19	2.12	2.06	2.02	1.96	1.87	1.81	1.78	1.72
	1%	7.64	5.45	4.57	4.07	3.75	3.53	3.36	3.23	3.12	3.03	2.90	2.80	2.71	2.60	2.44	2.35	2.30	2.18
29	5%	4.18	3.33	2.93	2.70	2.55	2.43	2.35	2.28	2.22	2.18	2.10	2.05	2.00	1.94	1.85	1.80	1.77	1.71
	1%	7.60	5.42	4.54	4.04	3.73	3.50	3.33	3.20	3.09	3.00	2.87	2.77	2.68	2.57	2.41	2.32	2.27	2.15
30	5%	4.17	3.32	2.92	2.69	2.53	2.42	2.33	2.27	2.21	2.16	2.09	2.04	1.99	1.93	1.84	1.79	1.76	1.69
	1%	7.56	5.39	4.51	4.02	3.70	3.47	3.30	3.17	3.07	2.98	2.84	2.74	2.66	2.55	2.38	2.29	2.24	2.13
40	5%	4.08	3.23	2.84	2.61	2.45	2.34	2.25	2.18	2.12	2.07	2.00	1.95	1.90	1.84	1.74	1.69	1.66	1.59
	1%	7.31	5.18	4.31	3.83	3.51	3.29	3.12	2.99	2.89	2.80	2.66	2.56	2.49	2.37	2.20	2.11	2.05	1.94
60	5%	4.00	3.15	2.76	2.53	2.37	2.25	2.17	2.10	2.04	1.99	1.92	1.86	1.81	1.75	1.65	1.59	1.56	1.48
	1%	7.08	4.98	4.13	3.65	3.34	3.12	2.95	2.82	2.72	2.63	2.50	2.40	2.32	2.20	2.03	1.93	1.87	1.74
125	5%	3.92	3.07	2.68	2.44	2.29	2.17	2.08	2.01	1.95	1.90	1.83	1.77	1.72	1.65	1.55	1.49	1.45	1.36
	1%	6.84	4.78	3.94	3.47	3.17	2.95	2.79	2.65	2.56	2.47	2.33	2.23	2.15	2.03	1.85	1.75	1.68	1.54

Appendix E

Values of r significant at .05 and .01 levels

DEGREES OF FREEDOM (df)	.05	.01	DEGREES OF FREEDOM (df)	.05	.01
1	.997	1.000	24	.388	.496
2	.950	.990	25	.381	.487
3	.878	.959	26	.374	.478
4	.811	.917	27	.367	.470
5	.754	.874	28	.361	.463
6	.707	.834	29	.355	.456
7	.666	.798	30	.349	.449
8	.632	.765	35	.325	.418
9	.602	.735	40	.304	.393
10	.576	.708	45	.288	.372
11	.553	.684	50	.273	.354
12	.532	.661	60	.250	.325
13	.514	.641	70	.232	.302
14	.497	.623	80	.217	.283
15	.482	.606	90	.205	.267
16	.468	.590	100	.195	.254
17	.456	.575	125	.174	.228
18	.444	.561	150	.159	.208
19	.433	.549	200	.138	.181
20	.423	.537	300	.113	.148
21	.413	.526	400	.098	.128
22	.404	.515	500	.088	.115
23	.396	.505	1000	.062	.081

Appendix F

Values of χ^2 significant at .05 and .01 levels

DEGREES OF FREEDOM	.05	.01
1	3.841	6.635
2	5.991	9.210
3	7.815	11.341
4	9.488	13.277
5	11.070	15.086
6	12.592	16.812
7	14.067	18.475
8	15.507	20.090
9	16.919	21.666
10	18.307	23.209
11	19.675	24.725
12	21.026	26.217
13	22.362	27.688
14	26.685	29.141
15	24.996	30.578
16	26.296	32.000
17	27.587	33.409
18	28.869	34.805
19	30.144	36.191
20	31.410	37.566
21	32.671	38.932
22	33.924	40.289
23	35.172	41.638
24	36.415	42.980
25	37.652	44.314
26	38.885	45.642
27	40.113	46.963
28	41.337	48.278
29	42.557	49.588
30	43.773	50.892

Values of r_s significant at .05 and .01 levels

N	.05	.01
5	1.000	—
6	.886	1.000
7	.786	.929
8	.738	.881
9	.683	.833
10	.648	.794
11	.619	.807
12	.591	.777
13	.566	.744
14	.544	.714
15	.524	.688
16	.506	.665
17	.490	.644
18	.475	.625
19	.462	.607
20	.450	.591
21	.438	.576
22	.428	.562
23	.418	.549
24	.409	.537
25	.400	.526
26	.392	.515
27	.384	.505
28	.377	.496
29	.370	.487
30	.364	.478
35	.336	.442
40	.314	.412
45	.295	.388
50	.280	.368
60	.255	.335
70	.234	.310
80	.221	.290

90	.208	.273
100	.197	.259
125	.176	.231
150	.161	.211
200	.139	.183
300	.113	.149
400	.098	.129
500	.088	.115
1000	.062	.082

Index

69 70 71 7 6 5 4 3 2